Inland Waterway Transport

T0384268

Inland waterways are a host for a mode of transport that is neither as visible to the general public, nor as widely used, as it once was. However, it is generally perceived to be very important to today's freight transport system. A closer look into the inland waterway transport system reveals the strengths and opportunities of this mode of transportation.

This book gives the reader a thorough understanding of the current role of inland waterway transport as a freight transport system and its conditions. Drawing on case studies from across Europe, this text explores the economic, logistic, technological and policy issues and challenges related to inland waterway transport. It also explores the strategies for the inland waterway transport sector to secure and then enlarge its role in the future of freight transport.

Inland Waterway Transport will be an invaluable resource for students and researchers of transport studies. In addition, the book will be useful to policy makers and practitioners in the field. It will also appeal to wider readers with an interest in the fascinating business of inland waterway transport.

Bart Wiegmans is senior researcher at the Faculty of Civil Engineering, Delft University of Technology, the Netherlands. He specializes in spatial and transport economics related to maritime and intermodal freight transport.

Rob Konings is senior researcher at the Faculty of Architecture, Delft University of Technology, the Netherlands. He is an economist specializing in spatial and transport economics.

Routledge Studies in Transport Analysis

1. **Maritime Logistics Value in Knowledge Management**
   Eon-Seong Lee and Dong-Wook Song

2. **The Management of Maritime Regulations**
   Hristos Karahalios

3. **Public Private Partnerships in Transport**
   Trends and Theory
   Edited by Athena Roumboutsos

4. **Climate Change and Adaptation Planning for Ports**
   *Edited by Adolf K. Y. Ng, Austin Becker, Stephen Cahoon,
   Shu-ling Chen, Paul Earl and Zaili Yang*

5. **Maritime Networks**
   Spatial Structures and Time Dynamics
   Edited by César Ducruet

6. **Inland Waterway Transport**
   Challenges and Prospects
   Edited by Bart Wiegmans and Rob Konings

Inland Waterway Transport

Challenges and prospects

Edited by Bart Wiegmans and Rob Konings

Routledge
Taylor & Francis Group

LONDON AND NEW YORK

First published 2017 by Routledge

2 Park Square, Milton Park, Abingdon, Oxfordshire OX14 4RN
52 Vanderbilt Avenue, New York, NY 10017

Routledge is an imprint of the Taylor & Francis Group, an informa business

First issued in paperback 2019

British Library Cataloguing in Publication Data
A catalogue record for this book is available from the British Library

Library of Congress Cataloguing in Publication Data
Names: Wiegmans, Bart, editor. | Konings, J. W., editor.
Title: Inland waterway transport : challenges and prospects /
Bart Wiegmans and Rob Konings.
Description: New York: Routledge, 2017.
Identifiers: LCCN 2016004655 | ISBN 9781138826717 (hardback) |
ISBN 9781315739083 (ebook)
Subjects: LCSH: Inland water transportation. | Inland navigation.
Classification: LCC HE617.W54 2016 | DDC 386–dc23
LC record available at http://lccn.loc.gov/2016004655

ISBN: 978-1-138-82671-7 (hbk)
ISBN: 978-0-367-87105-5 (pbk)

Typeset in Times New Roman
by Out of House Publishing

Contents

List of figures   viii
List of tables   xi
Notes on contributors   xiii

1 Inland waterway transport: an overview   1
ROB KONINGS AND BART WIEGMANS

  1.1 Introduction   1
  *1.2 Waterways: a precondition for inland waterway
     transport   3*
  1.3 Transport performance   5
  1.4 Important cargo flows for IWT   9
  1.5 Emerging markets: container transport   9
  1.6 Added value to society   12

**PART I
Economics and logistics**

2 The economic performance of inland waterway transport   18
BART WIEGMANS AND ROB KONINGS

  2.1 Demand and supply of inland waterway transport   18
  2.2 The role of costs and quality performances in IWT   21
  *2.3 Competitiveness of IWT with different transport modes
     and in different markets (dry bulk, liquid bulk, containers,
     others)   26*
  2.4 Major drivers to improve competitiveness   32

**3 The role of inland waterway transport in the changing logistics
environment**   35
TILMAN PLATZ AND GERHARD KLATT

  *3.1 Definition of the logistics environment of inland waterway
     transport   36*

3.2   *Integration of IWT into logistics chains   47*
3.3   *Outlook: opportunities and challenges for IWT in
      logistics   58*

**4   Managing capacity in the inland waterway sector:
      to intervene or not to intervene?**   **71**
EDWIN VAN HASSEL, THIERRY VANELSLANDER AND CHRISTA SYS

4.1   *Rationale and setting   71*
4.2   *Supply and demand characteristics of the IWT sector   73*
4.3   *Reduction of IWT barge capacity   78*
4.4   *The lack of bankruptcies   83*
4.5   *Which government actions were taken in the past?   88*
4.6   *The way forward: how to control capacity?   92*
4.7   *Conclusions   95*

**PART II
Infrastructure, nodes and fleet**

5   Existing waterway infrastructures and future needs   **99**
CORNELIS VAN DORSSER

5.1   *Introduction   99*
5.2   *Inland waterway characteristics   99*
5.3   *West European IWT system   104*
5.4   *Trends affecting the IWT system   112*
5.5   *Developing future-proof infrastructures   119*

6   Inland river ports   **125**
BRIAN SLACK AND CLAUDE COMTOIS

6.1   *Defining inland ports   125*
6.2   *Inland ports, the role of bulk cargoes   126*
6.3   *Inland ports, new traffic   131*
6.4   *Conclusions   138*

7   Developments in inland waterway vessels   **142**
ROBERT HEKKENBERG AND JIALUN LIU

7.1   *Inland vessels around the world   142*
7.2   *Innovation characteristics and innovation adoption
      in inland vessel design   148*
7.3   *The most influential innovations and developments
      of recent years   153*
7.4   *Impacts of these developments on the competitiveness
      of IWT   163*

PART III
Market developments and policies

8   A new wave for the inland waterways: palletized goods   168
    KOEN MOMMENS, DRIES MEERS, TOM VAN LIER AND
    CATHY MACHARIS

    8.1   *Pallets on the inland waterways?   170*
    8.2   *Market evolution   174*
    8.3   *Location Analysis Model for Barge Transport Of*
          Pallets   180
    8.4   *Conclusion   183*

9   Policies for inland waterway transport: needs and
    perspectives   188
    VLADISLAV MARAŠ

    9.1   *European IWT master policy programme: an*
          overview   189
    9.2   *An approach for the evaluation of European IWT policy*
          needs and perspectives   190
    9.3   *Findings of the European IWT policy evaluation   192*
    9.4   *Conclusion   212*

Index   218

Figures

1.1 Touristic narrow boats sailing on the UK canal network 2
1.2 IWT by commodity type for selected regions 10
1.3 Distribution of infrastructure investment between modes in Western European countries, 1995–2011 15
2.1 Beatrix lock and the Lekkanaal, prior to project commencement 24
2.2 Comparison of inland waterway closures, scheduled verses unscheduled, 1992–2006 25
2.3 Importance of barge subsectors in Europe: dry bulk is the main commodity group 30
3.1 Freight transport in Germany by the inland transport modes road, rail and inland waterway by type of good 42
3.2 ITS traffic information and services contributing to transport logistics 45
3.3 Physical goods flow and flow of information 48
3.4 Multimodal waterborne logistics chain (shipper to consignee) 49
3.5 Transport processes: planning – execution – completion 51
3.6 Useful RIS transport logistics services for logistics service providers 56
3.7 Fast and smart logistics chains supporting a floating stock concept for goods with changing demand patterns 62
4.1 Impact of increase in supply on the freight price 72
4.2 Overview of supply and demand in the dry cargo sector in Northwestern Europe 73
4.3 Development of supply and demand in the dry cargo fleet in Northwestern Europe at maximum allowable draught and at 2.99 m 75
4.4 Overview of supply and demand in the tank barge sector in Northwestern Europe 76
4.5 Evolution of ARA liquid bulk throughput and tank barge capacity 77

4.6	Demolition number of dry cargo vessels	79
4.7	Demolition age of dry cargo vessels	80
4.8	Demolition and export number of tank barges	82
4.9	Demolition age of tank barges	82
4.10	Overview of the tank barge sector	84
4.11	Overview of cash flow in the European inland shipping sector	85
4.12	Ratio of cost elements in the IWT sector	93
5.1	The relatively deep normalised Rhine	101
5.2	Push barge operation on the Oder	102
5.3	The effect of the beam on the capacity of inland container vessels	103
5.4	Frozen port of Moscow (a) and water hyacinths on Lake Victoria (b)	105
5.5	Rhine at Nijmegen (Braun, 1575)	106
5.6	'Trekschuit', ca. 1850	107
5.7	European inland waterways according to their CEMT-92 waterway class	111
5.8	Historical and expected development of new transport infrastructure networks	113
5.9	Illustration of watertruck concept	117
6.1	Layout of the port of Mannheim	130
7.1	A six-barge pushtow operating on the Rhine	144
7.2	A self-propelled dry cargo ship	145
7.3	A coupled unit	146
7.4	A tank ship	147
7.5	Container ships	148
7.6	A ship adapted for the transport of cars	149
7.7	Maximum, average and median values of deadweight of newbuilt ships	154
7.8	Numbers of newbuild ships vs length and beam	155
7.9	Top-down graph of Figure 7.8	156
7.10	Energy consumption in MegaJoules per tkm of transport	158
7.11	The *Mercurius Amsterdam*	162
7.12	The *River Hopper*, the vessel developed for the Distrivaart project	162
7.13	A typical aftship form of a self-propelled inland ship	164
8.1	World container traffic and throughput	169
8.2	Intermodal and unimodal transport chain for palletized goods and the related cost structure	172
8.3	From left to right: *Madagascar*, Pallet Shuttle Barge, *Fluviant* and *Patmar Z*	176

8.4   Optimal transhipment hub locations for Build-over-Water
      and ADSEI data, relative to the population density on the
      municipality level   183
9.1   Policy-theory of the NAIADES II action programme   191
9.2   IWT labour calculation model (IWT-LCM) – required vs
      available labour force   208

Tables

1.1	Total length of navigable waterways by country	3
1.2	Transport performance of IWT in selected regions, 1990–2013	5
1.3	Breakdown of IWT transport volume per corridor in Europe, 2008	6
1.4	Modal share in freight transport performance in selected regions	7
1.5	Transport performance of IWT in EU countries, 2013	8
2.1	Overview of efficiency levels and input, process and output	20
2.2	Data to define the factor costs of truck haulage	29
2.3	Indicative door-to-door prices and transit times, illustrative consignments	33
3.1	Relative strengths and weaknesses of road, rail and inland waterway transport	39
3.2	Costs and service quality criteria relevant to decision-makers in freight transport	40
3.3	Possible areas of intervention of RIS services for transport and logistics	53
3.4	RIS information for different actors	54
3.5	Provision of traffic information across all transport modes	57
5.1	CEMT-1992 classification for inland waterways west of the Elbe	109
5.2	Evaluation of loading efficiency for continental 45 ft containers	115
5.3	Calculation of required headroom	116
6.1	Largest ports on the four river systems, 2013	128
6.2	Container traffic at the ten largest Rhine ports, 2013	134
6.3	Container traffic at major Yangtze River ports, 2013	136
7.1	Fleet statistics	143
8.1	Transport service and goods' characteristics and their variations	173

8.2 Importance of commodity and supply chain characteristics
     for modal shift   174
9.1 Average utilization rates, available and required tonnage of
     the Western European inland navigation fleet   201

Contributors

Claude Comtois is professor of geography at the University of Montreal, senior member of the Interuniversity Research Centre on Enterprise Networks, Logistics and Transportation, and scientific advisor for Transport Canada's Port Working Group. His teaching and research are centred on ports and maritime transport. He currently supervises projects on the competitiveness of port systems, configuration of ocean shipping networks, and adaptation measures of maritime transport to environmental changes.

Cornelis van Dorsser is senior researcher on port economics and inland waterway transport at the Faculty of Civil Engineering of the Delft University of Technology, as well as a business developer at the Mercurius Shipping Group, a renowned Dutch IWT company. He graduated as a naval architect and transport economist on two innovative IWT projects and has worked as an IWT specialist in several IWT development projects throughout the world. He holds a PhD on the 'Very long term development of the Dutch IWT system' and wrote the shipping scenarios for the Dutch Delta Programme.

Edwin van Hassel is senior researcher at the Faculty of Transport and Regional Economics, Antwerp University, where he is also teaching three courses. He has an engineering degree in naval architecture and a PhD in applied economics. His main research interests and expertise are in inland navigation, port hinterland transport, ship design and transport modelling. He holds a PhD in the field of inland waterway transport. More recently the scope of his work has been extended to maritime cost chain modelling. He is also involved in several research projects ranging from logistics projects to infrastructure cost-benefit analysis and transport modelling projects.

Robert Hekkenberg is assistant professor at the Faculty of Mechanical, Maritime and Materials Engineering, Delft University of Technology. He is a naval architect specializing in inland ships. His main research interest and expertise is the conceptual design and optimization of inland ships. He holds a PhD in the field of naval architecture. He is involved in national and international research projects, supervises PhD candidates and dedicates a significant part of his time to the education of marine technology students.

Gerhard Klatt is senior expert at via donau – Österreichische Wasserstraßen-Gesellschaft mbH. He is a lecturer and supervisor at the University of Applied Sciences Technikum Wien. He holds a PhD in the field of business administration and specializes in inland navigation, transport and logistics, multimodal transport, IT in logistics, intelligent transport systems (ITS) and transport security. He has been involved in several European and national research and implementation projects.

Rob Konings is senior researcher at the Faculty of Architecture, Delft University of Technology. He is an economist specializing in spatial and transport economics. His main research interest and expertise is freight transport with a focus on intermodal transport and related topics. He holds a PhD in the field of intermodal inland waterway transport. More recently the scope of his work has been extended to sustainability issues regarding transport systems. He is a member of editorial boards of transport journals and a member of research networks. He has been active in several national and international research projects.

Tom van Lier is a postdoctoral research associate in the research group MOBI led by Prof. Dr. Cathy Macharis at the Vrije Universiteit Brussel, Belgium. His work focuses on evaluating the sustainability of transport solutions by means of external transport cost calculations. He has been involved in several research projects dealing with topics such as social cost-benefit analysis of transport options, external cost savings of freight bundling, carbon footprint calculations and life-cycle assessment of transport services. He earned his PhD in Applied Economics Business Engineering focusing on the development of an external cost calculator framework for evaluating the sustainability of transport solutions.

Jialun Liu is a PhD candidate at the Faculty of Mechanical, Maritime and Materials Engineering, Delft University of Technology. He has a background in navigation technology and transport information engineering. His PhD project concerns the impacts of rudders on inland vessel manoeuvrability. The goal of the project is to achieve a highly manoeuvrable inland vessel with minimal fuel consumption. He specializes in optimizing ship design with CFD tools and simulating ship manoeuvring behaviours. His research interest lies in the field of ship manoeuvrability, rudder design and Computational Fluid Dynamics.

Cathy Macharis is leading the MOBI research group (Mobility, Logistics and Automotive Technology Research Centre) and is chair of the BUTO department (Business Technology and Operations) of the Vrije Universiteit Brussel, Belgium. She is a professor at the Vrije Universiteit Brussel. She is also chairwoman of the Brussels Mobility Commission (RMC) and of the subcommission on freight transport. Her research focuses on sustainable logistics and urban mobility. She has been active in different national and international research projects.

Vladislav Maraš is assistant professor in the Faculty of Transport and Traffic Engineering at the University of Belgrade. He holds a PhD in technological sciences in the field of intermodal inland waterway transport. His main research interests and expertise are transport planning, fleet planning and operations, transport safety, and transport and environment with particular focus on inland waterway transport. He has contributed to several national, regional and EU projects. He is a member of the editorial board and a reviewer of several transport journals and conferences.

Dries Meers acquired an MSc in Urban Geography in a joint programme of the Universities of Leuven and Brussels. Currently, he is a researcher at MOBI (Mobility, Logistics and Automotive Technology Research Centre), led by Prof. Dr Cathy Macharis at the Vrije Universiteit Brussel. In his PhD, he focused on intermodal transport and the development of decision support methods to enhance a mental and modal shift.

Koen Mommens is a research associate in the research group MOBI (Mobility, Logistics and Automotive Technology Research Centre), Vrije Universiteit Brussel, led by Prof. Dr Cathy Macharis. He acquired an MSc in Geography at the Vrije Universiteit Brussel, in cooperation with Katholieke Universiteit Leuven. His PhD work focuses on the development of a freight transport model for Belgium and the modal shift of palletized goods. He therefore developed the LAMBTOP model, tackling the intermodal possibilities for transports of palletized goods, and TRABAM, a trimodal agent-based freight transport model considering different commodity types and loading units.

Tilman Platz is professor in the Faculty of Business at Baden-Wuerttemberg Cooperative State University, Mannheim. He is head of the freight forwarding, transport and logistics course. He received his PhD from the Radboud University Nijmegen. He has been involved in several national and European research and development projects. As a transport economist, his thematic focus is on inland waterway transport, intermodal transport, transport policy and sustainability in transport.

Brian Slack is Distinguished Professor Emeritus at Concordia University, Montreal, and a member of the Inter-university Research Centre on Enterprise Networks, Logistics and Transportation in Montreal. A geographer, he was educated at the London School of Economics and McGill University. His research focuses on maritime transport and intermodal transportation. He is a recipient of the Ullman Award from the American Association of Geographers for contributions to transport geography, and was awarded an honorary doctorate from the University of Le Havre, France. He consults regularly for governments and private institutions on issues relating to ports and shipping.

Christa Sys jointly graduated as a doctor in Applied Economics at the Ghent University and the University of Antwerp in 2010. Her doctoral research dealt with the competitive conditions, the concentration and the market structure of the container liner shipping industry. This research was awarded the General Manager Fernand Suykens Prize for Port Studies by the Section of Technical Sciences of the Royal Academy for Overseas Sciences.

Thierry Vanelslander graduated as a doctor in Applied Economics at the University of Antwerp in 2005. He is currently tenure track assistant professor at the Department of Transport and Regional Economics. Until 2013, he was holder of the BNP Paribas Fortis chair on transport, logistics and ports. Until midway through 2009, he was director of the Research Centre on Freight and Passenger Transport, hosted by the Department of Transport and Regional Economics, of which he is still a promoter. He is currently course coordinator for the courses 'Management of Innovation and Technology' and 'Port Economics and Business' at C-MAT, and 'Transport Economics' at the Faculty of Applied Economics. His research focuses on business economics in the port and maritime sector, and in land and air transport and logistics. His PhD dealt with cooperation and competition in seaport container handling.

Bart Wiegmans is senior researcher at the Faculty of Civil Engineering, Delft University of Technology. He specializes in spatial and transport economics related to maritime and intermodal freight transport. His main research interest and expertise is in performance research, cost modelling and competition issues. He holds a PhD in economics in performance conditions of intermodal container terminals. He is a reviewer of many scientific journals and is a member of several research networks.

1   Inland waterway transport

An overview

Rob Konings and Bart Wiegmans

1.1   Introduction

Transport on waterways is the oldest means of inland transportation and has been the only serious mode of transport for a very long time. In former times, roads barely existed and their quality was bad because they were not paved, but rather were made of sand and clay and railroads did not exist at all. Transport on waterways offered both for passengers and goods the best transport options. Initially inland waterway transport could only take place on natural rivers making use of wind as propulsion. Later canals were dug and for these waterways vessels were introduced that used a horse or man for propulsion. The gradual development of the road network was a first step in the development of road transport as a serious transport mode, but this transport system had to wait for its breakthrough until after the introduction of the combustion engine. Before that the emergence of railroads in the early nineteenth century led to the first real competitor for inland waterway transport. The technological developments in road and rail transport together with network developments paved the way for large improvements in the performances of these modes (in terms of speed and costs) and hence created complete new competitive conditions between road, rail and inland waterway transport. Since the last decades of the twentieth century the overall trend in Europe has seen an increase in road transport and a decrease in both rail and inland waterway transport. In other more developed economies around the world a more or less similar trend can be noticed. However, it is undisputed that the development and use of inland waterways for the transport of goods is still of utmost importance as part of our total freight transport system. Furthermore, inland waterways perform a number of non-transport-related functions that also have significant economic and societal value. Waterway transport differs in this respect from other transport modes, which do not have these additional functions.

First, waterways have an important function in water management. Canals and rivers are widely used to supply water. This may be water for drinking, but is often for industrial purposes (i.e. cooling) or agricultural uses (i.e. irrigation), with the water being returned to the canal or river after use. Waterways

Figure 1.1 Touristic narrow boats sailing on the UK canal network

are also used to transfer water between one part of the country and another, effectively acting as a pipeline. In addition, canals and rivers have functions in land drainage (Inland Navigation Commission, 2005).

Second, waterways also have a touristic and recreational value. Many people like to spend their leisure time on activities related to waterways, e.g. swimming, sailing, fishing and walking or cycling alongside waterways. Moreover, people also value the existence of waterways as part of cultural heritage for their historical infrastructure, for the settlements along the waterways (e.g. historical villages, old industrial buildings) and for their environmental and landscape values (Inland Navigation Commission, 2005). A good illustration of this historical value of waterways is found in England and Wales. The extensive network of small canals that was built centuries ago for freight transport lost its transport function, but is now extremely popular among tourists (see Figure 1.1).

In this chapter we elaborate on the transport function of inland waterways. The aim of this chapter is to give a broad overview of inland waterway transport as a mode of transportation and to serve as a general introduction to the following chapters of this book. It is of course not possible to cover all aspects of a transport mode here and particularly not since the characteristics of the inland waterway transport sector differ widely across the world. The

Table 1.1 Total length of navigable waterways by country

Country	Navigable length: km	Global share: %
China	110,000	18
Russia	102,000	16
Brazil	50,000	8
USA	41,009	7
Indonesia	21,579	3
Colombia	18,000	3
Vietnam	17,702	3
DR Congo	15,000	2
India	14,500	2
Burma	12,800	2
Argentina	11,000	2
Papua New Guinea	11,000	2
Bolivia	10,000	2
Peru	8,808	1
Nigeria	8,600	1
France	8,501	1
Bangladesh	8,370	1
Finland	7,842	1
Germany	7,467	1
Malaysia	7,200	1
Others	131,269	21
Total world	622,647	100
Total Europe	52,332	8

Source: CIA

chapter will touch on some of these typical geographical differences, describe the role and position of inland waterway transport in the total freight transport system and looks into the societal value of inland waterway transport.

1.2 Waterways: a precondition for inland waterway transport

The presence of waterways (rivers and canals) is together with their navigability an important precondition for inland waterway transport (IWT). Throughout the world there are over 600,000 km of navigable waterway networks (CIA, 2010). More than 50 countries have a navigable waterway network of more than 1,000 km in length, but in the majority of these networks IWT is underdeveloped (BVB *et al.*, 2009). The largest networks are located in China, Russia and Brazil (see Table 1.1).

China's network covers today more than 110,000 km of navigable waterways accounting for 5,600 different waterways (EICB, n.d.). However, only 50 per cent of these can accommodate vessels of about 50 m length; and only 6.5 per cent can take vessels that exceed 1,000 tonne capacity. All in all, the commercially significant waterways total 24,000 km (Amos *et al.*, 2009). The three longest rivers are the Yangtze (6,378 km), connecting the mid and southwest of China with the seaport of Shanghai, the Pearl river, a major hinterland axis between Hong Kong and southeast China, and the Yellow river, important for the accessibility over water of northwest China (see Peng *et al.*, 2010). Although the majority of the Chinese waterways are of minor significance in terms of handled volume they are important for local production and distribution to riparian communities (Amos *et al.*, 2009).

The major rivers in Russia are found in the European part of the country. That part of the network covers 6,500 km (with a guaranteed draught of 3.6 m and allowing vessels up to 5,000 tonne capacity) and includes the most important river in Russia: the Volga (3,530 km). Other waterways of interest are the rivers Kama, Don and Neva and some canals (Volga-Baltic, Volga-Don and the White Sea and Moskva canal).

Brazil has an extensive and ramified network of waterways since it covers almost all regions of the country. About 70–80 per cent of its total 60,000 km of waterways is navigable, while roughly 13,000 km are commercially used. In comparison with other countries with large river basins its waterway system is under-utilized (NEA *et al.*, 2011). Estimations indicate that the freight volume accommodated by the system has the potential to be four times higher (WWINN, n.d.). The basin of the Amazon River (3,150 km in Brazil) together with its tributaries (Madeira – Guaporé, Tapajos – Teles Pires and Negro) represent about half of the commercially exploited network. Other rivers of importance are Paraguai (1,321 km), Sao Francisco (1,371 km) and Parano – Tiete (1,660 km).

The US inland waterway system comprises 41,000 km of navigable waterways of which around 16,000 km is commercially significant (Amos *et al.*, 2009). The principal rivers are the Mississippi (3,780 km) and Ohio (1,580 km). Although the network is less extensive compared to other large countries the principal waterways are able to deploy the largest IWT transport units in the world (i.e. barges pushed by a towboat). On the Lower Mississippi, it is not uncommon to see 40 barges lashed together in a 5 × 8 configuration with a total length of 475 m and a width of 55 m. North of Saint Louis, Missouri, the normal barge configuration consists of 15 barges pushed by one towboat in a 3 × 5 configuration (297 m long and 33 m wide) (Lambert, 2010). This configuration provides the same cargo capacity as two railway trains over 1,845 m long or over 1,050 trucks (TTI and CPW, 2007). These possibilities create favourable conditions for very cost-efficient transportation.[1]

In Europe the size of the waterway network of all EU-27 countries combined measures about 52,000 km, but about 50 per cent of the total European network consists of the networks of France (14,900 km of which roughly half is navigable), Germany (7,500 km), the Netherlands (5,000 km) and Belgium (1,570 km). In terms of relevance for freight transport the size of the European waterway network is estimated at 8,000 km (Amos *et al.*, 2009). The backbone of this network consists of the two largest rivers, the Danube, flowing over a distance of 2,850 km from Germany through Austria, Hungary, Serbia and Romania to the Black Sea, and the Rhine (1,300 km), connecting Switzerland and important industrial regions in Germany with the seaport of Rotterdam in

Table 1.2 Transport performance of IWT in selected regions, 1990–2013

Region		*1990*	*2000*	*2010*	*2013*
China	Tonnes (millions)	706	994	3,208	4,886
	Tonne-kms (billions)	345	666	2,243	3,073
United	Tonnes (millions)	647	661	588	581
States*	Tonne-kms (billions)	514	525	450	437
EU-28	Tonnes (millions)	–	–	530	535
	Tonne-kms (billions)	119	134	156	153
Russia	Tonnes (millions)	–	–	–	–
	Tonne-kms (billions)	214	71	54	81

* Excluding coastal shipping and Great Lakes traffic.

Sources: Eurostat (2015, 2016), US Army Corps of Engineers (n.d.), National Bureau of Statistics of China (n.d.)

the Netherlands, together with the tributaries of the Rhine in Germany, i.e. the Mosel, Main, Neckar, the Ems, Weser, Elbe and Oder in the northern part of Germany, the Meuse streaming through France, Belgium and the Netherlands, the Seine and Rhône in France and the Rhine-Scheldt canal linking the seaports of Rotterdam and Antwerp. These waterways make major economic areas in Europe accessible by inland waterway transport. In addition, these waterways are complemented by lower-scale waterways, especially dense in the Netherlands and parts of Belgium, Germany and France, but much less elsewhere.

1.3   Transport performance

The performance of IWT differs significantly worldwide due to natural, geographical, economic and political differences between regions. For the purpose of presenting an overview and in view of the availability and consistency of data we present and compare IWT performances of mainly the countries of Europe (EU member states), the US, China and Russia. These are also the regions in which IWT plays a significant role.

1.3.1   *Traffic: tonnes and tonne kilometres*

The volume of goods (tonnes) transported over waterways in China are huge compared to that of the other regions (see Table 1.2). Measured in tonne-kms the contrast with EU is even bigger: China records 20 times the performance of the EU. It is striking that, in terms of tonne-kms, the EU also falls far behind the US. This has to do with a much smaller average transport distance in the EU which is about 290 km compared to 630 km in China and 750 km in the US. These differences can be partly explained by the contrasts in capacity and quality of waterways in these regions and the role of economic corridors.

Table 1.3 Breakdown of IWT transport volume per corridor in Europe, 2008

Waterway corridor	Share in total IWT
Rhine (Switzerland, France, Germany, Netherlands)	60%
Danube (Germany, Austria, Hungary, Serbia, Romania)	13%
Rhine-Scheldt canal (Netherlands, Belgium)	8%
Seine (France)	6%
Other	13%

Source: CE Delft *et al.* (2011)

In Europe IWT is heavily concentrated in the Rhine corridor (see Table 1.3). Although the Danube is another backbone of the European inland waterway network its role in freight transport is limited and under-utilized. Significant fluctuations in the water level, causing fairway depth limitations, and unreliability of locks, that result in unreliable logistic operations and unpredictable prices lead to limited interest among shippers. Moreover, the Danube flows through a less-developed economic region that generates smaller freight flows. Located along the Rhine axis, the Netherlands and Germany account for more than 70 per cent of the transport performance of inland waterway transport in the EU. Other EU countries that transport a substantial volume on waterways are Romania, Belgium and France. Together these five countries represent 92 per cent of the transport performance of IWT in the EU.

According to estimations about 80 per cent of all inland shipping in China is related to the Yangtze (NEA *et al.*, 2011). The Mississippi river system has a very similar dominant position in domestic IWT in the US,[2] as it has, for instance, a key role in the consolidation and long-distance transport of the Mid-Western grain harvest for export from gulf ports (Amos *et al.*, 2009). In Russia the Volga accounts for about half of all river freight traffic (WWINN, n.d.). On the other hand, there are several large rivers around the world that play a marginal role in freight transport due to geographic or economic conditions, but sometimes they have significant importance for passenger transport. A typical example is the Nile. Tourists make up the most important traffic (goods transport represents only 1 per cent). Moreover, it is also a vital waterway for the transport of local people and sometimes still provides the only means of transport, especially in Sudan when road transport is not possible during the flood season (WWINN, n.d.).

Apart from the impressive performance of IWT in China today the pace of growth of IWT has been spectacular over the last decade (see Table 1.2). Institutional changes at different levels of government have been important in enabling this growth (Li *et al.*, 2014). Furthermore, projections for China indicate a probable continuing growth of IWT. This is related to China's economic development boosting the demand for transport as well as the

Table 1.4 Modal share in freight transport performance (tkm) in selected regions (%)

	EU-28		United States		China		Russia	
	2013	*1995*	*2012*	*1990*	*2013*	*1990*	*2013*	*1990*
Road	72	67	47	30	47	19	5	6
Rail	17	20	31	37	24	59	44	44
IWT	6	7	6	12	26	19	2	3
Pipeline	5	6	17	20	3	3	50	47

Sources: Eurostat (2015), OECD/ITF (2012)

fact that the stage of China's economic development is causing a demand for the transport of raw materials that in particular favours the use of IWT. With respect to the EU, IWT volumes have slightly increased in the last decades, but long-term IWT developments in the US and Russia have been moving downwards. There are no indications of a strong revival of IWT in these regions, unless IWT is able to open up completely new product markets.

1.3.2   Modal shares

Table 1.4 shows the market share of the modes of road, rail, IWT and pipeline for the selected regions. The share of IWT is similar in the EU (6 per cent in 2013) and the US (6 per cent in 2012), but a major difference between these regions is that over a period of 20 years the IWT share in the EU has remained almost unchanged, while in the US a serious decline has been experienced. The relative role of IWT in Russia, having a share of 2 per cent (in 2013), is insignificant. In China IWT has been very successful in improving its market share and realized the second largest share (26 per cent) after road transport (47 per cent). It is interesting to notice that the increase in market share of road transport and IWT has been achieved while rail has experienced a dramatic loss.

In these aggregated data for these regions the modal share of IWT seems modest, but one should be aware that IWT can only compete and gain market share in transport corridors if there are waterways. So at a lower geographical scale different market positions emerge. For example, in Europe there is a wide range in the IWT share between countries (see Table 1.5).

The quality of waterways is also important, as it determines the possible size of vessels. For instance, France has an extensive network, but a relatively large part (about 75 per cent) consists of small waterways. This makes it more difficult for IWT to compete with road transport, because IWT cannot make the most of its scale advantages. Hence the market share of IWT in France is limited. On the other hand, although the Netherlands is a small country, and

Table 1.5 Transport performance of IWT in EU countries, 2013 (ranked by million tkm)

Rank	Region	Million tkm	Modal share	Share in EU IWT
1	Germany	60,070	13%	39%
2	Netherlands	48,641	39%	32%
3	Romania	12,242	21%	8%
4	Belgium	10,365	20%	7%
5	France	9,201	4%	6%
6	Bulgaria	5,374	15%	4%
7	Austria	2,353	5%	2%
8	Hungary	1,924	4%	1%
9	Slovakia	1,006	3%	1%
10	Croatia	771	6%	1%
11	Luxembourg	313	3%	0
12	Poland	91	0	0
13	Czech Republic	25	0	0

Source: Eurostat (2015)

domestic transport is over relatively short distances, IWT has a large share. The high density of the IWT network – comparable to the density of the Dutch highway network – allows many transport connections to use inland vessels.

Just as important as the size and length of the IWT network and the navigable quality of the waterways are their basins in terms of enabling access to cargo-generating regions, e.g. areas with dense populations and/or heavy industrial activities. For example the Rhine unlocks the Ruhr area (a conurbation with more than 5 million people) and major chemical and automotive industries in the middle part of Germany (Rheinland Pfalz). The role of the Volga basin in Russia is similar. It covers 40 per cent of the population, 45 per cent of the country's industry and 50 per cent of its agriculture (WWINN, n.d.). One of the best examples of the relevance of accessibility is Brazil. Although the country has one of the largest IWT networks worldwide (see Table 1.1) its main river networks are not located near existing centres of production and consumption. Consequently the share of IWT in Brazil is relatively modest. Explanations for differences in IWT between regions and countries may also be less directly related to the conditions for IWT, but rather to the performance of competing modes. Historically, in the US rail transport has developed strongly, in particular in those markets that are also addressed by IWT. The high performance of rail transport (in terms of speeds and rates) has thus marginalized the role of IWT in the US. In East European countries, too, governments have historically paid much more attention to rail transport, considering it the backbone of their national transport system and hence neglecting the potential of IWT.

1.4 Important cargo flows for IWT

Figure 1.2 summarizes the main types of commodities that are transported on inland waterways in the EU, United States and China, based on the available specific classification of commodity types. Although the classification and reference dates are not similar, making comparisons difficult, the overall picture indicates that IWT has a particularly strong position in the transport of bulk commodities.

IWT has a leading role in the transport of ores, coal, sand, gravel and chemical products. This can be explained by the combination of the characteristics of these commodities and their processing industries and the typical characteristics of this transport mode. These bulk commodities often involve large consignments, are not time sensitive, but because of their relatively low value per tonne are sensitive to transport costs. Barge transport is a mode that combines high-mass transport capacity with low operating costs, i.e. the line haul costs (per tkm) are low. It is a mode that also provides a high level of safety, which is a favourable condition for transporting dangerous goods. In addition, barge transport is known for its high reliability of transport services, because of the ample capacity of waterways that enables congestion-free transport. On the other hand, the inherent disadvantages of barge transport are its relative low speed and limited coverage of its infrastructural network compared to rail and road networks. Thus the relatively expensive transhipment of cargo to other modes (road or rail) usually restricts the transport connections for which barge transport is considered. The transport demand for ores and coal is a good fit for barge transport as it consists of large, long-distance (and in the EU international) transport flows to and from a limited number of transport nodes, i.e. from seaports to steel industries and power plants, which enables cheap transport using large vessels. The transport of chemical products, petroleum products in particular, has a more or less identical pattern. Transports are often seaport-related and involve large consignments, predominantly between refineries and chemical industrial complexes or as intermediate deliveries between chemical companies. Sand and gravel are generally not transported over very long distances, origins and destinations are much more dispersed and volumes are smaller, but still barge transport is the preferred mode for these items too.

1.5 Emerging markets: container transport

Cargo transport in containers has been a fast-growing market for IWT and probably represents one of the promising opportunities for future growth. The emergence of container barge transport can on the one hand be attributed to the spectacular growth of deep-sea container transport and on the other to the increasing capacity and congestion problems of the road and rail modes in moving containers to the hinterland of deep-sea container ports. However, no less important for its success, by exploiting its potential for large-scale

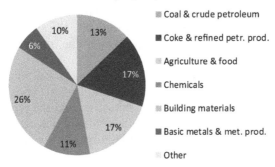

EU-28 (2013)

- Coal & crude petroleum
- Coke & refined petr. prod.
- Agriculture & food
- Chemicals
- Building materials
- Basic metals & met. prod.
- Other

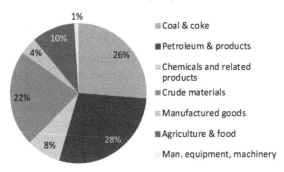

United States (2013)

- Coal & coke
- Petroleum & products
- Chemicals and related products
- Crude materials
- Manufactured goods
- Agriculture & food
- Man. equipment, machinery

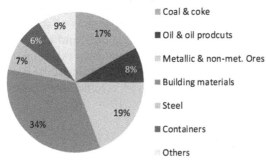

China (2006)

- Coal & coke
- Oil & oil prodcuts
- Metallic & non-met. Ores
- Building materials
- Steel
- Containers
- Others

Figure 1.2 IWT by commodity type for selected regions (Source: Eurostat, n.d.; US Army Corps of Engineers, 2014)

transport, ITW offers a cheap and cost-effective alternative to truck and train. Moreover, it adapts very well to shippers' needs, for instance, by offering fixed and regular sailing schedules to enable reliable transport services, total chain solutions (i.e. including terminal handling and drayage operations) as well as additional transport-related services (e.g. container storage) and even cargo-related services (e.g. value added logistics).

Container barge transport had its start in the late 1960s in Europe with services along the Rhine between the port of Rotterdam and US army bases located in Germany. Over the past 30 years container barge transport has experienced a tremendous growth in northwest Europe. Today the seaports of Rotterdam and Antwerp handle the largest volumes of barge containers (2.6 million TEU and 2.5 million TEU respectively in 2013) and have the largest share of barge transport in the modal split of hinterland container transport in Europe (about 33 per cent). The favourable location of these ports at the mouth of the Rhine has indisputably contributed to IWT's strong market position. It is interesting to note that container barge transport was initially assumed competitive only over long distances. However, nowadays Rotterdam and Antwerp domestic container barge traffic outnumbers international traffic along the Rhine.

Despite less favourable geographical and navigation conditions other major European container seaports also have container barge transport, but the volumes are still modest (e.g. Le Havre 170,000 TEU (7 per cent) and Marseille 59,400 TEU (6 per cent) in France and Hamburg 95,000 TEU (1 per cent) in Germany; all data for 2010). The total volume transported by barge in Europe was estimated at 4.5 million TEU in 2005. Now that recovery from the economic crisis has set in, it is likely that the volume has passed the 5 million TEU mark. Expectations are bright for barge transport capturing an increasing market share of container hinterland transport. However, the largest challenge for further growth lies in the development of continental transport. Some pioneering developments are now taking place.

The development of container barge transport in China has followed more or less the same model as in Europe, i.e. around the major seaports and similar to the Rotterdam operations (Amos *et al.*, 2009). Total barge container traffic reached about 8 million TEU in 2006, of which 3 million TEU were carried in the lower basin of the Yangtze and 3.5 million TEU in the lower basin of the Pearl river. Compared to Europe the container barge sector has developed very fast in a short period of time, benefiting from the tremendous growth in China's containerized trade. Over the last decade the growth of container barge traffic has been partly realized by moving containers much further inland, which has been made possible by improvements to the navigation infrastructure.

The situation and perspectives for barge container transport in the US are different to those in Europe and China, although the US has large rivers and huge container traffic volumes. For the last 30 years the US has tried to develop container barge traffic, but the volumes have to date been very modest (e.g. less than 100,000 TEU in 2004) (Konings, 2005). This can be explained by the fact that the waterway network is north–south oriented, while the container flows are predominantly east–west to and from the Pacific and Atlantic coasts. Other explanations include much higher terminal handling charges in the seaports for barges compared to trucks and train, which reduces the cost-competitiveness of IWT. Last but not least, IWT has to compete with highly efficient intermodal rail transport that can offer cheap rates and fast transit times. So although the hinterland container flows of Mississippi ports (e.g. New Orleans) are substantial, attracting IWT customers is difficult. Container barge transport will most likely remain a niche market (e.g. for low-value, time non-critical cargo and heavy container loads that are not allowed to be transported by road).

Due to the increasing penetration of the use of containers throughout the world, container barge transport is expected to increase in other regions of the world. For instance, possibilities for container barge transport in Brazil have recently been under consideration, for example a service over a distance of 300 km between seaport Rio Grande and Porto Alegre. While the container throughput in Rio Grande is substantial (over 600,000 TEU in 2013) it is, like in the start-up of any intermodal service, critical to have customer commitment in order to set up a regular service with competitive rates.

1.6   Added value to society

1.6.1   Direct merits

Inland waterway transport is an important activity from a societal point of view, as some data on employment, turnover and value-added of the IWT sector in the EU can illustrate. According to Eurostat the IWT sector employed more than 40,000 people in 2012. The total turnover of the IWT sector in the EU-28 was 7.1 billion euros in 2013. The Netherlands and Germany have the largest turnover (2.3 billion euros and 2.2 billion euros respectively). The direct added value of the sector was estimated at about one-third of the turnover, 2.4 billion euros in 2013. From the total added value about 70 per cent was realized from freight transport, while 30 per cent stemmed from passenger transport. It is not so easy to quantify the economic value of IWT, but some studies have tried. Taking an estimated $10–12 per ton shipper savings over the cost of shipping by alternative modes, Bray *et al.* (2011) come up with a figure of around $7 billion annually in transportation savings to the US economy.

1.6.2   Indirect merits

Important additional benefits for society come from the low cost and the high transport capacity of inland waterway transport. These features have great benefits for industries and are important for the economic competitiveness of these industries and even national economies. For instance IWT is an important mode for the energy production industry, in particular through the supply of raw materials for electricity production. In the US, 20 per cent of the coal used in electricity generation is shipped by water, while coal counts for 50 per cent of the nation's electricity production (US Army Corps of Engineers, n.d.). Furthermore, IWT is heavily involved in fuelling energy-intensive and raw material processing industries, for example the European steel industry. This industry can be competitive partly because of the low transport costs for raw materials made available by IWT. Consequently, the products of the steel industry can give added value to other industries, for instance the automotive and construction industries. Companies in the construction and chemical industries are often also suited to receive and deliver products by inland vessels.

The leading role of the US in the global grain trade can largely be attributed to cost-efficient IWT options for shipping grain to seaports. Its major competitor – grain producers in Brazil – is lacking such an asset. In the US nearly 80 million tons of grain are transported by water annually. More than 60 per cent of farm exports move on inland waterways such as the Lower Mississippi or Columbia rivers to ports such as New Orleans for shipment overseas (US Army Corps of Engineers, n.d.).

Seaports that have a well-developed waterway network into their hinterland can benefit greatly from IWT. The possibilities provided by cheap and large-scale inland waterway transport may induce shippers to route their goods through seaports having IWT access. As a result, those seaports often owe their success to throughput from the transhipment of bulk goods. Furthermore, the spectacular growth of container throughput in seaports and container transport in their hinterlands has brought another asset of IWT for seaports into the spotlight. Increasingly IWT is considered a mode to keep the seaport and its hinterland accessible, and since seaport competition in container handling is increasingly determined by the performance of hinterland chains, IWT is gaining strategic importance. In view of accessibility and liveability, i.e. air quality, the port of Rotterdam has even enforced an increasing role for both IWT and rail transport in its hinterland transport. As part of the concessions of the new container terminals at the Rotterdam Maasvlakte 2 area a modal split clause was introduced (De Langen *et al.*, 2012). By 2033 the terminal operators have to achieve a modal split of 35 per cent road, 20 per cent rail and 45 per cent water. Various other measures have also been taken to cut back road transport.

It is clear that the IWT sector can also benefit from the presence and performance of seaports because they generate large freight flows. The development of IWT for iron ore and coal between Rotterdam and the Ruhr area illustrates this. With the development in the last century of the port of Rotterdam as a major transhipment port for the Ruhr area, and since navigable conditions for the Rhine were improved, the way was opened for massive, low-cost transport by IWT (Schenk, 2015). Thus IWT defeated rail transport in this transport corridor and nowadays still has the dominant role.

This mutual interest also exists between the IWT sector and inland ports. IWT can not be a competitive mode without a well-developed network of inland ports and terminals. After all, inland ports and terminals are the places where vessels are loaded and unloaded. The necessity of a good network of inland ports and terminals has even increased due to the increase in intermodal transport, because this kind of transport involves more dispersed flows compared to the transport of bulk goods. In such a network the location of inland ports and terminals is important: nearby or offering easy access to industrial and logistics sites (see also Wiegmans *et al.*, 2015).

Although the primary function of an inland port or terminal is transhipping, its economic impact goes beyond this very specific activity. Inland ports and terminals contribute to the development of regional economies. A study conducted for the Dutch inland ports (Van der Enden, 2012) found that inland ports provide direct employment opportunities of over 66,000 jobs, a direct added value of 8.2 billion euros and a direct and indirect backwards added value of 13.2 billion euros. Wiegmans *et al.* (2015) revealed that besides the diversity in types of goods that are handled and port accessibility, the presence of a container terminal is important for the size and growth of an inland port. However, the economic impact of the container terminal is mainly indirect.

Taking a much broader societal view, IWT offers a relatively good environmental performance in terms of climate change mitigation, although it has lost its favourable performance in terms of air quality at the cost of road transport. This is not a global trend, but mainly noticeable in most developed regions (i.e. Europe) where legislation has forced the truck industry to significantly reduce emissions.

IWT is also a relatively safe mode of transport. A large proportion of the transport of hazardous materials takes places by water. This is much safer than by train or truck, because these types of transport often have to travel through urban areas in order to reach their destination.

Despite the fact that the advantages to society of IWT are acknowledged, obtaining strong political support for the promotion of the use of IWT remains difficult. One of the key conditions for raising interest in IWT is, as mentioned at the start of this chapter, having a proper waterway infrastructure. This means on the one hand raising its interoperability, i.e. creating similar technical features in terms of width, depth and size of locks for standard vessels to operate easily on different waterways. On the other hand opportunities for IWT would significantly increase by raising its interconnectivity, i.e. realizing missing links between major corridors (for example, the Rhone-Saone-Mosel link in Europe). In this way the geographical coverage of IWT could significantly increase. However, such extensions to networks are extremely rare and generally it is already problematic for sufficient maintenance to be conducted to avoid deterioration of the IWT network. Such problems are typically faced in the US

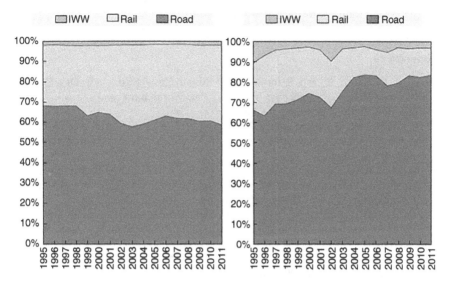

Figure 1.3 Distribution of infrastructure investment between modes in Western European countries,* 1995–2013 (Source: International Transport Forum at the OECD, n.d.)

and Europe. Locks and bridges need to be renewed and, in particular for the smaller European waterways, the permitted draught needs to be maintained. Lack of finance for upgrading the quality of the IWT infrastructure is a major problem, however. The rate of return on IWT projects is generally assessed much lower than for projects of other modes. The use of a waterway infrastructure is generally not at all or hardly charged and hence investments predominantly have to come from public funds. Since upgrading of the IWT system requires large budgets and the rate of return is often doubted, policy makers easily opt for investments in other transport modes. Looking at the European situation, investments in IWT have been disproportionally low compared to those in road and rail (see Figure 1.3). Except for the construction of the Seine-Nord canal it is unlikely that the inland waterway network will be extended significantly in the near future given the funding and also the planning problems that are encountered with infrastructure development (Tournaye *et al.*, 2010). At best, deferred maintenance and some bottlenecks can be resolved.

Notes

1 Hochstein (2003) reports that due to these favourable physical conditions the costs of IWT in the US are on average ten times less than trucks and four times less than rail. In addition, the IWT costs in Europe per tonne mile are on average five to ten times higher than in the US.

2 The Ohio river system accounts for about 54 per cent of the domestic Mississippi river system traffic (Grossardt *et al.*, 2014).

References

Amos, P., J. Dashan, N. Tao, S. Junyan and F. Weijun (2009) Sustainable Development of Inland Waterway Transport in China, The World Bank and the Ministry of Transport, People's Republic of China.

Bray, L.G., C.M. Murphree and C.A. Dager (2011) Toward a Full Accounting of the Beneficiaries of Navigable Waterways, Center for Transportation Research, University of Tennessee.

BVB (Dutch Inland Shipping Information Agency), (ECIB) Expertise and Innovation Centre Inland Shipping and (EBU) European Barge Union (2009) Inland Shipping an Outstanding Choice: The Power of Inland Navigation, Rotterdam.

CE Delft, MDS Transmodal, NEA, Planco, Via Donau (2011) Medium and Long Term Perspectives of IWT in the European Union, Final Report – Main Report, Zoetermeer.

CIA, The World Fact Book, Retrieved from www.cia.gov/library/publications/the-world-factbook/fields/2093.html [accessed 17 September 2015].

De Langen, P.W., R. van den Berg and A. Willuemier (2012) A New Approach to Granting Terminal Concessions: The Case of Rotterdam World Gateway Terminal, in: *Maritime Policy and Management*, 39(1), pp. 79–90.

EICB (Expertise and Innovatie Centre Inland Shipping) (n.d.) Binnenvaart in China [Inland Shipping in China], Retrieved from http://informatie.binnenvaart.nl/thema/china [accessed 9 September 2015].

Enden, J. van der (2012) Blue Ports: The Economic Impact of Dutch Inland Ports, Retrieved from http://hdl.handle.net/2105/12937 [accessed 14 October 2015].

Eurostat (2015) *EU Transport in Figures: Statistical Pocket Book 2015*, Luxembourg: Publications Office of the European Union.

Eurostat (2016) Inland Waterways Transport Measurement, Retrieved from http://ec.europa.eu/eurostat/data/database?node_code=iww_go_atygo [accessed 20 May 2016].

Eurostat (n.d.) http://ec.europa.eu/eurostat/data/database [accessed 27 December 2015].

Grossardt, T., L. Bray and M. Burton (2014) Inland Navigation in the United States: An Evaluation of Economic Impacts and the Potential Effects of Infrastructure Investment, University of Kentucky and University of Tennessee.

Hochstein, A. (2003) *Domestic Water Transport Comparative Review: USA and Western Europe*, New Orleans, LA: National Ports and Waterways Institute.

Inland Navigation Commission (2005) Economic Aspects of Inland Waterways, Report of Working Group 21 of the Inland Navigation Commission, PIANC, Belgium.

International Transport Forum at the OECD (n.d.) http://stats.oecd.org/Index.aspx?themetreeid=24&datasetcode=ITF_INV-MTN_DATA [accessed 17 September 2015].

Konings, R. (2005) Containerbinnenvaart in de Verenigde Staten nog geen 'booming' business, in: *Nieuwsblad Transport*, 18(42), pp. 8–9.

Lambert, B. (2010) The Economic Role of Inland Waterway Transport, in: *Proceedings of ICE, Civil Engineering*, 163(5), pp. 8–14.

Li, J.Y., T.E. Notteboom and W. Jacobs (2014) China in Transition: Institutional Change at Work in Inland Waterway Transport on the Yangtze River, in: *Journal of Transport Geography*, 40, pp. 17–28.

National Bureau of Statistics of China (n.d.) www.stats.gov.cn/english/ [accessed 17 September 2015].

NEA, EICB and Marin (2011) *Rivers of the World Atlas*, Rotterdam, Retrieved from www.riversoftheworld.nl/atlas [accessed 9 September 2015].

OECD/ITF (2012) Trends in the Transport Sector 1970–2010, Retrieved from http://observatoriotransporte.fomento.es/NR/rdonlyres/9539D9F0-0326-4A6E-A0E8-102164A5EBA2/123717/ITFTrendsinthetransportsector19702010.pdf [accessed 14 October 2015].

Peng, W., C.F. Shuai and X. Xin (2010) Yangtze River: China's Golden Waterway, in: *Proceedings of the Institution of Civil Engineers*, 163(5), pp. 15–18.

Schenk, J. (2015) A Rhine Economy, 1850–2000, Dissertation, Erasmus University Rotterdam, Rotterdam.

Tournaye, C., G. Pauli, D.M. Saha and H. van der Werf (2010) Current Issues of Inland Water Transport in Europe, in: *Proceedings of the Institution of Civil Engineers*, 163(5), pp. 19–28.

TTI (Texas Transportation Institution) and CPW (Center for Ports and Waterways) (2007) A Modal Comparison of Domestic Freight Transportation Effects on the General Public, US Maritime Administration, Department of Transportation, Washington DC.

US Army Corps of Engineers (2014) Waterborne Commerce of the United States, Calendar Year 2013, Part 5 – National Summaries, Alexandria, VA, Retrieved from www.navigationdatacenter.us/wcsc/pdf/wcusnatl13.pdf [accessed 27 December 2015].

US Army Corps of Engineers (n.d.) Inland Waterway Navigation: Value to the Nation, Retrieved from www.iwr.usace.army.mil/Portals/70/docs/VTN/VTNInlandNavBro_loresprd.pdf [accessed 14 October 2015].

Wiegmans, B., P. Witte and T. Spit (2015) Characteristics of European Inland Ports: A Statistical Analysis of Inland Waterway Port Development in Dutch Municipalities, in: *Transportation Research Part A: Policy and Practice*, 78, pp. 566–577.

WWINN (World Wide Inland Navigation Network) (n.d.) The Rivers, Retrieved from www.wwinn.org/nile [accessed 10 October 2015].

2 The economic performance of inland waterway transport

Bart Wiegmans and Rob Konings

This chapter focuses on the economic performance and the competitiveness of inland waterway transport. Both its own performance and the performance of inland waterway transport (IWT) versus single mode road transport (and rail transport if applicable) will be analysed.

2.1 Demand and supply of inland waterway transport

2.1.1 Demand for IWT

The demand for IWT originates from different actor groups. The three most important actors are the shippers (freight owners), the logistics service providers and freight forwarders (LSPs), and the inland waterway (IWW) terminal operators. These actors often can be regarded as simultaneously complementary and conflicting in their relationships with the other actors. The shipper is responsible for preparing the cargo for shipment and may be responsible for any costs associated with this. In addition, the shipper might also be responsible for ensuring all appropriate paperwork has been filed. The shipper may also be concerned with vessel turnaround times, so that it can plan its operations to match when the cargo should arrive, or when it needs to arrive, to manage their inventory costs. The shipper might either itself organize the IWT or opt for outsourcing to a LSP. LSPs are contracted by shippers to organize the transport for them. The LSP buys IWT capacity and handling capacities at IWW terminals in order to organize the total transport solution for the shipper. The IWW terminal operators also demand IWT. Often their focus is on a certain link connecting their terminal with a large maritime port. Certain terminals focus only on handling the cargo or the containers being supplied to them. Others have more involvement in other activities as well. Certain terminals might be involved in pre- and end-haulage, but terminals might also act as IWT providers and operate their own vessels. These different and often overlapping roles of the main actors lead to a diverse demand which is further complicated by the different IWT market segments (dry, liquid bulk, and containers). Furthermore the data required to further describe and analyse these actor groups is often quite limited due to confidentiality issues.

2.1.2 Supply of IWT

The supply of IWT is provided by the IWT operators. These are the actors responsible for managing the vessel while it is engaged in IWT. The transport operator secures the tonnage, crews the vessel, secures the cargo and is responsible for the vessel's safe passage. Normally, vessel transport operators make their money when the cargo is moving, and any delays, such as from lock outages, are considered detrimental to the bottom line.

The supply of IWT is provided by a large number of small operators with usually only one vessel and by a small number of larger companies with multiple vessels. In general, the small businesses strive to minimize their costs by limiting the crew to the minimum number allowed, by aiming for as much cargo as possible and by trying to realize fuel efficiency. Larger companies operating in the container segment of IWT also often strive for cost minimization. However, large IWT operators active in the dry and liquid bulk segment have another strategy. They often form part of a larger transport supply chain controlled by large energy or chemical companies. Their main aim is not cost minimization but output maximization in the sense that the transport supply chains controlled by these large companies operate as efficiently as possible. The continuation of supply and production is often more important to these companies than the minimization of the IWT cost. Besides acting on the demand side, the IWW terminal operator might also act on the supply side for IWT. In general, the terminal operator is the actor responsible for providing facilities for the loading/unloading of (containerized) cargo. But, increasingly, terminal operators operate their own vessels and in that respect also act as suppliers of IWT.

A last actor, not directly involved in the supply of IWT, is the infrastructure owner. For most countries with IWT infrastructure, the provision and maintenance of the infrastructure is important and performed by the public sector. The sector is responsible for ensuring that the locks and dams are constructed, maintained and operational. At the same time, the relevant agencies are often responsible for maintaining rivers and canals. For example, the navigation channel does not necessarily mean the whole river has to be dredged to a certain project depth, but the main shipping channel and the vessel will tend to stay within that channel to ensure the vessels do not ground out. In the US, the Corps of Engineers is responsible for the maintenance of the country's canals, rivers, locks and dams. In the Netherlands, the Ministry of Infrastructure and Environment takes care of these tasks, on which it spent 343 million euros in 2011 (https://data.oecd.org/transport/infrastructure-maintenance. htm#indicator-chart, accessed 16 December 2015).

2.1.3 Transport performance measurement options

IWT performance measurement is concerned with collecting, analysing and reporting information about individual vessel operators, the complete group

Table 2.1 Overview of efficiency levels and input, process and output

	Input	Process	Output
High efficiency	Minimizer		Maximizer
Efficient			
Low efficiency			

Sources: based on Kim and Marlow (2001), Sheffield Hallam University (2003)

of vessel operators (the sector) and the IWT system compared with other transport systems (such as rail and road). The goal is to analyse processes to see whether outputs are in line with, greater or less than those projected at the start of a certain period (usually a quarter or a year). The word 'performance' carries a certain judgement: a company can perform as planned, it can perform better than planned, or it can perform worse than planned. Performance can also be referred to as efficiency or being efficient. Kim and Marlow (2001) state that efficiency: 'refers to how well the resources expended are used'. Alternatively, efficiency can be defined as: 'the quality of being able to do a task successfully and without wasting time or energy' (Sinclair, 1992). Often – when referring to efficiency – there exists a relationship between input, process and output. Input consists of resources, such as money, power or workers, that are given to something such as operating a vessel. Process refers to the resources consumed in the procedure (relative to minimum possible levels) (Sheffield Hallam University, 2003). Output refers to the amount or value of goods or services produced according to specifications (Sheffield Hallam University, 2003). According to Ockwell (2001), efficiency is either a minimizer or a maximizer concept. Minimizing would then be applied to inputs, whereas maximizing could be applied to outputs. Efficiency levels can be combined with input, process and outputs to produce Table 2.1.

When analysing the efficiency of an IWT company, the focus will be on profitability depending on the company's ability to combine inputs efficiently to produce an output target leading to profits. Costs associated with the respective inputs of the vessel transport company – such as the vessel, the crew, fuel usage, deep-sea and inland port dues – influence the profits of the IWT company. The output – number of trips, transported cargo volume, distance covered, load factor, number and type of clients etc. – of the IWT company also influences the company's profits. In this respect, most of the data is focused on financial numbers and cargo and client characteristics in order to analyse the individual performance of the company.

When analysing the IWT sector, the focus will be on comparing the respective IWT companies with each other (also referred to as 'benchmarking'). Benchmarking – the process of determining who is the very best, who sets the standard and what that standard is – helps in making comparisons between companies and then learning the lessons that arise. The indicators that apply to individual company efficiency can also therefore be used to compare the respective IWT companies. The measurement of efficiency has received considerable attention in recent decades. Färe *et al.* (1994) showed how Data Envelopment Analysis (DEA)-like linear programs could be applied to construct non-parametric production frontiers. Charnes *et al.* (1981) developed DEA, a performance measurement technique which can be used to evaluate the relative efficiency of companies. Benchmarking can be performed on an indicator by indicator basis (also referred to as single-point benchmarking). Alternatively, more advanced benchmarking can be implemented by using, for example, DEA or Stochastic Frontier Analysis (SFA). The advantages of SFA over DEA are that it accounts for noise and it can be used to conventionally test hypotheses. But, the disadvantages are the need to specify a distributional form for the inefficiency term, the difficulty in accommodating multiple outputs and the need to specify a functional form for the production function. However, both methods can be used and their outcomes can then be analysed and compared. The IWT company's production technology can be characterized by a production function (and its corollary, the cost function), which gives the maximum possible output (minimum possible cost), given the inputs (output target). When an IWT company is not able to produce the maximum possible output (at the minimum possible cost), the firm is inefficient.

To analyse the performance of the IWT system, the focus is on the performance of IWT compared with rail and road transport. The core issue is which transport solution from origin to destination is the most effective. When considering IWT it is important to recognize that while often considered a silent industry, worldwide usage of IWT has increased. For example, in 1998, 16,698,393 million tonne-kms were moved on inland waterways. By 2010, that figure had increased to 42,490,083 million tonne-kms. Much of the growth in inland navigation over the past 13 years has occurred largely in China, which today is the largest user of inland navigation, ranked by tonne-miles (https://data.oecd.org/transport/freight-transport.htm#indicator-chart, accessed 16 December 2015). The important indicators in this respect are: tonnes, kms, tonne-kms and vessels.

2.2 The role of costs and quality performance in IWT

2.2.1 Decision-making in favour of IWT

Deciding on IWT is always a combination of the cost of an IWT solution and the qualities associated with that solution on a particular origin-destination combination. For companies offering the IWT solution it is important then to provide the customer with a solution that is competitive (in terms of cost and quality) not only within IWT but also when compared to road freight transport, which can be a substitute for IWT.

Buyers of IWT (usually shippers and LSPs) expect a certain transport quality for a certain transport cost (see e.g. Danielis and Marcucci, 2007). The importance buyers give to quality in relation to cost can differ, based on the buyer and the products to be transported. Analysing transport quality is a challenging task because different quality types exist. For example, Grönroos (1990) defines two quality types: (1) technical quality (actual outcome of the service) and (2) functional quality (how the service is delivered). De Vries *et al.* (1994) add relational quality (based on the person that delivers the service). Service quality can be measured by using service quality characteristics (De Vries *et al.*, 1994). These can include characteristics that might apply before even using the transport service (such as search characteristics). Thereafter, experience characteristics refer to the actual use of the transport service, while credence characteristics are based on trust before, during and after the service is used. Different buyers consider different service characteristics and also give different weights to the respective characteristics, which leads buyers to develop different quality profiles for the respective IWT service providers. The quality picture is further complicated by the possible distinction between expected, delivered and perceived quality. IWT service buyers have certain expectations about the transport quality, which can be linked to the characteristics. The expected quality can be considered the sum of a number of characteristics values, which are explicitly or implicitly required by the customer. The delivered quality relates to the buyer's judgement of the actual delivered service. The perceived service quality depends on the delivered service quality, but is further influenced by the buyer's personal experience of the service, by the information the buyer receives (from the provider or from other sources) and by the buyer's personal environment. Parasuraman *et al.* (1985) define service quality as the difference between the expected and perceived quality.

The characteristics of IWT service differ between different transport solutions, between clients and also between the different transport modes considered by shippers and LSPs. In general, IWT performs well on the following characteristics (Platz, 2008): transport cost per unit, ability to transport large volumes, predictability of transport processes, transport safety + transport security, greenhouse gas emissions, energy use per tonne-km, harmful substance emissions, noise and negative effects on ground water. IWT is expected to underperform (compared to rail and road transport) on the following characteristics: transport speed, network connectivity, convenience and flexibility, resistance to extreme weather conditions, and limitation of infrastructure capacity congestion. Transport frequency is regarded a neutral characteristic for IWT. The strong performance of road transport mainly results from its high speed, network connectivity and convenience and flexibility. From the customer's perspective, IWT solutions are mainly interesting for their low transport costs and if safety (i.e. dangerous goods) or large volumes are an issue. Although IWT scores positively on most characteristics, its relatively low market share reveals that those attributes apparently do not have a major impact on the decision of shippers and LSPs with regard to choice of transport mode. A important quality aspect that falls outside the focus of this chapter is that of the total supply chain. IWT quality contributes to the quality of the total transport supply chain and its quality should be analysed in this regard.

2.2.2   Costs of IWT

The costs of IWT can be distinguished between the costs of building and maintaining the respective transport infrastructure elements and the costs that are needed to operate the IWT service. In general, existing canals and rivers do not need to be expanded. However, IWT systems regularly face requirements for an increase in capacity (often for locks and bridges). When the IWT solution is extended to the deep-sea port and inland port areas, then terminal costs also form part of the total cost. In terms of infrastructure costs, IWT has an advantage over rail and road transport. Rivers and lakes are, in terms of infrastructure investment, 'free of charge'. For rail and road freight transport, however, large investments are needed, which place those transport modes at a disadvantage compared to IWT. In most instances, the ownership of the IWT infrastructure is public and the lifespan of the infrastructure is very long (centuries), leading to quite slow rates of change. However, while the IWT infrastructure is generally provided to the users 'free of charge', often at deep-sea and inland ports dues have to be paid. Ultimately, though, the economics of rivers, channels, locks and bridges are influenced by the water depth, channel design, maintenance requirements, operational considerations (e.g. low water, high water) and air draught restrictions.

2.2.3   Example of investment in an additional lock combined with a canal enlargement

The Beatrix lock was finished in 1938 and currently handles more than 50,000 ships (including vessels) per year, making it one of the busiest locks in the Netherlands. The project '3e Kolk Beatrixsluis' and enlargement of the Lekkanaal aims at increasing the vessels' speed and capacity of the Lekkanaal and at reducing the waiting times of the vessels at the Beatrix locks. The project consists of, among other things, the realization of a third lock, enlargement of the Lekkanaal and the creation of additional port and waiting positions for vessels. See Figure 2.1 for the situation prior to project commencement.

It is expected that building will start in September 2016 and will be finished in 2019. After that, the building consortium will hold a 27-year maintenance contract. The new lock will be 270 m long and 25 m wide. The two existing locks are 225 m long and 18 m wide. The new lock will be able to handle

Figure 2.1 Beatrix lock and the Lekkanaal, prior to project commencement

vessels up to 4 m draught. The new lock has been budgeted at 216 million euros, and aims to solve an important congestion point on the second busiest inland waterway in the Netherlands, connecting Amsterdam, Antwerp and Rotterdam.

2.2.4 *Maintenance example*

Next to investing in the IWT infrastructure, maintaining it is important and can be a time-consuming and expensive task. As an example, take the inland navigation industry in the United States, which consists of a system of 196 commercially active lock sites, with 241 lock chambers (multiple chambers at some sites), providing a minimum 2.7 m navigation channel on nearly 17,700 miles of inland and intracoastal waterways. This system is operated and maintained by the US Army Corps of Engineers (the Corps) as part of its civil works programme. In the US, over the past ten years, locks have been experiencing increased delays, as both scheduled (announced and planned) and unscheduled outages have increased, leading to additional costs to the IWT system (see Figure 2.2). For instance, a study of costs to the industry was conducted after the unscheduled closure of the Greenup Lock on the Ohio River. The resulting costs amounted to a $13 million loss to towing companies and an additional loss of $62 million to shippers (based on carrier and shipper surveys).

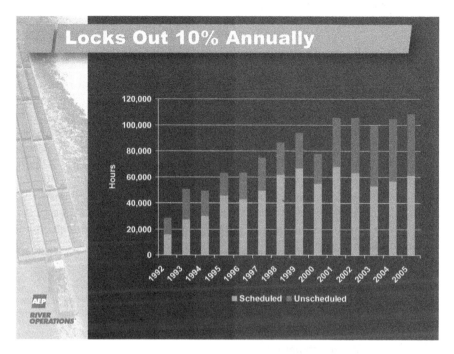

Figure 2.2 Comparison of inland waterway closures, scheduled verses unscheduled, 1992–2006 (Source: AEP River Operations, n.d.)

2.2.5   Cost of operation of the IWT service

Transport service costs relate to the costs needed to produce the IWT service. In most instances, the operation of the IWT service is private and the lifespan of the transportation means is intermediate (decades), leading to relatively higher rates of change. IWT service providers (those who use the infrastructure) have costs of which infrastructure (often only the deep-sea and inland ports) is one aspect. IWT service costs can be split into fixed and variable costs, of which fixed costs are typically most important. The fixed costs consist largely of capital costs – in particular the depreciation and interest costs of the vessel – and labour costs. Capital costs include – aside from depreciation and interest – insurance, repair and maintenance, port dues and other costs (administration, communication, certificates, overheads and others). A consequence of the relatively high fixed costs is that a vessel will require a high load factor to achieve low transport costs per load unit. In addition to the vessel's load factor its utilization rate is highly important. This rate is closely related to the vessel's roundtrip time and its effective use of this time. An effective roundtrip time enables more roundtrips in the same period. Major determinants of the roundtrip time are the passage time at locks and bridges (if they need to be opened) and the handling and waiting times at terminals (Wiegmans and Konings, 2015). Moreover, bridges may also influence the cost performance of IWT because the bridge clearance may limit the number of layers of containers that can be transported. The labour costs are influenced by the type and length of vessel and by the type of operations (day operations or continuous operations).

The variable costs consist of fuel and maintenance and repair. Fuel costs depend on the fuel consumption and on the price of fuel. Numerous conditions influence fuel consumption, i.e. sailing speed, size and shape of the vessel, force of the current, installed engine power and specific characteristics of the engine. Therefore, fuel costs will vary at different waterways, which actually makes fuel costs to some extent trip-specific. In addition, the load factor of the vessel is of particular importance for fuel consumption. Repair and maintenance costs are, however, only partially fixed, since these costs will increase if a vessel is used more intensively. Overall, the resulting cost for an IWT service will be quite specific depending on the origin-destination combination and further trip details.

2.3   Competitiveness of IWT with different transport modes and in different markets (dry bulk, liquid bulk, containers, others)

2.3.1   Distortions in competition

When the Treaty on European Union came into force in 1992 it became clear that competitive conditions for IWT operators (but also the operators in other transport modes) were pretty different between countries, and between West European and East European countries in particular. As this unification implied free market access across the EU territory, these distortions became effective because previously the national markets were more or less protected. Even now there are still several such distortions that need to be resolved (see also Chapter 9).

IWT operators face different forms of competition: within the IWT-sector – domestic and international – and with operators in other transport modes. Their competitiveness will on the one hand be determined by their entrepreneurial skills and the relative inherent strengths of the IWT mode for a specific transport compared to alternative modes. However, on the other hand their competitiveness may be influenced by conditions that disturb the possibility of free competition taking place on a fair and level playing field. As a result transport prices may not reflect the real costs of transport services, i.e. costs are being borne by others than the transport operator (e.g. governments or society). Such distortions can take place nationally and internationally and within and between transport modes. Moreover, the causes of these distortions have different backgrounds. Political factors including transport policies are likely the most dominant cause.

In the competition between IWT and rail in many European countries rail has been favoured by governments. Part of the explanation for this is that railways are often run by (former) state or state-owned companies. So governments have an interest in maximum cost recovery for rail and tend to formulate their transport policies to favour the economic success of the railways. Alternatively, governments may use transport as an instrument to support other transport policy objectives or even policy objectives outside the transport sector. For example, in Germany rail transport in the hinterland of the German seaports has been favoured to improve the competitiveness of these seaports compared to the seaports of Rotterdam and Antwerp that mainly rely on IWT in serving their hinterland in Germany.

International trade is one of the main pillars of the economy of the Netherlands and in view of that its international road transport sector is strongly developed. As a result, the Netherlands is rather conservative in revising policies that may change the competitiveness of road transport compared to other modes. Although the Netherlands may have a special interest in road transport, in most other European countries road transport is also of key importance for social and economic development. For this reason national governments remain rather reluctant to develop profound policies to combat the environmental damage that is caused by transport and by road transport in particular. Studies indicate that if the environmental costs of transport were incorporated into transport tariffs, the competitive position of the different modes would change.

2.3.2   Cost comparison between IWT and rail and road transport

The majority of transport decisions are mainly determined by the transport cost. This means that any comparison between different transport solutions operating in the same mode (e.g. a number of different truck transport solutions) or between modes (e.g. rail, IWT and truck solutions) is mainly based on the cost of the respective solutions. Of course, quality aspects such as reliability, safety, security etc. also play a role, but to a lesser extent than costs. Comparing costs between different modes is extremely difficult and average transport costs, which are often used, are definitely not sufficient. This is because many different variables influence the transport cost per unit load. Transport costs for a certain origin-destination pair are influenced among other things by: volume, distance, speed, single-trip or round trip, transport mean capacity, congestion, but also different kinds of regulation such as motor sustainability (e.g. Euro 3 or Euro 6). All these variables show that comparing costs between and also within transport modes is an extremely sensitive and complicated issue.

2.3.2.1   A short description of cost structure: rail transport + cost levels

The cost of rail transport can be distinguished in the cost for building and maintaining transport and handling infrastructure and in the costs that prevail in needing to operate the rail transport service. One of the main disadvantages of rail freight transport is the large investments needed. Both the transport infrastructure (on the links) and the rail terminal infrastructure (in the nodes) are expensive and lead to large fixed capital costs, often placing rail transport at a disadvantage when compared with IWT and trucking. This disadvantage can be reduced by sharing the infrastructure with passenger transport, but then rail freight transport often has the second right of way leading to unreliable transport solutions. The rail infrastructure, which is publicly owned and has a very long lifespan (centuries), is provided to users for a 'user charge' that enables the infrastructure provider to recoup a part of its investment in the infrastructure. Furthermore, rail terminals charge a transhipment cost for handling and other possible services provided. Important cost categories associated with the operation of rail services are the cost of locomotives, wagons, interest and labour. The transport services are provided by two important groups of providers: (1) rail freight transport operators and (2) intermodal rail freight operators (often also operating their own rail freight transport services).

2.3.2.2   *A short description of cost structure: road transport + cost levels*

The cost structure of road transport differs from the cost structure of IWT and rail transport as the infrastructure costs play a less prominent role in the total costs. Road freight transport operations can be divided into fixed and variable components. Fixed road transport costs comprise road taxes (e.g. general taxes and Eurovignet), depreciation, interest and insurance, and variable costs include maintenance, fuel and tyres. In the road transport cost structure, both the variable (or kilometre costs) and the fixed (or time costs) are important (Konings, 2008). There are two driving forces behind road freight transport trips. On the one hand, the aim to minimize the number of empty vehicle kilometres in order to reduce the variable costs as much as possible and strive for the lowest possible costs; on the other hand, the aim to maximize resource productivity (labour and equipment) and strive for the maximum possible sales (having well paid trips). An example of a possible cost outline for road freight transport can be found in Table 2.2.

2.3.2.3   *Competitiveness in different market segments*

The competitiveness of IWT compared with rail and road transport differs for different markets or products to be transported due to different transport requirements. Generally in bulk transport the most important factor that determines the choice of transport mode is the transport price (per tonne). Although low transport costs are almost always of great importance in opting for IWT, reliability is often a condition *sine qua non*. In addition to this, transit time and flexibility are often also important in the transportation of containers and other manufacturing and consumer goods. Rather than

Table 2.2 Data to define the factor costs of truck haulage (reference date: 2011)

	Tractor	Trailer
Purchase price	75,000	23,000
Depreciation period (in years)	7	12
Rest value (in % of purchase price)	10	10
Number of tyres	6	6
Tyre purchase price	380	380
Tyre lifetime (in km)	200,000	200,000
Repair + maintenance (per km)	0.05	0.02
Insurance costs (per year)	4,000	215
Motor road taxes (per year)	768	–
Eurovignet (per year)	1250	–
Other costs	p.m.	–
Fuel consumption (litres/km)	0.4	–
Fuel rate (in euros) (January 2011)	1.10	–
Interest rate (%)	5	–

Sources: Adapted from TLN (email from Mr van den Heuvel of TLN, 21 June 2011), Dorsser (2005)

the actual speed of vessels the total door-to-door transit time of the chain (including transhipment and pre- and post-haulage (PPH)) is important. In discussing the competitiveness of IWT it is useful to distinguish the following market segments in view of the dominant appearance of products transported in these segments: (1) dry bulk consisting of the power generation industry, the steel industry and the agri industry, (2) liquid bulk consisting of the petroleum and chemical industries and (3) containers, a remaining product category which does not represent a specific industry, but has an appearance across many industries (see Figure 2.3 for an overview of the market shares of the largest IWT market segments).

2.3.2.3.1   DRY BULK

Power generation industry: coal. The main customers for coal transport are power generation plants that require reliable coal delivery from seaports. Therefore, IWT coal shuttles with dedicated vessels are often in operation. They continuously supply large coal volumes from seaports to the power plant and directly return without payload for the next coal shipment. The decision to choose IWT for coal transport is cost-driven – shippers have an incentive to use large dry bulk transport units realizing significant economies of scale. In Europe, large push convoys consisting of a push boat and up to six vessels are used, carrying coal from seaports to destinations along the Rhine such as Duisburg. These convoys provide capacities of up to 18,000 tonnes, hence producing a low transport rate per tonne. In the US, these convoys are

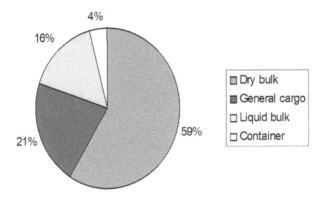

Figure 2.3 Importance of barge subsectors in Europe: dry bulk is the main commodity group (Source: European Commission, 2002)

even larger – from 15 vessels up to 40 vessels (Lambert, 2010). Depending on waterway dimensions and fairway depth the size and load of the transport units may be limited, affecting the transport costs. In this market segment the only alternative to IWT is rail. However, rail and IWT are complementary rather than competitive. While IWT is the prevailing mode, rail is used whenever customers (mainly power generation plants) do not have suitable waterway access.

Steel industry: iron ores. IWT is a major mode for the transport of raw materials to steel plants. Generally dedicated vessels run to ensure a reliable supply, which is important to avoid costly halts in production. Thus, among those modes with sufficient reliability, costs dominate transport decisions. Therefore large transport units are operated to achieve low transport costs per unit. Where waterways can accommodate them, push vessel convoys are used, otherwise self-propelled vessels. The latter dominate the transport of break-bulk products. The share of IWT in the transport of raw materials for the steel industry depends on the location of the steel plants with respect to waterways and seaports. For instance, along the Rhine corridor, the IWT costs from Rotterdam to steel plants are lower than the rail transport costs due to the fact that very large push barge convoys can operate. When the size of the transport units is limited by waterway capabilities rail transport becomes more cost-competitive. Despite this, the higher reliability often remains a decisive factor favouring IWT.

Agri industry: grains, animal fodder and fertilizers. In the agribulk sector the main products transported are grains, animal fodder and fertilizers. Despite being bulk goods, freight flows of these products are generally less massive than the flows of coal or ores. Part of the agribulk flows are also often related to seaports, since the products are imported or exported overseas, but the shippers and receivers are much more numerous and hence dispersed than in the power generation and steel industries. As a result, transport flows are also much more dispersed and the fleet to transport this type of cargo generally consists of motor vessels (small and medium-sized vessels). However, push barge convoys also operate, mainly in flows to or from seaports. A typical example is the export of grain in the US. As a result of the dispersed flows the size of shipments may be limited and origins and destinations are more distant from waterways. These conditions favour road transport, causing serious competition for IWT in some parts of the agribulk sector.

2.3.2.3.2 LIQUID BULK: PETROLEUM AND CHEMICAL INDUSTRY

The transportation of liquid bulk is strongly related to the petroleum and chemical industry. In general, this market segment is heavily seaport-oriented. Large volumes are being transported from seaports to chemical plants in the hinterland but also between plants. For this purpose large tank vessels are used and often these vessels are commodity-specific, because the cost-intensive cleaning of tanks is required before carrying other commodities. In particular regarding large freight flows between seaports and industrial sites, IWT may face competition from the existence of a pipeline connection. For liquid products that can be transported by pipeline, this is the superior mode. IWT's strong market position in commodities related to the chemical industry can partly be explained by the fact that several of these commodities are classified as dangerous. For safety reasons there are restrictions on transporting such goods by road and rail. The relevance of speed for transport decisions increases with the finishing of products along the supply chain. Among the finished products, packed chemicals account for a larger share. Furthermore, increasing volumes of chemicals are shipped in (tank) containers. Road and rail transport dominate the transport of packed chemicals and tank containers, while IWT accounts for a small share of volumes.

2.3.2.3.3 CONTAINERS

Containerized cargo covers a wide range of products, initially mainly finished products, but nowadays many semi-finished products are also transported in containers. The decisions on mode choice in the container transport sector are therefore not universal, but vary according to product characteristics, shipment size and logistical requirements. Sometimes, e.g. to catch up on production delays or previous delays in the transport chain, speed is the only thing that matters and road transport is the only option. However, in general there is a more balanced trade-off in the performances of different modes regarding costs, transport time, reliability and, as far as IWT (or rail) is concerned, the frequency of services. The relative importance assigned to the performance of modes in these attributes may vary greatly between shippers and according to specific circumstances. For instance, Rotaris *et al.*

(2012) found that shippers located close to their main market appear to have a preference for faster transport.

IWT's competitive edge in container transport is basically its low costs and reliability. The frequency of services is also important. To some extent a high frequency of service can compensate for the disadvantage of longer transport times in IWT. Nowadays IWT only competes with road and rail transport in seaport hinterland transport, with varying success in Europe, China and the US. The conditions for competing in the continental freight transport market are much less favourable. The deployment of large vessels of containers enables low-cost operations and thus competitiveness. However, it is also possible to deploy relatively small vessels competitively, since in many services in Western Europe vessels that have a capacity in the range of 75 to 200 TEU are used. Even the operation of smaller vessels (up to 50 TEU) appears viable in short-distance services in the Netherlands and Belgium. Instead of the vessel size, it is the load factor and the utilization rate of vessels that are decisive factors. With regard to the load factor, bridge clearance is of particular importance. In Europe three layers of containers are generally required to achieve cost levels that are competitive with rail and road transport, but two-layer container services are also in operation. Apart from the cost advantages, IWT success in container transport can also be attributed to the use of inland terminals as storage facilities for containerized cargo. To ensure on-time delivery, containers that have arrived at the inland terminal by IWT can be delivered on demand by trucks serving the region around the inland terminal. This is an ideal solution for IWT to overcome its inherent disadvantages of a slower speed and lower flexibility in comparison with a unimodal solution based on road-only transport.

Buck Consultants (Buck Consultants International *et al.*, 2004) made some indicative comparisons of door-to-door transit times and costs for a number of IWT routes and commodities in Europe (not only the Rhine). The examples, cited in the PINE report, included containers from Rotterdam Port to Heidelburg (a road distance of 500 km), bulk liquids from Rotterdam Port to Vienna (a road distance of 1,200 km) and motor vehicles from Vienna to Romania (a road distance of 1,250 km). The comparisons are given in Table 2.3. They show that IWT operating with larger, more efficient vessels can have a substantial cost advantage over other transport modes, although the total transit time is usually longer.

2.4   Major drivers to improve competitiveness

The demand for IWT is diverse and originates from different actor groups. The three most important actors are the shippers (freight owners), the logistics service providers and freight forwarders (LSPs) and the IWW terminal operators. Furthermore the supply of IWT is diverse in type of actor (small versus large) and also in transported cargo (dry bulk, liquid bulk, containers etc.). When supply and demand meet, prices and performances result. In theory, analysing

Table 2.3 Indicative door-to-door prices and transit times, illustrative consignments

		Road	*Rail*	*IWT*
Rotterdam-Heidelberg Container (1.44 TEU)				
Transport cost	Index	100	105	73
Transit time	Days	1.5	2.5	3.5
Rotterdam-Vienna Bulk liquids				
Transport cost	Index	100	80	67
Transit time	Days	2	4	8
Austria-Romania Motor vehicles				
Transport cost	Index	100	93	35
Transit time	Days	3	6	7

Source: Adapted from Amos *et al.* (2009) based on Buck Consultants International *et al.* (2004)

the performance of IWT could be executed in several ways. However, data availability is very limited which usually only enables the comparison of average IWT performances with other transport modes such as rail and road transport.

The final decision to opt for a certain freight transport solution is always made on a combination of cost and quality aspects. IWT performs well in terms of cost (low cost) and in many cases its specific quality dimensions might also be suitable to the buyers of the service.

Each of the transport modes has its own combination of strengths and weaknesses leading to a certain performance. Road transport is often characterized as being fast and reliable but a little expensive. IWT transport can be characterized by its reliability, low speed and low costs. In Europe, rail transport is not always regarded as being very competitive with low average speed, relatively high cost and low reliability. But when distances are long and IWT is not available, rail transport could be an option.

References

AEP River Operations (n.d.) Comparison of Inland Waterway Closures, Scheduled verses Unscheduled, 1982 to 2006, Jeffersonville, IN.

Amos, P., J. Dashan, N. Tao, S. Junyan and F. Weijun (2009) Sustainable Development of Inland Waterway Transport in China, The World Bank and the Ministry of Transport, People's Republic of China.

Buck Consultants International, ProgTrans, VBD European Development Centre for Inland and Coastal Navigation, Via Donau (2004) Prospects of Inland Navigation within the Enlarged Europe (PINE), Final Concise Report, Nijmegen.

Charnes, A., W.W. Cooper and E. Rhodes (1981) Evaluating Program and Managerial Efficiency: An application of Data Envelopment Analysis to Program Follow Through, in: *Management Science*, 27(6), pp. 668–697.

Danielis, R. and Marcucci, E. (2007) Attribute Cut-offs in Freight Service Selection, in: *Transportation Research Part E: Logistics and Transportation Review*, 43(5), 506–515.

Dorsser, C. (2005) Amsterdam Barge Shuttle, Economische haalbaarheid van het AMS barge project [Economic Feasibility of the AMS Barge Project], afstudeerscriptie [Master's thesis], Zwijndrecht.

European Commission (2002) Volumes per Commodity Group in Million Tonnes in 2001, Brussels: European Commission.

Färe, R., S. Grosskopf, M. Norris and Z. Zhang (1994) Productivity Growth, Technical Progress, and Efficiency Change in Industrialised Countries, in: *American Economic Review*, 84(1), pp. 66–83.

Grönroos, C. (1990) *Service Management and Marketing: Managing the Moments of Truth in Service Competition*, Lexington, MA: Lexington Books.

Kim, S.Y. and P. Marlow (2001) The Measurement of Efficiency and Effectiveness in Distribution Channels, Report presented at the 9th World Conference on Transport Research, Seoul.

Konings, R. (2008), Drayage and the Competitiveness of Intermodal Freight Transport, Proceedings of the 87th Annual Transportation Research Board Annual Meeting, Washington, DC.

Lambert, B. (2010) The Economic Role of Inland Water Transport, in: *Proceedings of the Institute of Civil Engineers*, 163(5), pp. 8–14.

Ockwell, A. (2001) *Benchmarking the Performance of Intermodal Transport*, Paris: OECD Division of Transport.

Parasuraman, A., V.A. Zeithaml and L.L. Berry (1985) A Conceptual Model of Service Quality and Its Implications for Future Research, in: *Journal of Marketing*, 49, pp. 41–50.

Platz, T. (2008) Market Perspectives for Inland Waterway Shipping in Intra-European Intermodal Transport, Proceedings of the European Transport Conference, 2008.

Rotaris, L., R. Danielis, I. Sarman and E. Marcucci (2012) Testing for Nonlinearity in the Choice of a Freight Transport Service, *European Transport*, 50, pp. 1–22.

Sheffield Hallam University (2003) *Benchmarking Methods and Experiences*, Sheffield, UK: Sheffield Hallam University.

Sinclair, J.M. (1992) *English Language Dictionary*, London: Harper Collins.

Vries Jr., W. de, H. Kasper and P.J.C. van Helsdingen (1994) Dienstenmarketing, Educatieve Partners Nederland BV, Houten.

Wiegmans, B. and J.W. Konings (2015) Intermodal Inland Waterway Transport: Modelling Conditions Influencing Its Cost Competitiveness, *Asian Journal of Shipping and Logistics*, 31(2), pp. 273–294.

3   The role of inland waterway transport in the changing logistics environment

Tilman Platz and Gerhard Klatt

Inland waterways consist of navigable rivers, lakes and canals. Together with roads, railway lines, and pipelines, they represent the surface transport infrastructure and can be used for the transport of goods. In the European Union (EU-28), the inland waterway transport network comprises ca. 37,000 km of inland waterways. As for today, 21 member states have navigable inland waterways, and 13 member states are directly interconnected through inland waterways. In 2013, 535 million tons were carried by inland waterway transport (IWT). The transport performance accounted for 153 billion ton-kms. Consequently, the average transport distance was 286 km (Eurostat, 2016).[1] While this forms only a smaller part of the total EU transport network and activity, it is worth considering that the amount of cargo transported by IWT is rather high in relation to the length of its infrastructure network. The network of inland waterways provides ample additional capacity and, unlike the road and railway network, can accommodate far more traffic. The spare capacities as well as the favourable environmental performance of IWT with regard to energy efficiency and greenhouse gas emissions are reasons why IWT is promoted by the European Commission (European Commission, 2012b, pp. 4–5). It has often been argued that, in order to gain a higher share in the freight transport market, this transport mode has to meet today's logistical requirements and has to be integrated into logistical concepts. Changing market conditions result in the need for new or amended IWT logistics services. Hereby most important is that IWT is capable of being an integral part of multimodal transport chains, ideally supported by smart Intelligent Transport Systems of the waterway infrastructure and information technologies for its logistics operations. As the majority of the European IWT network is represented by interconnected waterway systems of different countries and as there is ever more cargo to be shipped across borders, IWT operations become transnational, too, demanding internationally available and harmonized infrastructure and logistics services. An efficient and reliable inland waterway transport infrastructure, complemented by smart electronic infrastructures and services (here: River Information Services), is a prerequisite for modern IWT. Besides innovation in the field of technologies, market opportunities have to be taken. Mega trends coming from the European transport logistics sector itself (i.e. changing markets and types of goods, synchromodality) must be considered when planning and managing IWT today and in the future. Then, this mode of transport can be employed to a much larger extent.

3.1   Definition of the logistics environment of inland waterway transport

3.1.1   Logistical features of inland waterway transport

Each of the land transport modes has specific relative strengths and weaknesses regarding the decision factors that are relevant for modal choice. While the criteria relevant to logistical decision-makers will be presented in the next subsection, in the following the relative strengths and weaknesses of IWT with regard to intermodal competition will be addressed. IWT has qualitative features that make it suitable for the transport of goods which are sensitive to transport costs while not being sensitive to transport time, i.e.:

*   a high capability to achieve the transport of large volumes (bulk handling capacity);
*   a slow transport speed.

This explains why IWT has a high share in the transport of bulk goods: raw materials such as coal, ore and crude oil as well as minerals have lower demands on transit time. This is because they have a lower value density (e.g. expressed in EUR/kg) and because they are rather continuously needed for production processes. Furthermore, this type of goods cannot cope with a large proportion of transport costs in relation to its value. IWT is a cost-efficient mode of transport due to the economies of scale (low unit transport costs), so it is the preferred mode for bulk shipments. In this respect it is important to note that the cost advantage of IWT only appears when the transport capacity is exhausted (high-capacity usage of the inland vessels) (Konings, 2009, p. 53).

In addition to the high transport volume of bulk, because of its cost advantage, IWT participates in the growing market of containerized loads. It has gained a high share in the hinterland transportation of maritime containers to and from the most important European container ports (North Sea ports). The disadvantage of the slow transport speed of inland vessels does not have a negative impact on these carriages: sailing time in deep sea container shipping is most often more than a month (e.g. between Southeast Asia and Europe), so the additional transport time resulting from the slow sailing speed of inland vessels marginally increases the lead times of these containerized trades. For hinterland transportation of import/export containers destined for/originating in Europe, punctuality and predictability are more important than transport speed. In this context, inland waterways offer plenty of additional transport capacity and, unlike road and railway transport, IWT does not suffer from congestion. For IWT, this results in a high predictability of transport processes.

While this predictability of transport processes is particularly needed when it is required to meet the departure of a deep sea container vessel in the seaport, the disadvantage of the slow transport speed of IWT can be partly offset by a high frequency of departures of the IWT container transport services. Making use of different vessel sizes, it is possible for the IWT sector to provide a high transport frequency. In this regard, it is important to note that a high transport frequency requires large shipment sizes (quantities to be shipped together) and cargo bundling in order to operate the vessels efficiently. Furthermore, IWT is suitable for the transportation of dangerous goods (hazardous material) like chemicals or petrochemical products because of its high level of transport safety. There is a low accident rate (average), and the use of double-hull tanker vessels can prevent leakage, so dangerous liquids can be carried safely. Moreover, when cargo is carried along rivers and canals, there is a lower risk of theft and damage. Neither the transport vehicle nor the cargo can be stolen en route. So another qualitative feature of IWT is a high level of transport security.

Generally speaking, the geographical situation of inland waterways across the European continent often impedes a consideration of IWT in logistics chains,[2] for instance in the case of the transport of palletized goods from Latvia to Italy. Additionally, if IWT can be involved, in most cases, the consignor and/or the consignee will not have their premises alongside rivers and canals. Whenever an origin or destination of a logistics chain is not located along an inland waterway, in addition to the cargo handling procedure, pre- and/or on-carriage by another transport mode is required (resulting in multimodal transportation). This pre-/on-carriage may be time-consuming and has to be organized; additional costs are incurred. In many cases, the pre-/on-carriage forms the most expensive transport leg. Multimodal transport is more complex than unimodal transport and implies higher demands on transport planning and transport execution. This makes this form of transportation inconvenient for logistical decision-makers. Furthermore, suitable cargo handling facilities (terminals) are needed, and cargo handling has to be arranged. So further qualitative features of IWT, which are not in favour of this mode of transport, are (Platz, 2009, p. 4 and p. 284; via donau, 2013, p. 17):

- a limited network connectivity;
- a higher complexity of multimodal transport chains with high demands on transport planning and execution as well as terminal planning;
- a certain inconvenience for the logistical planners and decision-makers.

Additionally, the limited network connectivity causes problems whenever inland navigation is halted. It may either be the case that inland waterways are blocked or that IWT is impeded. On the one hand, this can be the result of unfavourable weather conditions (periods of high water levels or extremely low water levels, icing), caused by nature. On the other hand, this can result from human action (e.g. unplanned events like accidents,[3] planned events like waterways preservation and maintenance works). For these cases, special arrangements have to be made between logistics service providers and the logistics service clients, and/or backup transportation has to be arranged and secured. So there is the challenge that IWT has

- a very limited robustness to extreme weather conditions;
- the need for backup transport solutions.

The limited network connectivity and the low robustness in relation to extreme weather conditions limit the flexibility of IWT: it is difficult to change the waterborne routing of shipments when certain events such as blockages occur. But, as IWT is not bound to time slots to access transport infrastructure (except for locks and terminals where advance notification is mandatory), there is flexibility with regard to the times of departure. Plus, there are different vessel sizes and vessel types available to carry different types of cargo on different routes. In addition to that, some of the events that may hinder inland navigation can be anticipated and considered in transport planning. For instance, the mid-term weather forecast and current water levels can be used to calculate future water levels. Icing can also be anticipated, and preservation and maintenance works along inland waterways are known in advance. It may be concluded that there is limited flexibility in the system.

Furthermore, it should not be omitted that there are environmental benefits of IWT when it comes to energy consumption (e.g. expressed in MJ/ton-km) or greenhouse gas (such as CO_2) emissions, traffic noise and land consumption.[4] The CO_2 emissions of IWT are significantly lower than those of road transport. For example, in door-to-door container transport between Rotterdam and Duisburg the estimate of the difference in CO_2 emissions is approximately 50 per cent in favour of an intermodal transport chain using an inland vessel (Den Boer *et al.*, 2011, p. 70 and p. 97). In other cases, the difference may even account for 75 per cent or more (Schweighofer, 2013, p. 29, p. 46 and p. 66). A major concern is the poor progress made on reducing the emission of air pollutants and in particular the emission of nitrogen oxides (NOx) and particulate matter (PM2.5) (Den Boer *et al.*, 2011, p. 95). The trend towards 2020 shows an increasing gap between the emission performance of engines in inland vessels and the emission performance of engines in trucks. Road transport already uses more modern and, therefore, cleaner engines. Due to the quick modernization of the fleet of trucks in Europe the emission per ton-km will in many cases also be better for road haulage compared to IWT. Notably, the continuous progress in transport technology and

Table 3.1 Relative strengths and weaknesses of road, rail and inland waterway transport

Feature	Road	Rail	Inland Waterway
Transport costs per unit	3	2	1
Ability to achieve the transport of large volumes	3	1	1
Transport speed	1	2	3
Network connectivity	1	2	3
Predictability of transport processes	2	2	1
Transport frequency	1	2	3
Transport safety	3	1	1
Transport security	3	2	1
Transport flexibility	1	3	2
Convenience	1	3	3
Robustness to extreme weather conditions	3	2	3
Limitation of infrastructure capacity, congestion	3	2	1
Energy use per ton-km	3	2	1
Emission of harmful substance, air quality	2	2	2
Emission of greenhouse gas	3	1	1
Noise, negative effects on ground and water	3	3	1

Note: (1) relatively good performance, (2) medium performance, (3) relatively poor performance (compared to the other transport modes)

Source: Based on Platz (2009, p. 12)

the development of, and compliance with, environmental standards help to improve the environmental performance of all land transport modes. These aspects should be taken into account when considering the integration of IWT into logistics chains. To sum up, the relative strengths and weaknesses of the land transport modes are given in Table 3.1.

3.1.2   Criteria relevant to logistical decision-makers

When considering the use of IWT, logistical decision-makers need information on several decision factors. These decision factors and their feature characteristics are provided in Table 3.2. With its specific strengths and weaknesses, IWT can be favourable or unfavourable regarding these decision factors. For instance, given that a sufficient volume of cargo is available the bulk handling capacity of IWT results in a comparably low freight rate along the waterborne stretch of the door-to-door transport, thus reducing door-to-door transport costs (1) (via donau, 2013, p. 17). In contrast to this, the fact that the points of origin and/or points of destination are most often not located along inland waterways plus the small degree of connectivity of the inland waterway network incurs costs for pre- and/or on-carriage. As far as the second decision factor is concerned, the high predictability of transport processes and the unused capacities of the transport infrastructure as well as

Table 3.2 Costs and service quality criteria relevant to decision-makers in freight transport

Decision factor	Dimensions
(1) Door-to-door transport costs	IWT freight rate Transhipment costs Costs incurred for pre-/on-carriage Additional transport costs
(2) Transport reliability	Punctuality Transport safety Prevention of loss and damage (delivery quality and delivery accuracy) Compliance with security regulations
(3) Transport flexibility	Frequency of departures Departure times (time frame) Capability to deal with varying shipment sizes Availability of transport capacities at short notice Recoverability in case of delays Backup transport solutions / possibility to switch to other transport modes
(4) Transit time	Transport speed Transhipment time Order processing time
(5) Readiness of information	Timetables/schedules Information on available transport capacity Booking procedure, status of transport requests Tracking and tracing of shipments Environmental impact
(6) Complementary additional services offered	Additional transport-related services (e.g. cleaning of transport vehicles and loading units, container depot service) Additional other logistical value-added services (e.g. warehousing, order-picking, distribution planning, order delivery) Additional other non-logistical value-added services (e.g. finishing of goods)

Source: Based on Platz (2009, p. 370)

the high level of transport safety and security cater for transport reliability (2). While theoretically a high transport frequency can be provided, there is only a reduced capability to deal with small shipment sizes, taking into account the economic viability of the transport. As stated in 3.1.1, IWT shows a limited robustness to extreme weather conditions, causing restrictions with regard to departure times. Backup transport is not only often required, but also more difficult to arrange than for purely transport by road, so different dimensions of transport flexibility (3) are affected, too. For another example, the low sailing speed of inland vessels has a negative impact on door-to-door transit time (4).

A review of literature and the empirical testing via questionnaires distributed among logistical decision-makers revealed that door-to-door transport costs (1) are most relevant to decision-makers considering the choice of IWT ('all-in') (Platz, 2009, pp. 213–216 and p. 370). This is in line with more recent findings where increased efficiency and productivity of logistics processes is regarded as the most important strategic target of the private actors relating to freight transport in Europe (Ruesch *et al.*, 2012, p. 15). This economic aspect is followed by criteria concerning transport service quality. In the context of service quality criteria, transport reliability (2) is most important, followed by transport flexibility (3). Whether transit time (4) is decisive depends on the features of the specific shipment (transport relation, type of cargo, specific needs of a shipper etc.). To a certain degree, a longer transit time, when using IWT, can be offset by a reduced level of transport costs and an improved reliability (i.e. there is a trade-off). Readiness of information (5) has become a central requirement (must have condition) in the transport sector (Platz, 2009, p. 216 and p. 370). This involves, among others, the capability of logistics service providers to provide relevant information on the status of shipments all along the logistics chain. Additionally, information on environmental parameters like energy consumption and carbon dioxide emissions is increasingly demanded. For this reason, tools for the calculation of the carbon footprint and the external costs of freight transport have been developed (COFRET, 2011, pp. 11–14).[5]

3.1.3   General logistics trends

The significance of the specific aspects logistics clients take into account when thinking about an integration of IWT into their logistics chains as well as the demands of shipments vary over time. For the last decades, certain logistical megatrends are reported (Aberle, 2009, pp. 91–98). These are:

Goods structure effect: This effect implies that the goods which are to be transported in a highly-developed, service-oriented economy are different from the goods that are to be carried during industrialization processes (at a lower stage of economic development) (SPECTRUM, 2012, pp. 30–31). For instance, the customization of products, the rise in e-commerce, the shift of production sites to other regions and other related developments result in a smaller amount of bulk cargo, while more general cargo (including containers) is carried. 'As a trend for the transport industry, this means that the cargo consists more and more of smaller and lighter goods' (SPECTRUM, 2012, p. 31). Moreover, the containerization of all kinds of goods (and even bulk) increases the share of unitized loads. For example, in Germany, the share of vehicles, machinery, semi-finished and finished products as well as cargo carried in intermodal loading units such as containers fairly continuously rose from 10.8 per cent in 1995 to 19.3 per cent in 2009, whereas the share

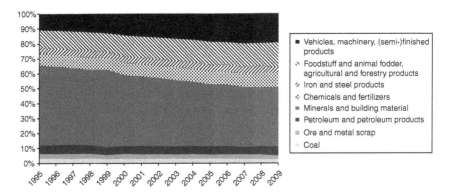

Figure 3.1 Freight transport in Germany by the inland transport modes road, rail and inland waterway by type of good (Sources: BMVBS, 2011, pp. 250–251, pp. 254–255 and p. 258; BMVBW, 2001, p. 240)

of minerals and building material in the overall transport volume of the land transport modes dropped from 53.5 per cent in 1995 to below 40 per cent in 2009 (see Figure 3.1). In the Federal Republic of Germany, coal used to be the most important type of good in surface transport. Its role declined in line with the economic development (or change). Its share diminished from more than 34 per cent in the early 1950s to about 2.5 per cent in 2009 (BMV, 1991, p. 352; see also Figure 3.1).

What can also be observed is a higher value of freight (value density). In essence, the goods structure effect is not in favour of IWT: inland vessels have a high loading capacity. While the cargo hold of inland vessels can basically be separated to accommodate several shipments, still a high amount of cargo is needed to exhaust the transport capacity in order to operate the vessels efficiently. On the other hand, the IWT industry could partly compensate for this by gaining quite a share in the transport of containerized (meaning unitized) loads. As far as the higher value density of freight is concerned, interest accrues for goods of higher value. Aiming at a reduction in both capital costs and lead times transport processes need to be speeded up, which makes it less probable that IWT (representing the slowest of the transport modes) is chosen.

Integration effect: The emergence of larger economic areas resulting from the extension of the EU, WTO initiatives (free trade agreements etc.) and the globalization of economic activities both on the supply and the demand side lead to a rise in overall transport volume, higher average transport distances and a higher share of international transport. In line with this development, logistics chains have become more complex.

Beneficiaries of this development were sea freight and airfreight (due to a stepping up of intercontinental trade) as well as road transport. Compared with rail freight transport IWT could better cope with this development because it is easier for inland vessels to operate across borders. But it should not be disregarded that inland vessels are bound to a limited network of inland waterways, so there is only a limited potential to participate in logistics chains over longer distances.

Logistics effect: Today's logistical and production concepts such as lean production, a concentration on core competences related with outsourcing of other value-adding processes, inventory reduction and the just-in-time/just-in-sequence (JIT/JIS) provision of materials, as well as the centralization of distribution systems, require a higher frequency of transport services (more frequent departures), on-time delivery and shorter lead times. Materials logistics and distribution logistics have become more time-sensitive, so has logistics in general (Muilerman, 2001, p. 212). Additionally, relating to the increased frequency of shipments/deliveries, shipment sizes have decreased.[6] Flexibility and readiness of transport-related information have become crucial in order to deal with the increased complexity of the supply networks. On the one hand, there are higher requirements on Information and Communication Technology (ICT). On the other hand, the technical development of ICT partly enabled and accelerated this development. Regarding the logistics effect, because of its features IWT was negatively affected by smaller shipment sizes and higher demands on transit times (Muilerman, 2001, p. 215). Moreover, there is only a limited flexibility in the IWT transport system, for instance concerning re-routing. Though, a 'true' just-in-time philosophy strengthens the role of punctuality instead of transit time, so, theoretically, IWT can fit JIT/JIS materials supply concepts. The current practice of JIT has been questioned anyway, and experts expect a redesign of supply chains, with an emphasis on savings in energy consumption (EIRAC II, 2011, p. 14). But only in the case of the application of suitable cargo bundling concepts (e.g. 'floating stock') can IWT be integrated into such logistics chains.

Customization effect: The substitution of publicly supplied transport services by individual transport means in line with the deregulation and liberalization of the transport market plus the socio-economic development made several logistics service providers adapt their transport vehicle fleets and their logistical facilities to the demands of the logistics clients. In surface transport, this caused an individualization of loading space/cargo holds and vehicle characteristics. In particular, this can be observed in the road transport sector where, in contrast to standardization activities and to the striving for an industrialization of transport processes, the transport vehicles are often laid out according to the individual purpose of certain logistics clients. So transport by truck became the beneficiary of this development. Apart from these long-term megatrends, further recent (mid-term) trends in the transport and logistics sector should be mentioned:

Major role for Intelligent Transport Systems: Technology has been fundamental to transport throughout human history, but recent rapid advances in information technologies promise to transfer transport management in ways that would have been inconceivable until recently. Nowadays, technology plays an essential role both for vehicle and infrastructure allowing an upgrade of safety standards as well as of the efficiency performance (UN/ECE, 2012, p. 10 and p. 18). Apart from ICT for in-house operations of commercial enterprises, Intelligent Transport Systems (ITS) play an important role in shaping the future of mobility and the transport sector. The huge potentials and benefits, however, can only be reaped if ITS solutions are put in place and internationally harmonized as much as possible (UN/ECE, 2012, p. 10 and p.18; European Parliament / Council of the European Union, 2010, pp. 1–2). Intelligent Transport Systems exist for every mode of transport, such as the air traffic management system of the future (SESAR), the European rail traffic management system (ERTMS) and rail information systems, maritime surveillance systems (SafeSeaNet), River Information Services (RIS), Intelligent Transport Systems (ITS) and interoperable interconnected solutions for the next generation of multimodal transport management and information systems (including for charging) (see Figure 3.2) (European Commission, 2007, p. 4).

In order to compete with – or complement, as part of a transport chain – transport modes like road and rail, traffic management in inland navigation has to provide additional services to allow for an optimization of the traffic flow and to increase the transparency of cargo flows. Modern logistics management requires intensive information exchange between partners in logistics chains. RIS facilitate inland waterway transport organization and management. 'River Information Services (RIS) are modern traffic management systems enhancing a swift electronic data transfer between water and shore through in-advance and real-time exchange of information' (RIS Portal, 2015). Through information exchange, transport operations (such as trip schedules and terminal/ lock operation plans) can easily be optimized, providing advantages for inland navigation and enabling it to be integrated into the intermodal logistics chains (European Commission (Directorate-General for Mobility and Transport) / Transport Research Knowledge Centre, 2010a, p. 3). In the late 1990s, several countries started to work on information systems for inland navigation. European and national research projects paved the way towards full deployment. After the publication of the Directive 2005/44/EC, comprehensive RIS deployment projects started in all European countries with connected inland waterways. RIS are

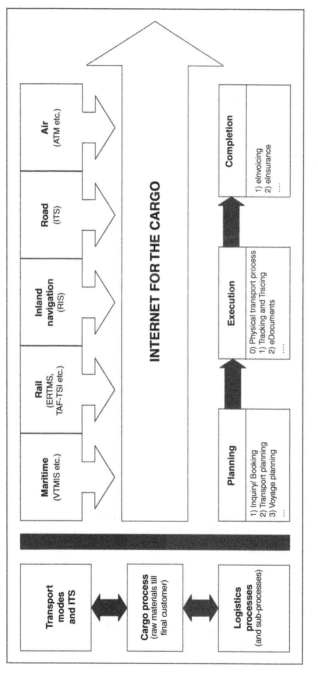

Figure 3.2 ITS traffic information and services contributing to transport logistics (Source: Reprinted from Transport Research Arena – Europe 2012, Procedia – Social and Behavioral Sciences 48 (2012), Schilk, G. and Seemann, L., p. 629, Copyright (2015), with permission from Elsevier)

defined as a concept of harmonized information services to support traffic and transport management in inland navigation, including interfaces to other modes of transport. RIS are regulated under Directive 2005/44/EC (European Parliament and Council of the European Union, 2005), which defines binding rules for data communication and RIS equipment as well as the minimum level of RIS Services for future RIS implementations. The Directive provides a Europe-wide framework for the harmonized implementation of the RIS concept and the compatibility and interoperability of current and new RIS systems across Europe. The implementation of RIS will not only improve safety and efficiency in inland waterway traffic but enhance the environmental friendliness of transport operations in general (European Commission (Directorate-General for Mobility and Transport) / Transport Research Knowledge Centre, 2010a, pp. 1–2).

Green logistics: The environmental performance of logistics operations has become a major topic since about 2008/2009. There were push factors as well as pull factors causing this development. On the one hand, legislation and political pressure made logistics managers think of their current supply chains in the context of sustainability. For instance, on different levels (UN, EU, national, regional, local), a reduction of greenhouse gas emissions is aimed at (recently called 'decarbonization' of supply chains [EIRAC II, 2011, p. 9]). It is expected that one day costs related to the carbon footprint of logistics processes will be allocated to the causer, leading to an internalization of external costs (EIRAC II, 2011, p. 14). Another example is that tenders and concessions require the compensation of negative impacts of the construction of additional transport infrastructure by certain measures helping to reduce energy consumption, to shift transport to transport modes and vehicles that are more environmentally friendly etc.[7] Currently, the focus of the public opinion is on emissions reduction, limited climate change and on the conservation of natural resources (Ruesch *et al.*, 2012, p. 19). On the other hand, on a micro level, there seems to be a mental shift with regard to the importance of the environmental performance of economic activity in general. This can be observed not only for consumers, but also for the manufacturers and their suppliers committing themselves to comply with environmental regulations and environmental management systems. A simple 'greening' of the supply chains or 'greenwashing' of transport operations for marketing purposes has become insufficient to meet the market requirements. As regards transport logistics, various technical and organizational measures have been proposed to make the transport sector more sustainable, such as the development and deployment of cleaner engines for vessels. Also, a modal shift from road to more sustainable transport modes like rail and IWT has been suggested. Generally speaking, because of its features, IWT can benefit from this trend towards green logistics. It should not be disregarded that a greening of the logistics chain requires measures to be taken to improve the environmental friendliness of the other transport modes, too. The reason for this is that IWT most often represents just one part of a multimodal transport chain. Consequently, the environmental performance of a transport chain depends on the environmental performance of all its legs.

Synchromodality: In many parts of Europe, the continuous growth in freight transport causes congestion of the transport infrastructure. And freight transport in Europe, which is carried out mainly by road, is expected to grow further (Capros *et al.*, 2013, pp. 38–39). In particular, densely populated agglomerations are affected. Road congestion has a negative impact on both the economy and the environment: transit times are increased, punctuality is hampered and the reduced roundtrip productivity of trucks, trailers and drivers results in higher rates. From an environmental perspective, the growth in transport and road congestion leads to higher emissions of greenhouse gas and harmful substances. On the other hand, the transport system is to become more sustainable to achieve the goals of environmental policy. In this context, the concept of 'synchromodality' has been developed. 'Synchromodality exists when supplies of services by different modes of transport are synchronized to the extent that all together they are seen as one coherent transport product' (SPECTRUM, 2012, p. 33). The synchromodal transport services are designed to meet the criteria relevant to logistical decision-makers, i.e. door-to-door transport costs, transport reliability, transport flexibility, transit time, readiness of information, plus, taking into account the striving for greener logistics chains, sustainability. Synchromodality also aims at an improved usage of transport infrastructure capacity. Concerning freight transport public actors consider the ideal utilization of transport infrastructure to be a highly important strategic target (Ruesch *et al.*, 2012, p. 19). Taking into consideration that particularly the waterways offer plenty of unused capacities, the emphasis on synchromodal transport planning might be in favour of IWT.

3.2   Integration of IWT into logistics chains

3.2.1   *Definition of the logistics chain*

In transport logistics, the physical goods flow is always related with a flow of information. Either the information accompanies the freight (e.g. shipping note), or there is advanced notification of transport-related information (e.g. electronic transport document), see Figure 3.3 where t (1), t (2) and t (3) represent the lapse of time. There is also a transport-related flow of information after the physical transport process has taken place (e.g. invoicing, acknowledgement of receipt of payment). So there are physical transport processes and related information processes taking place before, during and after the transport

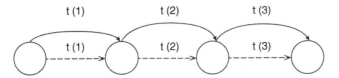

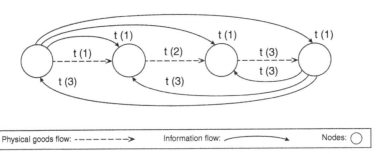

Figure 3.3 Physical goods flow and flow of information (Source: Based on Ihde, 2001, p. 194)

execution. As explained in Section 3.1.2, readiness of information has become a central requirement for transport operations. The continuous progress in ICT systems allows for the timely provision of information in an electronic form. Moreover, in addition to the ICT systems of the companies, RIS provides a new information and communication infrastructure that can be used for logistical purposes. The provision of adequate infrastructure in terms of RIS and the use of this information on board and on shore have been identified as a main field of action to stimulate IWT (Sys and Vanelslander, 2011, pp. 220–223). It is expected that IWT can only gain a higher share in the transport market if the potential provided by these systems can be exploited to a larger extent. ICT and RIS are also important for a further integration of this mode of transport into logistics chains.

A logistics chain can be defined as a part of a supply chain where products are transferred from a supplier to a customer. This transfer does not only involve transport processes, but also cargo handling and temporary storage. Typical transport logistics-related elements of a supply chain are (COFRET, 2011, p. 5):

• transport
  • transport by any mode
  • shunting, idling, empty driving

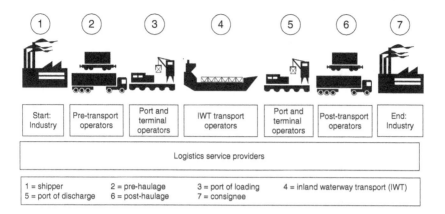

Figure 3.4   Multimodal waterborne logistics chain (shipper to consignee) (Source: Own
   representation based on RISING, n.d.)

- transhipment
  - loading and unloading of a transport vehicle
  - handling other than loading and unloading (stuffing/stripping of loading units, labelling, intra-terminal sorting and repositioning of loading units)
  - special cargo handling, e.g. refrigerated cargo
  - warehousing: intermediate storage (between transport processes)
- information handling and data management.

In many cases, and whenever the origin or destination of a logistics chain is not located along an inland waterway, other transport modes (namely road or railway transport) have to be engaged along the logistics chain. Then, this transportation by two or more modes of transport is called 'multimodal transport'. A typical (generic) logistics chain involving multimodal transport is shown in Figure 3.4, in which IWT constitutes the main carriage, while road and rail carry out pre- and/or post-carriage. Indeed, mostly road transport is used for pre- and post-transport operations, but in some cases also rail transport is being used – this especially for internal transport of bulk and heavy cargo between production and transhipment sites for accessing inland navigation.

In the following subsections, the integration of IWT into logistics chains will be shown from a process-based point of view (3.2.2) and an actor-based point of view (3.2.3), which corresponds to well-known scientific methodologies for characterizing transport logistics processes. While the first methodology places emphasis on the presentation and optimization of comprehensive process cycles, the second focuses on the particular view point of one dedicated business entity.

3.2.2   Information and communication processes in IWT: perspectives on process levels

Multimodal-based IWT processes require the involvement and interactions of numerous transport operators, like cargo owners, vessel and/or fleet operators, skippers, road/railway operators for pre- and post-carriage actions, inland port and terminal operators, logistics service providers and eventually further operators (container operators, transhipment operators, sea port), which are denominated differently depending on which literature source is being consulted. In former European projects, such as FREIGHTWISE and eFreight, the inherent large number of different types of involved businesses and administrations in transport logistics processes has been allocated to four main cluster groups: (1) Logistics Client, (2) Logistics Service Provider, (3) Regulator and (4) Transportation Network Manager (eFreight (MARINTEK), 2010, p. 10, and FREIGHTWISE (MARINTEK), 2010, pp. 14–16):[8]

1   Logistics Client: This legal business entity represents any enterprise that searches for logistics services, for instance to book logistics services for letting cargo transported from point A to B. It also provides the Logistics Service Provider with instructions and detailed information about cargo and transport to be considered for the logistics processes. Here, with regard to IWT, for instance, cargo owners and shippers/senders can be identified, who want to transport their cargoes by IWT.
2   Logistics Service Provider: This business actor plans and executes logistics services. The requirements for the services are collected from the Logistics Client. The Logistics Service Provider communicates with the Transportation Network Manager and the Regulator during planning and execution of the logistics services. It also has the responsibility of providing the Logistics Client with status information during the execution of the transport services. With regard to IWT both a forwarding agent and an IWT vessel/fleet operator can be subsumed under this important role, as both parties are responsible for the transport of the cargo. While the forwarding agent is mainly responsible for the planning and steering of the entire IWT- and multimodal-borne processes, the IWT vessel/fleet operator is mainly responsible for the IWT-borne transport process between the port of origin and the port of destination.
3   Regulator: The Regulator is the administrative role that receives all mandatory reporting in order to ensure that all transport services are completed according to existing public rules and regulations. With regard to IWT, for instance, an inland port authority receives and manages reports received from incoming inland vessel operators.
4   Transportation Network Manager: This administrative entity extracts all information available regarding static and dynamic traffic infrastructure (road, rail, inland waterways etc.) related to planning and executing

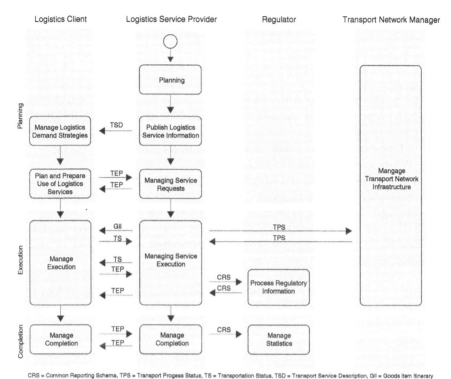

Figure 3.5 Transport processes: planning – execution – completion (Source: Vennesland/
SINTEF)

transport and makes this information available to the Logistics Service
Provider. With regard to IWT, River Information Service (RIS) providers
can offer available traffic infrastructure information (i.e. water level and
prediction data, lock operation data and fairway data), which also supports transport logistics decision-making processes.

Transport processes consist of both physical transport processes and
information processes, which accompany and support the former. Transport
processes in general can be divided into three sub-phases: (1) planning phase,
(2) execution phase and (3) completion phase (Figure 3.5). The same applies
for IWT-borne transport processes, which are today increasingly supported
by new ICT and ITS.

1   IWT-borne transport planning phase
    The planning process starts always first although during the physical
    transport process also re-planning actions might appear. During this
    transport planning process phase, voyage and route planning, resource
    planning and other actions like ordering and booking are fulfilled.

ICT support: For instance, the usage of unimodal and/or multimodal route planning applications as well as transport and voyage planning applications, reservation and booking applications.

2   IWT-borne transport execution phase
     The execution phase follows the planning phase and contains all actions from start to end of the physical transport process, such as the transport of goods from point A to point B with one or more modes of transport.
     ICT support: For instance, identification and positioning technologies for tracking and tracing or the calculation of the Estimated Time of Arrival (ETA), document and data transmission and clearing systems etc.

3   IWT-borne transport completion phase
     The final phase is named the completing phase and closes transport processes with typical actions such as invoicing, payment, but also insurance management in case of incidents occurred during transit.
     ICT support: For instance, ICT applications for efficient invoicing, eventual claiming and payment processes as well as sensors in goods (= smart cargo) and vehicles.

River Information Services can contribute to all three main transport logistics process phases:

1   RIS can support transport planning by providing inland waterway infrastructure-based information (i.e. water levels/predictions, vertical clearance information about road/rail bridges, lock operation status) to logistics personnel enabling them to consider this information for the multimodal transport planning work.

2   RIS has the potential to support the transport execution phase by offering its users position information in relation to inland vessels and/or unpropelled inland vessels as well as tracking and tracking services for following the respective transport. Hereby, RIS can also support port and terminal operators on their day-to-day operational work such as berth planning, transhipment, but also the optimization of pre- and post-carriage.

3   RIS can also support the completion phase by providing information, which becomes essential once the IWT-borne transport process has been accomplished. Hereby, available tracking and tracing information can also be used for managing vessel accidents that occurred en route. Besides, available tracking and tracing information can also foster the invoicing and payment processes by indicating faster and more transparently where and when the IWT-borne transport process has been finalized.

Table 3.3 shows these possible areas of intervention of RIS services for transport and logistics.

The different types of transport logistics operators have interests in divergent kinds of information they need both for planning and managing their

Table 3.3 Possible areas of intervention of RIS services for transport and logistics

Logistics processes	Possible areas of intervention of RIS services for transport and logistics operations	
Planning phase	• Transport planning based on waterway infrastructure data (ETA calculation support, water levels and prognoses, vertical/bridge clearance information, lock operation status information etc.)	
	• Voyage planning and fleet management	Electronic
Execution phase	• Tracking and tracing of (unpropelled) inland vessels	data exchange and document
	• Event management of on-going inland waterway transport	management (all phases)
	• Port and terminal (berthing, transhipment, pre- and post-carriage etc.)	
Completion phase	• Invoicing and controlling processes	

Source: Based on European Commission (Directorate-General for Mobility and Transport) / Transport Research Knowledge Centre (2010a, p. 29)

transport operations. For instance, RIS information can help logistics service providers by informing them about current and (to a degree) future water levels, which are needed for optimizing transport efficiency and capacity (see Table 3.4). Whether a vessel can pass under a bridge depends on the bridge clearance above the water level and the highest point of the vessel (via donau, 2013, p. 56), which differs depending on whether the vessel is fully loaded or empty. In some cases it might happen that a fully loaded vessel can pass a certain bridge on its way to the port of destination, but after unloading all transported cargo at this port there might be a problem to pass the bridge again. Therefore vertical clearance information about bridges (i.e. road, rail, pipelines, energy networks) are essential for inland vessel/fleet operators, but might be of interest also for the logistics service providers, when planning the multimodal-based IWT transport orders.

3.2.3 Information and communication processes in IWT: perspectives on stakeholder levels

In line with the different actors presented in the preceding subsection, in the following, the individual interests of these sectors regarding ICT processes are outlined in more detail:

1 IWT operators
2 inland port and terminal operators
3 logistics service providers (road and rail operators).

Table 3.4 RIS information for different actors

RIS information for (…)	Inland vessel and fleet operators	Inland ports and terminals	Logistics service providers
PLANNING			
Position data	1	1	1
ETA calculation	1	2	2
Vertical clearance (bridges, …)	1	3	2
Water level / prognoses	1	3	2
Lock operation information	1	3	2
Lock reservation	1	3	3
Voyage planning	1	3	3
EXECUTION			
Tracking and tracing	1	2	1
Berth occupancy	2	1	3
Cargo operation	2	1	3
Vessel operation	2	1	3
Fleet management	1	3	3

Note: (1) High interest; (2) For information only; (3) Less interest

Source: RISING (2012, p. 5)

3.2.3.1   IWT operators

For efficient communication processes modern ICT technologies are a prerequisite. Regarding ICT for IWT operators the availability of a computer or similar hardware device and access to the Internet are important preconditions for exchanging information with the shore. According to several surveys, with almost 900 to 1,600 respondents per survey, conducted by the Federal Water and Shipping Administration of Germany regarding equipment on board inland vessels in the years 1998, 2003 and 2008, the penetration of computer equipment on board has steadily increased, from ca. 34 per cent in 1998, to ca. 70 per cent in 2003 and ca. 77 per cent in 2008 (Federal Water and Shipping Administration of Germany, 2008, p. 1). In parallel the Internet equipment on board has been growing from ca. 12 per cent in 1998, to ca. 39 per cent in 2003 and ca. 59 per cent in 2008 (Federal Water and Shipping Administration of Germany, 2008, p. 1). About 14 per cent also make use of water depth information, whereas almost 10 per cent use this information also for their vessel loading (Federal Water and Shipping Administration of Germany, 2008, p. 1). These selected examples demonstrate the high importance of the provision of waterway infrastructure information to transport logistics operators enabling them to optimize their business efficiency. Apart from infrastructure and traffic information, RIS can also manage voyage and cargo-related information for IWT operators. Regarding electronic reporting for instance, electronic reporting on dangerous goods is frequently used in Austria, while electronic reporting of containers is common on the Rhine today.

3.2.3.2 Inland port and terminal operators

Inland vessels leave and enter inland ports and terminals during their voyages. In this context inland ports act as transhipment hubs for IWT-borne transport, where cargo is loaded and unloaded to/from inland vessels and vessels from/ to road, rail or maritime modes of transport.

Inland ports and terminals need certain transport information to prepare and manage their operational processes. On the one hand ports and terminals can use standardized or proprietary transport software solutions for increasing the efficiency of yard planning, storage capacity etc. On the other hand ports and terminals can also make use of traffic information, based for instance on RIS, for further optimization of their businesses.

For example ports and terminal operators might have an interest in the following traffic-related information for optimizing their port facilities (i.e. terminal, quay, transhipment equipment and personnel, pre- and post-carriage traffic in ports) in an efficient manner:

- position data of ingoing vessels, based on RIS data
- ETA of ingoing vessels, enriched by RIS data
- vessel tracking and tracing of ingoing vessels, based on RIS data
- cargo tracking and tracing of ingoing vessels, based on RIS data
- electronic arrival/ departure service
- berth management
- vessel management in ports/ terminals etc.

Business example
An inland port/terminal arrival and departure service allows an inland port to carry out monitoring of in-going and out-going inland vessels automatically. In order to set up such a service based on RIS, a 'Geofence' function is necessary to build a virtual electronic fence around all port basins. The arrival and departure service automatically generates a message when a vessel enters or leaves one of the port basins. The automatically generated message will be sent to the responsible person of the competent port authority of the particular inland port. If a vessel passes the marked area, an event will be triggered and the competent authority will be informed by email when the vessel arrives in or departs from the port facilitating reporting formalities. The benefits for an inland port and terminal operator are improvements in the allocation of its in-house resources, measureable in terms of fewer time resources and lower costs, due to more efficient transaction processes with ingoing and outgoing inland vessels inside the port and terminal areas. This RIS service can also be the basic service for further value added services, such

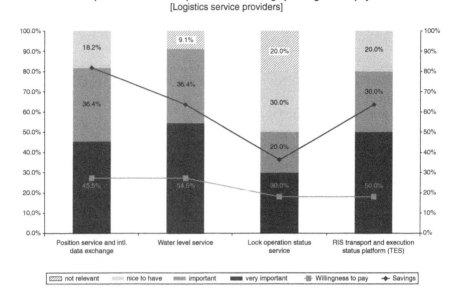

Figure 3.6 Useful RIS transport logistics services for logistics service providers (Source: RISING, 2011, p. 32)

as vessel and cargo tracking and tracing for which, besides exact position data, also data about the vessel arrival and departure locations and times are essential.

3.2.3.3   *Logistics service providers*

The architects of the entire transport and logistics chain – meaning logistics service providers, forwarding agents etc. – also need information for managing their businesses. According to a study of the European project RISING, in which 42 interviews with stakeholders from the European IWT transport logistics sectors have been conducted, logistics service providers are also interested in receiving ITS traffic information, such as RIS for their commercial actions (Figure 3.6).

Logistics service providers are mostly interested in receiving the position data of inland vessels (ca. 82 per cent), ideally from all river corridors based on international RIS data exchange, and in water level information (ca. 91 per cent) including, besides current values, also prognosis data. With the receipt of position data logistics service providers are at least informed about the current position and status of an IWT-based multimodal transport, based on which estimated times of arrival (ETA) at the port of destination can be calculated. This is highly important for road and rail transport operators engaged for pre- and post-carriage, because they need this information as an

Table 3.5 Provision of traffic information across all transport modes

	Safety	Efficiency	Environment
Improved quality of traffic management and traffic information	X	X	X
Increased level of transport safety through alerts in case of events, well-informed rescue service, maintenance service and ITS users	X		
Improved suggestions for, and information on, events (e.g. infrastructure congestion), modal choice, route planning, ease of intermodal transfer options		X	X
Savings in cost and time for ITS users		X	

Source: Based on bmvit (2011, p. 8)

input for their transport and resource planning (e.g. fleet management, route planning). For railway undertakings engaged in on-carriage, when trains have to wait for the cargo to be loaded onto the wagons, wagon demurrage may be charged in case of a delayed arrival of the relevant inland vessel(s). And road haulage operators engaged in container terminal trucking to and from inland container terminals expect to spend less than half an hour for a pickup in a terminal (or delivery, respectively). Generally speaking, in order to enhance collaboration between the transport modes and to increase the efficiency of the multimodal transport chain, ITS traffic information should be made available to users of other transport modes as well (bmvit, 2011, p. 8). This measure helps to make transport more sustainable (Table 3.5).

By making use of river infrastructure data, such as water level information and prognosis, logistics service providers, as well as inland shipping companies, can calculate the optimal transport volumes to be loaded on vessels or eventually to be transhipped between inland vessels during transit, if water levels are critical. Just as important for logistics service providers as the position data of inland vessels are services related to inland vessel and cargo tracking and tracing (80 per cent), here named the 'RIS transport and execution status platform (TES)', where not only inland vessels can be monitored, but also the transported cargoes, which contributes to the approach of 'floating stock': the cargo loaded onto inland vessels represents pipeline inventory; then, the cargo hold of the inland vessels can be regarded as a floating warehouse. Consequently, for the period of a vessel's voyage, warehousing costs are replaced by transport costs. Particularly in the bulk sector major cargo owners manage their inventory taking into account pipeline inventory, so they request information on where the cargo is.

As can also be seen in Figure 3.6, only 50 per cent of all interviewed logistics service providers are interested in receiving information about locks and their current service levels. The main reason for this relatively low rate of interest in this RIS traffic information could be the circumstance that IWT vessel/fleet operators are rather the primary addressees and beneficiaries of these data using them for their day-to-day voyage planning and vessel operation processes than logistics service providers who are mainly interested in transport and logistics data. The majority of all logistics service providers have recognized the potential savings to be made by making use of such new RIS transport logistics services for their in-house process flows and transactions, but only a minority of the interviewed stakeholders is also willing to pay for such services (see again Figure 3.6). We can conclude therefore that logistics service providers would mostly be interested in the following kinds of information, which can also be partly delivered and/or enriched by ITS services:

- position data of inland vessels (ideally available on a transnational level)
- Estimated Time of Arrival (ETA) of in- and outgoing vessels
- vessel tracking and tracing
- cargo tracking and tracing
- river traffic infrastructure information, such as:
  - water level and prognosis data
  - lock status information.

3.3   Outlook: opportunities and challenges for IWT in logistics

3.3.1   *Market opportunities for IWT*

IWT is widely used for the transport of dry bulk, liquid bulk and the carriage of maritime containers to and from the seaports. But taking into consideration the findings of the previous sections it can be stated that the logistical features of IWT basically allow for the further exploitation of additional market potential. 'The IWT sector offers many opportunities for technological innovation in vessels and new logistical concepts, whereby the vessel becomes part of new or existing supply chains' (De Vries, 2009, p. 43). In recent decades, from the perspective of the IWT sector, the following market segments could be addressed:

> **Transport of project cargo**: With the generous dimensions of vessel cargo holds, IWT is suitable for the transportation of heavy and outsized goods. Examples are rotor blades for windmills, large-sized transformers, machinery etc. Limitations for the transport of project cargo along the road and rail network and the relatively simple installation of terminals along inland waterways make IWT attractive for this type of goods. Normally, there is pre-/on-carriage by another transport mode. For this kind of multimodal IWT-based logistics chain a high predictability of transport processes is demanded. RIS can provide relevant information for related transport planning and execution. On the other hand, the high degree of flexibility provided by road transport is not required for this

kind of cargo because in the planning of the transport of investment goods there is usually a longer preparation time.

Integration of IWT into reverse logistics chains: IWT has been engaged for the carriage of scrap metal for a long time. In some European conurbations IWT-based logistics chains have now been developed for the transport of household waste and recyclable material such as glass and paper. In these cases special containers are used for intermodal transport solutions, with pre-/on-carriage by road. Waste is sensitive to transport cost and does not require fast delivery, so this type of goods fits the features of IWT. Given there is sufficient storage space at the yard there is the possibility for cargo bundling to fill the vessels' capacities (in order to reduce transport costs). Increased urbanization of the population and the related consumption of goods will increase the market opportunities for IWT in this segment, albeit rather on a regional level. Moreover, the disposal of industrial waste has also been carried out by IWT. In this context, in addition to the low level of transport costs, in case of dangerous goods disposal the high level of transport safety is in favour of IWT, too. More generally, it is expected that the scarcity of resources will increase the relevance of reverse logistics systems and the related logistics services, implying an expanding market for logistics services.

Transport of new road vehicles by IWT: The high level of transport safety and security as well as the punctuality provided by IWT allow for transport solutions where newly built cars, vans, trucks, buses, and agricultural machinery are distributed using IWT. This form of transport is based on roll-on/roll-off vessels allowing for fast horizontal transhipment. Such logistics chains can only be operated in an economically viable manner if the vessels offer sufficient capacity to achieve economies of scale in IWT operation and if pre-carriage distances to rivers and canals are short (high costs are incurred for pre-carriage by road). Fortunately, in Europe, the geographical locations of major car distributors and/or manufacturers can be found alongside inland waterways. Although the production capacity of the car manufacturing industry is not expected to be significantly increased, and although there is competition from the rail freight sector, in this segment IWT can deal with the implications of the logistical trends, i.e.:

- There is an increased share of vehicles and machinery in the growing total land transport volume, resulting in an additional market potential for IWT despite a possible stagnation of the automotive sector (goods structure and integration effect).
- Transport services for new road vehicles have been established on the free flowing rivers (Rhine and Danube), which means that there are no locks that have to be passed during the voyage. Consequently, on medium distances transit times are competitive as against transport by road and by rail. Thus, the capital costs incurred for in-transit

inventory resulting from the high value of this type of cargo are more or less the same and do not represent a reason to prefer other modes than IWT in modal choice (goods structure and logistics effect).

- The high quality performance of IWT allows for on time delivery without a risk of theft or damage to the cargo. This is particularly important for this type of freight (logistics effect).
- There are dedicated vessels accommodating rolling cargo (customization effect).
- The development and use of RIS supports the need for the provision of updated information during all stages of the transport process (major role for Intelligent Transport Systems).
- As an environmentally friendly transport mode offering plenty of additional capacity IWT can cope with the concepts of green logistics and synchromodality.

Hinterland transport of maritime containers on shorter distance: In its White Paper the European Commission aims at a modal shift of 30 per cent of road freight over 300 km to other modes such as rail or waterborne transport by 2030 (European Commission, 2011, p. 9). In doing so, the European Commission expects that transport over short and medium distances will considerably remain on trucks (European Commission, 2011, p. 7). As far as container hinterland transport is concerned, there may be additional transport volume being carried over shorter distances that can be shifted to IWT: Many inland waterway container transport services have been set up in the hinterland of major European seaports on shorter distances (<50 km). While in former times IWT of containers to and from the seaports was said to be cost-efficient on longer distances only, it was found that for IWT it is not a minimum break-even distance, but the roundtrip productivity of inland vessels and the deployment of vessels of a proper size that are decisive for the economic viability of the transport service. As far as the launch of short-distance IWT container transport services is concerned, the most important requirements that are to be fulfilled are: suitable transport bundling concepts; collaboration of shippers, deep sea container terminals, inland container terminals and IWT container operators; timeliness regarding the exchange of relevant information; organizational re-design of the logistics chains.

Transport of palletized loads in continental intermodal transport: Along certain transport routes in Europe, IWT is engaged for the transport of palletized cargo. Thereby, either continental intermodal loading units are carried in a transport system similar to the inland waterway container transport services in the hinterland of the seaports, or the underlying logistical concepts are based on the deployment of pallet-carrying vessels. A large market potential has been identified, but several requirements have to be met: efficient cargo bundling, easy intermodal load transfer, guaranteed lead times, backup transportation in case of events, the provision of complete transport-related service packages, plus the reliance on intermodal loading units providing the loading capacity of a standard semi-trailer (Platz, 2009, p. 373). The general logistics trends increase the market potential in this segment, but there are high quality requirements of the logistics clients that have to be considered by logistics service providers, and IWT has to compete with door-to-door road transport with its specific strengths like network flexibility, transport speed, connectivity, continuous cargo monitoring etc. One prerequisite is that logistics clients need to adjust their current logistics systems in accordance with the features of waterborne continental intermodal logistics chains. In practice it could turn out to become a major challenge.

For palletized raw material, semi-finished products and industrial goods, the emphasis in just-in-time-based materials logistics concepts should be set on punctuality (timeliness) while allowing for longer lead times. Inland ports and terminals with their storage capacity can act as buffers from where the goods are delivered just-in-time. For palletized consumer goods showing peaks in demand the floating stock concept could be implemented in a way that minimum demand is covered by pre-orders that are sustainably shipped via inland waterways ('SMART'). The information on additional demand can be provided by merchandise information systems (MIS), resulting in reorders that are speedily shipped via road ('FAST'). In the end, this will lead to a parallel use of the land transport modes for certain supply chains. As can be seen in Figure 3.7, decentralized warehousing and the provision of relevant information to the supplier (like sales volumes and inventory on hand) will then be necessary for the proper transport planning.

Urban freight logistics: The environmental benefits of IWT, the congested roads and restrictions on freight transport as well as the scarce availability of areas for goods distribution centres in urban areas led to the development of intermodal transport solutions where IWT is used for the distribution of goods of higher value, even on shorter distances. For example, there are short-distance logistics chains where IWT is used for the supply of pubs, restaurants and supermarkets in cities, served from regional distribution centres (RDC). For another example, IWT is reported to be engaged for parcel delivery services, with a sorting of parcels for last-mile delivery tours during waterway transportation. Combined with other environmentally friendly transport vehicles engaged in delivery tours such as bikes, e-bikes and electric cars, low-emission logistics operations should be supported. The short distance where IWT is used allows for next-day deliveries in urban areas (i.e. meeting the demands of time-based logistics). If intermodal terminal infrastructure is lacking, the vessels can be equipped with on-board handling equipment like cranes ('self-loading inland vessels').

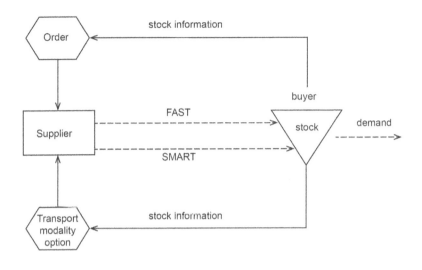

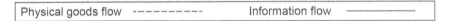

Figure 3.7 Fast and smart logistics chains supporting a floating stock concept for goods
 with changing demand patterns (Source: Based on De Vries (2009, p. 55))

Supply of urban construction sites: While IWT has always been involved
in the transportation of construction material such as sand, gravel etc.,
in some agglomerations IWT has become a preferred mode of transport
for the supply of construction sites. For this purpose, temporary load
transfer facilities have been established in urban areas which will be used
until the work is completed. This helps to avoid inbound and outbound
truck trips. There is limited market potential, though. The reason is that
the building industry does not have so many major building projects in
highly-developed countries.

Transport of sensitive goods: There have been successful trials where
sensitive goods such as plants and horticultural products or perishables
such as fruit and vegetables are carried by IWT. Reefer container
technology allows for a conditioning of temperature and climate
surrounding the cargo. In these logistics chains, IWT is chosen mainly
because of its reliability. Information about the status of the vessel's
voyage and the cargo are of high relevance.

Transport of biomass: As the sources of energy are subject to changes
the reduction in the IWT of fossil sources of energy such as coal, oil and
gas could partly be compensated for by the transport of other sources of
energy such as pellets for heating systems and biomass destined for power
stations, to name but a few. This has to be seen in the context of the goods

structure effect. The IWT industry has already recognized the market potential for this type of cargo and can refer to its relevant capabilities regarding the transport of biomass (via donau, 2015, pp. 6–7).

This list of emerging market segments for IWT shows that there are chances for the industry to attract new business in spite of the change in overall goods structure, current freight transport and logistics requirements, and the geographical relocation of businesses and logistics chains. The trends towards green logistics, synchromodality and the promotion and use of ITS to improve transport logistics operations can be taken up. Nonetheless, certain challenges will have to be faced to achieve a further integration of IWT into logistics chains.

3.3.2   Legal conditions, frameworks and limitations

According to the results of recent research and development (R&D) projects, to open up new markets for IWT, particularly in the segment of intermodal transport two preconditions have to be fulfilled (Kwak and van de Kamp, 2013, p. 12): vertical and horizontal cooperation along the supply chain and the effective exchange of information between the cooperating partners. This also includes the willingness to share relevant information, so the information can be jointly used. Both information stemming from ICT systems of the private sector and ITS/RIS are concerned. Are there any legal conditions and/or limitations to be considered, when making use of modern information and communications technologies in the field of European inland waterway transport? The following, selected examples should highlight the current and eventual future issues still left open with respect to legal affairs.

> **Personal data**: Nowadays, discussions about the protection of personal data are increasing on a general societal level. This becomes relevant not only for natural persons on the Internet, but also for enterprises when using human resources in their daily business. With regard to the European IWT sector, there is currently an ongoing discussion on the protection of personal data when using Inland Automatic Identification System (AIS) devices and AIS-borne data in the IWT industry sector. Some European countries deem AIS information to be personal data, because in many cases in inland navigation these data can be associated with individuals (CCNR, 2014).
> **Publishing data**: An international organization in the field of maritime transport has highlighted the risk to the security of vessels as a result of publishing vessel related information on freely available and public websites (IMO, 2004, p. 50: subsections 5.63 and 5.64). Existing technologies already enable the identification of maritime vessels as well as of inland vessels, which can be accessed and monitored not only by the

public authorities, but also by enterprises, which makes such vessel data available on Internet websites for commercial purposes.

Legal framework: The exchange of inland vessel- and/ or cargo-related data to be processed by new IT-based services, such as for vessel and cargo tracking and tracing, requires a robust legal framework among the involved participating legal entities, such as: IWT vessel/fleet operators, RIS providers and transport logistics users, i.e. inland port/ terminal operators, logistics service providers and others. Ideally a legal framework is being established between the IWT vessel/fleet operator, the RIS provider and the users of RIS data:

1 An 'authorization agreement' needs to be set up between the IWT vessel and/or fleet operator(s) and RIS provider(s) to empower the RIS providers to receive vessel, voyage and also cargo data from the IWT fleet and vessel operator(s) to be used by the RIS providers themselves, but also to be distributed to the pre-defined transport logistics users.

2 A 'data usage agreement' needs to be signed between the RIS provider(s) and the transport logistics user(s) to ensure that the pre-defined transport logistics users are handling the received RISING data accordingly. Based on such or similar legal agreements, the basic conditions are given for exchanging vessel position, ETA, tracking and tracing data with further transport and logistics operators.

Prerequisites on future data structures and exchange services are:

•   Harmonized services: Intelligent Transport Systems (ITS), such as information systems that allow freight operators to make informed decisions when planning their international trips, can contribute to the improved efficiency of freight transport at the European level. For this there is a need to develop interoperable traffic information services at the European level which build on harmonized and standardized data structures and exchange services (European Commission (Directorate-General for Mobility and Transport) / Transport Research Knowledge Centre, 2010b, p. 10). In this context also the UN demands that ITS solutions in place should be internationally harmonized as much as possible (UN/ECE, 2012, p. 10 and p. 18).

•   Transnational services: As door-to-door multimodal IWT-based transport logistics chains do not stop at national borders, the electronic information flows, which accompany and support first ones, must not stop there either. In other words, transnational cargo flows also require cross-border information exchange and services – this both for commercial in-house ICT as well as for ITS services.

•   Secure services: Data security and protection will have an increased impact on our daily lives, but also on businesses in the future. With respect to the European IWT sector, in this commercial sector legal challenges also come up, which need to be tackled to ensure secure data exchange among the involved legal entities covering both public and private actors.

Furthermore, there are additional legal conditions and/or limitations that have to be considered with regard to the logistics environment of IWT. These additional conditions deal with regulation and policy on energy issues, sustainability in transport, the relief of congested transport infrastructure, additional mandatory security measures and liability issues. It is challenging to anticipate the future development regarding these aspects, but new regulations and initiatives belonging to the political framework of IWT are likely to occur on the following topics:

Energy policy: While the energy efficiency of IWT will remain a major incentive to use this transport mode, current energy policy strives for the use of electric vehicles, in order to rely on renewable energies. Inland vessels used for goods transport fitted with electric engines can hardly be found (e.g. in Utrecht), whereas in the road transport sector, more and more examples of logistics chains are reported where electric vehicles are used, including vans and light trucks. For the time being, the propulsion of inland vessels is likely to be based on the combustion of fossil energies such as gas oil and liquefied natural gas (LNG), with propulsion systems based on fuel cells being an option that is currently being explored.

Sustainability in transport: Today, in intermodal competition, IWT is favourable because of its environmental benefits. This is also true for the emission of harmful substances ('regulated emissions'). One recent challenge in Europe in this regard is that IWT has to comply with stricter emissions regulations, while the vessels that are currently in use show difficulties in achieving this. Either, the engine will have to be replaced (an investment causing additional costs), or the vessels' engines will have to be supported by catalysts (likewise causing additional investment). In some European countries there is public financial support for the technological upgrade of vessel engines (retrofit). Aside from the movement of the vessels, electric power is demanded on board the inland vessels during their stay at the ports and terminals. In this context, the provision and standardization of onshore power supply for mooring inland vessels has recently become a topic. The aim is to reduce the local influence of pollutants by turning off the vessels' engines during the mooring period.

Decongestion of transport infrastructure: The co-modality approach of the European Commission, the transport policy of several of the EU member countries as well as the strategic transport plan in China intend to make better use of the transport infrastructure and, thus, promote the increased use of IWT. Inland waterways provide plenty of additional capacity to accommodate the increasing freight transport. In this respect, it should be borne in mind that an upgrade of IWT infrastructure takes a lot of time, and there are only a few related projects. New inland waterway links are unlikely to be built. This is in contrast to the development of road infrastructure. The road network is being extended, and ITS support a better usage of the road infrastructure. In road and railway transport, there are ongoing initiatives to increase productivity through the operation of longer train compositions. The effect on IWT is still to be examined, taking into account that IWT represents mostly just one leg in multimodal logistics chains. Besides, as a kind of push factor towards a redesign of logistics chains, several conurbations restrict the access of trucks to the city centres (via road toll or delivery time slots) in order to decongest the inner city road network.

Additional mandatory security measures: To date, the IWT sector has managed to comply with security regulations and standards that came into force (e.g. ISPS Code, C-TPAT and AEO). Considering the different prevailing risks that appear on the regional and global level and affecting security in freight transport, such as contraband or illegal immigration, there may be more security regulations yet to come. This will predominantly concern intermodal container transport (EIRAC II, 2011, p. 27). While legislative security requirements at the EU level have addressed maritime transport and aviation there is the intention to develop a legal framework on transport security for the land transport modes and IWT as well (European Commission, 2012a, p. 8 and pp. 11–12). As far as multimodal transport and logistics chains are concerned, common EU rules for end-to-end supply chain security are suggested.

Multimodal liability regime: Different liability regimes apply to multimodal transport on a national and international level. These should be harmonized for multimodal transport on an international level. So far, a world-wide harmonization of the liability issue could not be agreed on. For cross-border logistics chains this deficit is regarded as an obstacle for the development of multimodal transport concepts (including IWT).

Abbreviations

AEO	Authorised Economic Operator
AIS	Automatic Identification System
CO2	carbon dioxide
C-TPAT	Customs-Trade Partnership Against Terrorism
ETA	Estimated Time of Arrival
EU	European Union
EUR	euro
ICT	Information and Communication Technology
ISPS Code	International Ship and Port Facility Security Code
ITS	Intelligent Transport Systems
IWT	Inland Waterway Transport

JIT	just in time
JIS	just in sequence
R&D	research and development
RIS	River Information Services
RISING	River Information Services for Transport and Logistics
UN	United Nations
WTO	World Trade Organization

Notes

1 The average transport distance is calculated by dividing the freight transport performance by the freight transport volume.
2 A logistics chain forms the part of a supply chain where a product is transported from a supplier to a customer. Typical processes occurring along a logistics chain are described in Section 3.2.
3 Blockages of inland waterways resulting from accidents can last for a couple of weeks, as happened in the past on the Rhine.
4 Thus, for IWT the external costs of transport are low, see via donau (2013, pp. 18–19).
5 There are several calculation tools available, and many of the tools are available online. As far as air pollution and climate change are concerned, the Marco Polo Calculator provided by the European Commission calculates the external costs of road, rail, inland waterway and short sea transport in the context of a potential modal shift (see European Commission, 2013).
6 If Q represents the overall transport volume within a certain time frame and n the number of departures within the same time frame, the average shipment size q will be calculated as follows: $q = \frac{Q}{n}$. An increase in n equals an increased frequency of departures. If Q is fixed, the average shipment size q will consequently decrease.
7 For the case of the Netherlands and the port of Rotterdam, see Tieman (2011, pp. 160–161).
8 The FREIGHTWISE/e-Freight Framework has been continuously developed, so the names of the roles have been adapted slightly over time.

References

Aberle, G. (2009) *Transportwirtschaft: einzel- und gesamtwirtschaftliche Grundlagen*, 5th Edition, München/ Wien: Oldenbourg.
BMV Bundesminister für Verkehr (ed.) (1991) *Verkehr in Zahlen 1991*, Vol. 20, Bonn.
BMVBS Bundesministerium für Verkehr, Bau und Stadtentwicklung (ed.) (2011) *Verkehr in Zahlen 2010/2011*, Vol. 39, Hamburg: DVV.
BMVBW Bundesministerium für Verkehr, Bau und Wohnungswesen (ed.) (2001) *Verkehr in Zahlen 2000*, Vol. 29, Hamburg: DVV.
bmvit Bundesministerium für Verkehr, Innovation und Technologie (2011) IVS-Maßnahmenkatalog 2011- Anhang zum IVS-Aktionsplan Österreich; available at www.bmvit.gv.at/service/publikationen/verkehr/gesamtverkehr/downloads/ivsmassnahmen2011_lang.pdf (accessed 02.01.2015).
Capros, P. *et al.* (2013) *EU Energy, Transport and GHG Emissions: Trends to 2050 – Reference Scenario 2013*, Luxembourg: Publications Office of the European Union.

CCNR Central Commission for the Navigation of the Rhine (2014) Protection of Personal Data When Using Inland AIS Devices, Summary Report: Review of National Regulations as at 15 April 2014; available at www.ccr-zkr.org/files/documents/ris/rp14_10en.pdf (accessed 29.10.2014).

COFRET (2011): D 2.1 Existing Methods and Tools for Calculation of Carbon Footprint of Transport and Logistics; available at http://cofret-project.eu/downloads/pdf/COFRET_Deliverable_2.1_final.pdf (accessed 20.11.2014).

De Vries, C.J. (2009) *The Power of Inland Navigation: The Future of Freight Transport and Inland Shipping in Europe 2010–2011*, Rotterdam: Dutch Inland Shipping Information Agency (BVB); available at www.bureauvoorlichtingbinnenvaart.nl/pageflip/UK/pageflip/ (accessed 02.01.2015).

Den Boer, E., Otten, M. and van Essen, H. (2011) *STREAM International Freight 2011: Comparison of Various Transport Modes on a EU Scale with the STREAM Database*, Delft: CE Delft.

eFreight (MARINTEK) (2010) D1.3b e-Freight Framework – Information Models; available at www.efreightproject.eu/uploadfiles/e-Freight%20D1.3b%20e-Freight%20Framework.pdf (accessed 17.10.2014).

EIRAC II (2011) The Next EIRAC Strategic Agenda 2010–2030+; edited by European Intermodal Research Advisory Council (EIRAC); available at www.eia-ngo.com/wp-content/uploads/2012/09/EIRAC-II-Strategic-Intermodal-Research-Agenda.pdf (accessed 05.01.2015).

European Commission (2007) Communication from the Commission COM 2007 – The EU's Freight Transport Agenda: Boosting the Efficiency, Integration and Sustainability of Freight Transport in Europe, COM (2007) 606 final, © European Union, http://eur-lex.europa.eu/; available at http://eur-lex.europa.eu/LexUriServ/LexUriServ.do?uri=COM:2007:0606:FIN:EN:PDF (accessed 22.03.2016).

European Commission (2011) White Paper Roadmap to a Single European Transport Area – Towards a Competitive and Resource Efficient Transport System, COM(2011) 144 final; © European Union, http://eur-lex.europa.eu/; available at http://eur-lex.europa.eu/legal-content/EN/TXT/PDF/?uri=CELEX:52011DC0144&from=EN (accessed 23.06.2015).

European Commission (2012a) Commission Staff Working Document on Transport Security, SWD (2012) 143 final, Brussels; available at http://ec.europa.eu/transport/themes/security/doc/2012-05-31-swd-transport-security.pdf (accessed 14.01.2015).

European Commission (2012b) Commission Staff Working Document Towards 'NAIADES II', Promoting, Greening and Integrating Inland Waterway Transport in the Single EU Transport Area, SWD (2012) 168 final, Brussels; available at http://ec.europa.eu/transport/modes/inland/promotion/doc/2012_0168_final_swd.pdf (accessed 28.10.2015).

European Commission (2013) Marco Polo – Call Documents 2013; available at http://ec.europa.eu/transport/marcopolo/getting-funds/application-packs/2013/index_en.htm (accessed 19.06.2015).

European Commission (Directorate-General for Mobility and Transport) / Transport Research Knowledge Centre (2010a) River Information Services: Modernising Inland Shipping through Advanced Information Technologies, Brussels; available at www.transport-research.info/Upload/Documents/201104/20110405_145853_15995_Brochure_RIS_web.pdf (accessed 18.06.2015).

European Commission (Directorate-General for Mobility and Transport) / Transport Research Knowledge Centre (2010b) Towards an Integrated Transport

System – Freight Focus: Research Contributing to Integration and Interoperability across Europe, Brussels.

European Parliament / Council of the European Union (2005) Directive 2005/44/EC of the European Parliament and of the Council of 7 September 2005 on harmonised river information services (RIS) on inland waterways in the Community, © European Union, http://eur-lex.europa.eu/; available at http://eur-lex.europa.eu/legal-content/EN/TXT/PDF/?uri=CELEX:32005L0044&from=EN (accessed 22.03.2016).

European Parliament / Council of the European Union (2010) Directive 2010/40/EU of the European Parliament and of the Council of 7 July 2010 on the Framework for the Deployment of Intelligent Transport Systems in the Field of Road Transport and for Interfaces with Other Modes of Transport, © European Union, http://eur-lex.europa.eu/; available at http://eur-lex.europa.eu/legal-content/EN/TXT/PDF/?uri=CELEX:32010L0040&qid=1420130758500&from=DE (accessed 01.01.2015).

Eurostat (2016) Inland Waterways Transport Measurement; available at http://ec.europa.eu/eurostat/data/database?node_code=iww_go_atygo (accessed 20.05.2016).

Federal Water and Shipping Administration of Germany (2008) Ergebnisübersicht, from 2008; available at https://www.elwis.de/Service/Ergebnisse-der-Umfragen/Telematikumfrage-2008/ergebnis.pdf (accessed 10.05.2016).

FREIGHTWISE/MARINTEK (2010) FREIGHTWISE Framework Architecture, release 4, Deliverable D13.2 of the FREIGHTWISE project; Public Document, licensed under the Creative Commons Attribution 3.0 Unported License (CC BY 3.0); available at http://freightwise.tec-hh.net/Deliverable_D13.2_WP13_Freightwise_Framework_Architecture_release_1.pdf (accessed 01.01.2015).

Ihde, G.B. (2001) *Transport – Verkehr – Logistik*, 3rd Edition, München: Vahlen.

IMO International Maritime Organization – Maritime Safety Committee (2004) Report of the Maritime Safety Committee on its Seventy-Ninth Session, MSC 79/23, 15 December 2004, 5.63 and 5.64; available at www.crs.hr/Portals/0/docs/eng/imo_iacs_eu/imo/msc_reports/MSC79-23.pdf (accessed 28.10.2014).

Konings, J.W. (2009) *Intermodal Barge Transport: Network Design, Nodes and Competitiveness*, TRAIL Thesis Series Volume T2009/11, Delft: Delft University Press.

Kwak, R. and van de Kamp, J. (2013) Supply Chain Partners Give Impulse to Inland Shipping, edited by Rijkswaterstaat; available at www.rijkswaterstaat.nl/images/The%20final%20results%20of%20the%20private%20sector%20initiatives%20IDVV_tcm174-368195.pdf (accessed 05.01.2015).

Muilerman, G.-J. (2001) *Time-based Logistics: An Analysis of the Relevance, Causes and Impacts*, TRAIL Thesis Series Volume T2001/2, Delft: Delft University Press.

Platz, T. (2009) *The Efficient Integration of Inland Shipping into Continental Intermodal Transport Chains: Measures and Decisive Factors*, TRAIL Thesis Series Volume T2009/7, Delft: the Netherlands TRAIL Research School.

RIS Portal (2015) River Information Services Portal; available at www.ris.eu (accessed 10.11.2015).

RISING (RIS Services for Improving the Integration of Inland Waterway Transports into Intermodal Chains) (n.d.) Usage of River Information Services (RIS) for Transport Logistics Services; available at www.rising.eu/web/guest/logistics-focus (accessed 08.01.2014).

RISING (RIS Services for Improving the Integration of Inland Waterway Transports into Intermodal Chains) (2011) Validation of the Business Concepts and Implementation Plan for RIS Transport Services, Vienna.

RISING (RIS Services for Improving the Integration of Inland Waterway Transports into Intermodal Chains) (2012) RISING Services; available at: www.rising.eu/c/document_library/get_file?p_l_id=10520&folderId=57308&name=DLFE-2004.pdf (accessed 16.10.2014).

Ruesch, M., Bohne, S., Huschebeck, M. and Eichhorn, C. (2012) Main Challenges in Freight Logistics, BESTFACT (Best Practice Factory for Freight Transport) Deliverable 2.1, V1.0 (22.05.2012); available at www.bestfact.net/wp-content/uploads/2013/08/BESTFACT_D2_1.pdf (accessed 19.06.2015).

Schweighofer, J. (ed.) (2013) D7.3 Environmental Impact, Final Report, Deliverable D7.3 of the MoveIT! Project; available at www.moveit-fp7.eu/assets/d7.3_move-it-final-report.pdf (accessed 17.06.2015).

SPECTRUM (Solutions and Processes to Enhance the Competitiveness of Transport by Rail in Unexploited Markets) / PANTEIA (2012) SPECTRUM – Logistics and market analysis – Deliverable D1.3, Final (19.11.2012); available at www.spectrumrail.info/component/jdownloads/summary/25-deliverables-public/67-d1-3-logistics-and-market-analysis-final-report?Itemid=473 (accessed 05.01.2015).

Sys, C. and Vanelslander, T. (2011) Scenarios and Strategies for the Inland Navigation Sector, in: Sys, C. and Vanelslander, T. (eds) *Future Challenges for Inland Navigation: A Scientific Appraisal of the Consequences of Possible Strategic and Economic Developments up to 2030*, Brussels: University Press Antwerp, pp. 217–231.

Tieman, R. (2011) Regulation in Inland Navigation, and How to Optimally Stimulate New Technologies, in: Sys, C. and Vanelslander, T. (eds) *Future Challenges for Inland Navigation: A Scientific Appraisal of the Consequences of Possible Strategic and Economic Developments up to 2030*, Brussels: University Press Antwerp, pp. 157–170.

UN/ECE United Nations (Economic Commission for Europe) (2012) Intelligent Transport Systems (ITS) for Sustainable Mobility; available at: www.unece.org/fileadmin/DAM/trans/publications/Intelligent_Transport_Systems_for_Sustainable_Mobility.PDF (accessed 17.06.2015).

via donau (ed.) (2013) *Handbuch der Donauschifffahrt*, Wien: via donau – Österreichische Wasserstraßen-Gesellschaft mbH.

via donau (2015) Arbeitsinitiative: Nachwachsende Rohstoffe mit dem Binnenschiff – Argumentarium 2012–2014; available at: www.viadonau.org/newsroom/publikationen/broschueren/ (accessed 23.06.2015).

4   Managing capacity in the inland waterway sector

To intervene or not to intervene?

Edwin van Hassel, Thierry Vanelslander and Christa Sys

4.1   Rationale and setting

The current inland waterway transport (IWT) markets are characterized by surplus capacities. The supply of loading capacity in both the dry and liquid bulk markets have increased much more than demand. This chapter deals with the underlying reasons. A distinction is made between the dry cargo market and the tanker market because both markets function differently. A common problem is the influx of additional capacity which will remain operational for a long period (50 years). According to supply and demand, freight prices increase in times of high demand for loading capacity. In a perfectly competitive market, an increase in freight rates attracts more IWT barge operators bringing more IWT vessels into the market. Moreover, if a further growth in demand is expected, then more vessels will be ordered and built. Because there is a large time lag between ordering and delivering new tonnage (± 1.5 years), the barge operator tends to run a high risk of overshooting the demand for IWT shipping capacity. From the supply side, there is also the problem that the IWT market is unable to decrease capacity. So, excess supply results in overcapacity. The inefficiency due to overcapacity is more difficult to eliminate. In a perfectly competitive market, this leads to the situation shown in Figure 4.1.

The supply function in Figure 4.1 is not only influenced by the number and size of vessels active in the sector, but also by the sailing speed, the type of operation (round-the-clock or semi-continuous) and the varying water level. This last element in particular characterizes the situation for larger vessels. A significant reserve capacity to balance fluctuations in supply, which are a result of, for instance, low water levels and seasonal peaks, is typical in this sector. Structural overcapacity, however, keeps freight tariffs permanently low (Beelen, 2011). The freight prices can become lower than the average cost, so that ship owners cannot, in the long run, fulfil their repayment of the loans to the bank and will default. When this situation occurs, and is recorded by a large majority of the vessel owners, then the sector experiences structural overcapacity. To effectively address overcapacity, the sector may choose to reduce capacity and/or wait until demand increases while capacity remains

Price

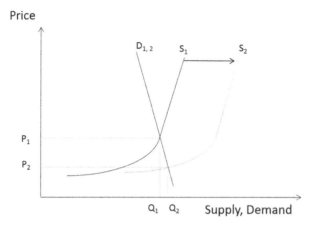

Figure 4.1 Impact of increase in supply on the freight price

constant (no more additional capacity), so that supply and demand will be more in balance.

The main problem of the IWT sector is that when there is excess capacity, it can hardly be reduced without government interventions. This is valid both in terms of loading capacity (number of vessels) as in operational terms. It will lead to overcapacity, which will be prominent in the market for a long time. At the same time, there is not (yet) a track record of a market-based supply reduction in the IWT sector. It is the Western European member states that intervened in the 1970s and the European Commission (EC) that intervened in the 1990s via the demolition rules (EEG/1101/89) and old-for-new regulation (EEG/844/94) to manage capacity. Meanwhile, it is known that influx of additional capacity in this sector cannot just be reduced via demolitions or lay-ups through bankruptcies or be controlled in times of overcapacity. Against this background, the central question becomes whether there is a need for regulation to manage capacity? Or is it part of the free market system bringing demand and supply in equilibrium? And how can all this be explained and changed? These questions are answered in this chapter. To do this, the remainder of the chapter focuses on two markets, namely the dry cargo market and the tank barge market. For each market, firstly, Section 2 analyses the evolution of supply and demand and studies the supply side in detail. Section 3 examines capacity reduction measures. Section 4 explains the underlying principles of the observed build-up and decrease of supply by analysing IWT sub-markets. Section 5 evaluates past initiatives for dealing with overcapacity. The final two sections draw lessons and suggest concrete solutions for current overcapacity problems.

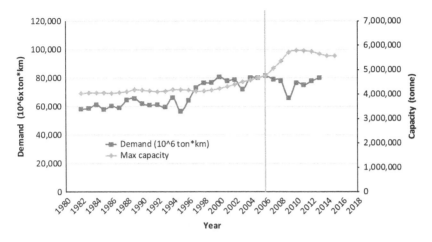

Figure 4.2 Overview of supply and demand in the dry cargo sector in Northwestern
Europe

4.2   Supply and demand characteristics of the IWT sector

This section addresses subsequently the supply and demand characteristics of the
IWT dry cargo and liquid bulk sector. The scope of the analysis is limited to the
self-propelled IWT ships transporting dry cargo. The large push barge convoys,
a separate market with its own characteristics, are left out of this analysis.

4.2.1   Dry cargo sector

A problem of overcapacity has arisen in the Western European[1] dry cargo
IWT fleet.[2] Figure 4.2 shows the development of the tonne-kilometres
undertaken by the dry cargo fleet[3] (left-hand axis) and the development of the
total loading capacity of the same fleet on the basis of the standard draught
(right-hand axis). According to CCR (2014), the total dry cargo fleet in 2012
consisted of 8,000,000 tonnes of loading capacity (all push barges included).
In Figure 4.2, the total loading capacity in 2012 is found to be 5,740,000
tonnes. The difference can be explained by the total push barge capacity in
the Western European fleet, which, as said, are excluded from this analysis.

The evolution of supply and demand can be divided into two periods: the
period up to 2006 and the period after 2006. The former period is characterized by a gradual increase in loading capacity, combined with a rise in
tonne-kilometres transported from 1994–1995 onwards. The sub-period
1989–2003 corresponds to the period when dry cargo loading capacity was
controlled by the demolition rules (2000) and old-for-new rules (2003). This
means that supply and demand developed at more or less the same pace. For

the latter period, from 2007 onwards, Figure 4.2 shows that a significant discrepancy arises between supply and demand.[4] Demand declines as a result of the 2008 financial and economic crisis and struggles to recover while supply has increased dramatically. An explanation can be found in the fact that after the abandonment of the old-for-new regulations in 2003, capacity could be added to the fleet without restrictions. Up to 2006, the increase in the fleet capacity was rather moderate. At the same time, the economic forecasts were very positive. The problem of the surplus of shipping capacity was created at the moment that the forecast demand was not met and vessels were already on order, to be delivered to the market with a delay of 1 to 1.5 years.

Regarding the second period, the total net loading capacity of the self-propelled dry cargo vessels has increased by more than 950,000 tonnes over the period 2006–2009. After 2009, the supply was quite stable while the demand has decreased by 1.7 per cent (2006–2013). The new tonnage consists mainly of large vessels (288 vessels of 110 and 135 m) and the intensity of use also increased (van Hassel, 2013). The evolution of the maximum capacity suggests the beginning of a new period in which the total loading capacity is decreasing. This decrease in capacity is mainly due to the outflow of small IWT vessels (<86 m). Many of these smaller vessels are old and exit the market (van Hassel, 2013). However, the problem of overcapacity in the segment of the large IWT vessels may not disappear. The impact of overcapacity cannot be examined without studying the influence of the fluctuations in the water levels on the total loading capacity of the fleet. Most large dry cargo vessels sail from the Dutch and Flemish ports to Germany. The German part of the Rhine has a large fluctuation in water levels. Assuming that an average voyage of a large IWT vessel takes roughly three to four days (typical trip time from Antwerp or Rotterdam to Germany), the minimum water level on three and four days is used to calculate the maximum allowable draught. Based on the KAUB[5] data, two medians are then calculated (2.00 m for three-day voyages and 1.98 m for four-day voyages[6]). This results in a permissible average draught for IWT of 2.99 m.[7] Significant peaks can be observed in the water levels. The peak is 6.81 m (maximum draught) and the trough 0.48 m (draught 1.48 m). It is therefore important to correct the total loading capacity of the entire fleet for this divergence. Figure 4.3 once again presents the total loading capacity of the fleet, but in this case with a permissible draught for IWT vessels of 2.93 m (the average permissible draught).

Figure 4.3 clearly shows the difference between the loading capacity at standard and at 2.93 m draught, corresponding to about 46,000 tonnes in 1982. This difference rises to around 600,000 tonnes in 2013. A large proportion of the overcapacity that has developed in the IWT dry cargo market is therefore variable and thus largely depending on water depth. However, it is noted that the water levels can fluctuate much and in case of low water levels, less cargo can be transported with inland ships due to draught restrictions. These fluctuations could increase in the future due to climate change, with more wet winters and dryer summers (Jonkeren *et al.*, 2007).

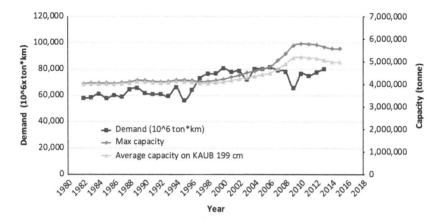

Figure 4.3 Development of supply and demand in the dry cargo fleet in Northwestern Europe at maximum allowable draught and at 2.99 m

To calculate the loading capacity, taking into account a limited water depth, the loading capacities of vessels shorter than 86 m were kept constant. These vessels have a draught of between 2.50 and 2.80 m, meaning that a draught restriction up to 2.93 m is not impacted on by varying water levels. For larger vessels, the loading capacity was calculated when a draught restriction were to apply. In van Hassel (2013), a data set was compiled of the draughts of dry cargo vessels longer than 86 m. For vessels with a loading capacity of more than 3,000 tonnes, the design draught is between 3.00 and 4.50 m for the largest vessels. An additional element here is that the empty draught (draught when the vessel is empty) of these large vessels has also increased. This means that these vessels are able to carry less cargo when the water level is low. These large vessels (with large design draughts) therefore cause the total capacity to rise when the water level is high and the loading capacity to fall when the water level is too low. It should be pointed out here that the draught restrictions for container transport are smaller. In that case, it is a matter of volume rather than mass transport; and therefore the impact on the actual draught is smaller.

4.2.2   Tank barge sector

In the tank barge sector, a similar trend can be observed as in in the dry cargo sector (Figure 4.4). The net tank barge loading capacity has doubled during the last seven years. So, a large part of the existing capacity is very young (less than ten years). However, the underlying principles why this happened in the tank barge sector are different from the dry cargo sector. In Figure 4.4, a line (marked with triangles) was added in order to reconstruct the supply function

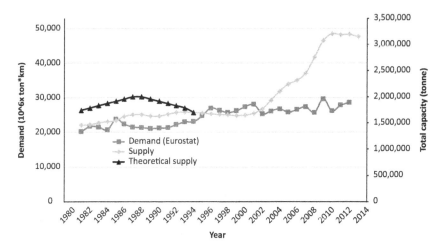

Figure 4.4 Overview of supply and demand in the tank barge sector in Northwestern Europe

over the period 1980–1996. The EC (1999) states that the tank barge sector consisted of 2,000,000 tonnes of loading capacity in 1990 and 1,600,000 tonnes in 1999/2000. This capacity was reduced mainly due to the demolition and old-for-new rules in the same period.

Figure 4.4 shows that the build-up of capacity already started in 2003. But until 2011/2012, the tank barge sector was not characterized as a sector with very low or negative margins. On the contrary: the sector was performing very well. The question arises how that good performance could co-exist with the observed demand/supply gap in Figure 4.4. Van Hassel (2014) cites two reasons.

Firstly, due to legislation, single-hull tank barges were forced to exit the market. This capacity was replaced by new double hull capacity. There is an accepted level of overcapacity of single-hull barges which was phased out by the end of 2015. Van Hassel (2014) gives an overview of several sources with the number of single-hull barges (IVR, 2013; CCR, 2013; Luman, 2013; etc.).[8] There are large variations between the different sources. Therefore, an attempt was made to determine the number of single-hull barges still in use in 2014 with the help of the fleet list of tank barge operators and logistics service providers. Based on this new data set, the loading capacity of single-hull barges was estimated at 390,000 tonnes. This finding suggests that there is much more capacity being added than merely the replacement investments of single-hull barges. The total single-hull fleet is only 12 per cent of the total tank barge capacity. So, taking these vessels off the market will not compensate for the total surplus of tank barge capacity that has been added in the last ten years.

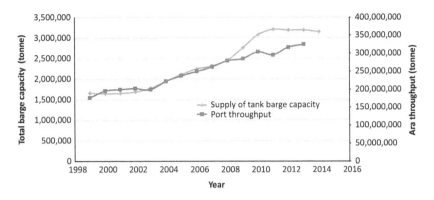

Figure 4.5 Evolution of ARA liquid bulk throughput and tank barge capacity

Secondly, there is a problem with the main indicator to determine demand, namely the ton-kms performed by tank barges in Europe. When tank barges are used for floating storage, then the performed ton-kms are low or even zero, even though the majority of the tank barges are in use. This is what happened between 2006 and 2010. On the one hand, there was an increase in demand for storage of liquid bulk in the Amsterdam-Rotterdam-Antwerp (ARA) region, while, on the other hand, the quay wall capacity was limited and started to expand with a time lag of two years. This means that the queueing time at the tank terminals increased, so that the productivity of the tank barges was reduced. However, the waiting time may be offset by demurrage. Furthermore, a lot of intra-ARA traffic was happening. Oil and fuel oil was shuttled between Antwerp and Rotterdam when traded. This trade was again spurred by the contango[9] period on the oil market (van Hassel, 2014). In sum, from 2006 until 2008, a lot of money could be earned with tank barges, even without actually transporting cargo. It can also be shown that the increase in tank barge capacity is closely linked to the port throughput of liquid bulk in the four main ARA ports (Antwerp, Rotterdam, Amsterdam and Ghent) (Figure 4.5).

In 2015, the demand for floating storage was lower. This is mostly due to the fact that the quay wall tank storage capacity increased by 71 per cent between 2004 and 2015 in the ARA region (van Hassel, 2014) and due to the weak oil market (backwardation[10] period). This means that most vessels that were used for floating storage are now available for transportation, resulting in overcapacity. For the tank barge sector, the impact of the fluctuating water levels is less than for the dry cargo vessels. As said before, most of the traffic with tank barges takes place in the ARA region and the water depth of the IWT network in this region is such that the load capacity of IWT tank barges is not affected by changing water levels. Another important feature that both the dry cargo sector and the tank barge sector have in common is that the investment decision to buy and to operate a new ship is taken at captain-owner level. The former professional IWT companies are almost all gone. The main reason for the disappearing of the shipping companies is the fact that the operating cost (i.e. manning and repair and maintenance cost) of an individual captain-owner is lower than the operating cost of a shipping company. The last remaining shipping companies were found in the chemical tank barge sector (TON, 1997). These shipping companies were needed due to the fact that a shipping company could guarantee safety. But, by the introduction of the European Barge Inspection Scheme (EBIS) system in 1998, the need for a shipping company disappeared because the safety of the vessels was guaranteed at ship level (= captain-owner level). Due to the fact that investment decisions are taken at captain level, it is very difficult to control and manage the inflow of new capacity. As a result, there is a high probability of creating overcapacity. The above analysis clearly shows that both the dry and liquid bulk sector suffer from overcapacity. The issue of overcapacity is more structural in the tanker barge sector. The next section will deal with the different means of reducing capacity and the associated bottlenecks.

4.3   Reduction of IWT barge capacity

While the previous section analysed the build-up of capacity of dry cargo and tank barges, this section concentrates on capacity management measures, and more in particular with a focus on reducing capacity. There are two main ways in which overcapacity can be reduced: (hoping for) an increase in demand and/or a reduction of the shipping capacity. Here, the focus is on the latter. Four different forms of reduction of capacity are distinguished:

1   demolition or scrapping
2   export of capacity to other regions
3   laying up vessels
4   operational adjustments.

The next subsections consecutively deal with the way and extent to which such measures have been taken for dry and liquid bulk IWT markets.

4.3.1   Self-propelled dry cargo IWT market

This section deals with the capacity reduction measures in the dry cargo IWT fleet, taking into account only the self-propelled vessels, not the push barges.

4.3.1.1   Scrapping and exporting dry cargo capacity

Scrapping and exporting dry cargo capacity are the first two capacity management solutions. The impact of such measures can be studied by the number, the type and the age of the ships. First, Figure 4.6 provides

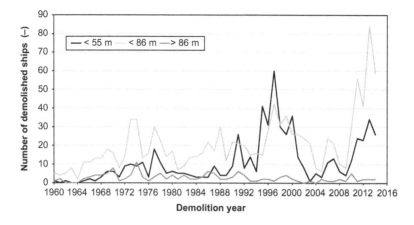

Figure 4.6 Demolition number of dry cargo vessels

an overview of the number of dry cargo vessels that have been scrapped to date. It can be observed that there was a large peak in demolitions of small and medium-sized vessels in the period between 1990 and 2000. This is the period in which the demolition rules were active. After 2003, which is the moment of the abandoning of the old-for-new rules, there was again an increase in the number of demolitions. This new peak in demolitions is now not supported by large interventions in the sector but by the market. Second, a lot of small dry cargo vessels of the types 'Spits' and 'Kempenaar' did exit the market and no newbuildings of these types of vessels have been reported since the 1960s (van Hassel, 2011). It can also be observed that most of the encountered demolitions involve vessels shorter than 86 m. Large vessels also get demolished, but not in the same numbers.

Ultimately, Figure 4.7 gives an overview of all the dry cargo vessels that were scrapped between 2008 and 2013 and that were found in the database of Vereniging de Binnenvaart including the scrap age of the vessels. It has to be mentioned that in order to determine the age of an IWT vessel, the official rule is used of letting the oldest part of the hull construction determine the age of the vessel. When a vessel was built in 1960 and was enlarged from 86 m to 100 m in 2000, the age of the vessel is still 54 years (and not 14). From Figure 4.7, it can be observed that there is a large spread in demolition ages of dry cargo IWT vessels. There are vessels with a hull age of over 100 years! The minimum demolition age is 40 years. This means that a dry cargo IWT barge will last for at least 40 years! So once capacity is added, it will stay in the market for a very long time. Furthermore, there is no decrease in the vessel demolition age between 2008 and 2013. In a period of overcapacity, vessels are being demolished, but always based on the age of the vessel. So, older vessels (mostly smaller ones) are taken off the market while the bulk of the

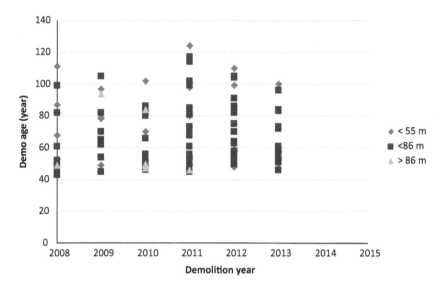

Figure 4.7 Demolition age of dry cargo vessels

newly-built large vessels (110 m and the 135 m plus push barges) are not taken off the market.

There are little to no recordings of dry cargo vessels being exported to other sailing areas such as West Africa or China. In the tank barge sector, this is being observed as will be shown in Section 4.3.2.

4.3.1.2   Laying up vessels

For laying up vessels, vessels are taken from the active freight market and are 'parked' in a port. This is an effective way of reducing capacity but hardly used in the IWT sector. An explanation can be found in the fact that this sector is very fragmented. Almost 96 per cent and 98 per cent of the Dutch and respectively Belgian vessel owners own only one vessel (or motor vessel with one push barge) (Beelen, 2011). This means that the vessel owner who decides to lay up his vessel will contribute to the reduction of the capacity. This could lead to an increase in the freight price in case enough vessel owners would do the same. The ones benefiting from this increase are the ones who are still sailing. So, there is a negative incentive to lay up and therefore the individual interest of the vessel owners will prevail.

4.3.1.3   Operational adjustments

With respect to the operational adjustments, there is also the problem of the large fragmentation of the sector. In long periods of low freight rates, due to a surplus of capacity, the earnings are also low. This means that the individually operating owner will work more in order to increase his earnings (reduce downtime, increase sailing speed or even change sailing regime). This means that more effective capacity is added to the fleet. As a result, in the long run, the prices will be reduced even further (Dullaert *et al.*, 1998). Interestingly, this behaviour was also observed during the Great Depression in the 1930s (Beelen, 2011). Not much has changed in 85 years. So, the main reason for the IWT sector being unable to adjust supply in operational terms is the large fragmentation. Van Hassel (2013) has suggested the dry cargo sector create pools.[11] These large pools could be able to adjust supply by laying up vessels and by intervening in the operations of the vessel. Basically, the structure is copied from the bulk and tanker markets in the maritime sector where these measures can be taken, not always successfully either (Haralambides, 2003).

4.3.2 *IWT tanker barge market*

4.3.2.1 *Scrapping and exporting tank barges*

For the tank barge sector, there was a large peak of demolition in the period between 1990 and 2000 (Figure 4.8[12]). This goes along with the demolition rules (see also Section 6). The tank barges that got demolished in this period are the medium-sized ones (between 55 m and 86 m). A new peak of demolitions is reached from 2010 onwards. Besides demolitions, also a new form of capacity reduction occurred: exporting tank barges. These exports concern mostly large (> 86 m) single-hull barges which are transported to West Africa (Sierra Leone, Nigeria etc.). These vessels are not demolished but are taken off the European market and can therefore be considered a capacity reduction. This latest increase in vessel removals is now not supported by a government intervention but is done by the market.

In line with Figure 4.7, Figure 4.9 gives an overview of the demolition age and exporting age of tank barges between 2008 and 2014. A split is made between three different vessel sizes (<55 m, 55–86 m and >86 m).

From Figure 4.9, it can be concluded that there is a large range in the demolition (and exporting) age. There are two large tank barges which have a considerably lower exporting age than average.[13] Except those two outliers, it can be observed that the minimum demolition (or exporting) age is between 20 and 30 years. The minimum demolition age of tank barges is lower than that of dry cargo barges. This is due to the installed technical installations such as pumps, pipes and tanks. These wear out faster than the installations on a dry cargo vessel (Beelen, 2011).

4.3.2.2 *Lay-up of vessels*

In different maritime shipping sectors (container shipping, bulk shipping etc.), also a temporary form of capacity reduction is used. There is an option

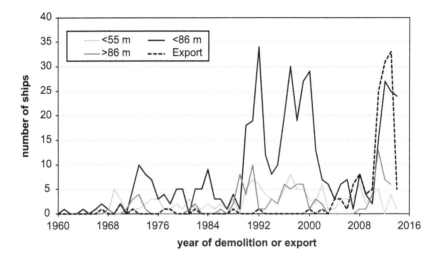

Figure 4.8 Demolition and export number of tank barges

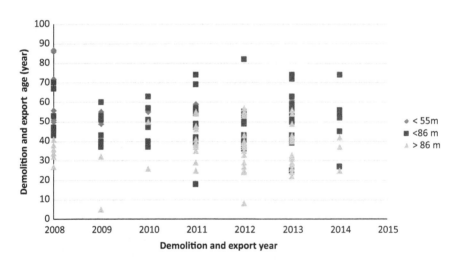

Figure 4.9 Demolition age of tank barges

of laying up vessels and also of reducing the sailing speed (slow steaming) to reduce capacity. Just like in the dry bulk market, this is hardly used either. The same reasons as for the dry cargo market apply.

4.3.2.3   *Operational adjustments*

The tank barge sector is a little less fragmented than the dry cargo sector. Due to the compulsory European Barge Inspection Scheme (EBIS), set up by the oil and chemical shippers, most vessel owners are more linked to a freight broker to allow their compulsory checks. Figure 4.10 gives an overview of the Western European tank barge sector.[14] In this overview, some companies are purely freight brokers, while others have a double function: they act as freight broker for their own vessels and for other vessels.

However, these freight brokers are not able to influence the operational parameters of the tank barges they do not own. They are also not able to decide whether a tank barge must be laid up. Hence, in terms of capacity management, only the individual vessel owner can make these decisions. And as already described above, the individual vessel owner is trapped and not capable of reducing the operational capacity on its own.

Section 4.3 has shown that it is very difficult if not impossible to reduce the existing capacity. In such a situation, in the long run, captain owners are expected to go bankrupt, although this hardly happens. The next section will go into the detail on why bankruptcies are not common in the IWT sector.

4.4   The lack of bankruptcies

An explanation for the overcapacity observed in the previous sections might be found in the functioning of the IWT market. One of the problems is that vessels are not taken away from the market in times of too much supply. In order to further analyse this phenomenon, different submarkets of the IWT market are examined in detail. Following Stopford (2010) and van Hassel (2011), these different sub-markets are:

- freight
- newbuilding
- second-hand
- demolition
- export.

In Figure 4.11, the schematic overview is presented of the cash flow of these five IWT sub-markets, including the position of the bank. The bold lines in the figure represent the cash flows in and out of the total IWT system. The thin black lines represent the delivery of vessels from a shipyard to the shipping market or from the shipping market to the scrap market or export

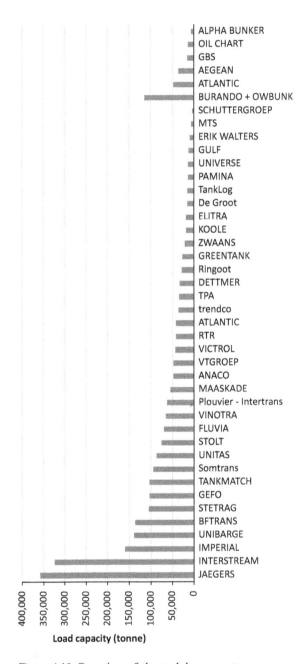

ALPHA BUNKER
OIL CHART
GBS
AEGEAN
ATLANTIC
BURANDO + OWBUNK
SCHUTTERGROEP
MTS
ERIK WALTERS
GULF
UNIVERSE
PAMINA
TankLog
De Groot
ELITRA
KOOLE
ZWAANS
GREENTANK
Ringoot
DETTMER
TPA
trendco
ATLANTIC
RTR
VICTROL
VTGROEP
ANACO
MAASKADE
Plouvier - Intertrans
VINOTRA
FLUVIA
STOLT
UNITAS
Somtrans
TANKMATCH
GEFO
STETRAG
BFTRANS
UNIBARGE
IMPERIAL
INTERSTREAM
JAEGERS

400,000 350,000 300,000 250,000 200,000 150,000 100,000 50,000 0

Load capacity (tonne)

Figure 4.10 Overview of the tank barge sector

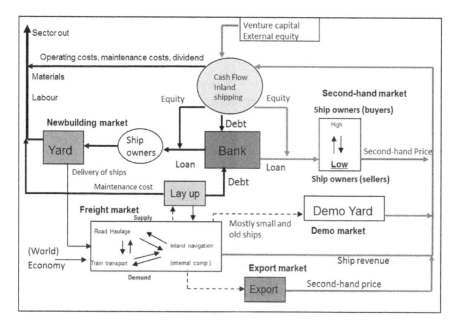

Figure 4.11 Overview of cash flow in the European inland shipping sector

market. The grey lines represent the cash inflow in the IWT sector, while the black lines are cash flows out of the IWT market.

In the freight market, inland vessels are competing with other inland vessels but also with other modes of transport, predominantly road for short distances and rail for longer distances. In the freight market, it is possible to make operational adjustments to the inland fleet (i.e. speed reductions). In that market, it is also possible to lay up vessels. Vessels are taken, temporarily, off the actual freight market. Laying up a vessel incurs costs such as fixed costs (debt repayments) and maintenance costs. So, laying up a vessel will have to be done in cooperation with a bank.

In the freight market, revenue is being generated. The prices are determined by the demand for transport (world economy) and the supply of shipping capacity (number of vessels and the exploitation of these vessels). When the earnings are larger than the operating and maintenance cost and the repayment of the loan, equity can be generated. This equity can be built up by the IWT companies as a reserve, or the equity together with a loan granted by a bank can be used to purchase a new vessel. These new vessels are delivered to the freight market where more capacity will be added. In this process, cash disappears from the IWT sector and is transformed into a fixed asset (the ship). This process can take up to two years, depending on the order books of the shipyards. It is also possible that an IWT vessel is sold from one owner to another (second-hand market). The value of the vessel depends on the future earning potential and is linked to the developments in the freight market and the expectations of the developments of the economy. In this market, money is shifted from one owner to another, which implies that the cash remains in the IWT sector.

Normally, starters in the sector buy a (smaller) second-hand ship, earn money with that ship in the freight market and later sell that ship to a new starter. Owners who sell their ship obtain cash from selling their ship and with this cash, plus the cash obtained from the freight market and a loan from a bank, they can buy a larger second-hand or a newbuilding vessel.

The fourth market is the demolition market. In this market, existing vessels are scrapped and taken off the market. Shipping capacity is reduced and vessels are transformed into cash. This cash is then flowing back into the IWT sector. In the seagoing shipping market, the scrap market is also used to reduce excess capacity. The average scrapping age has decreased from 32 years in 2008 to 27 years in 2014. Also, the age of the youngest demolished vessels has reduced from 15 to 10 years. Equally, during the crisis years of 2009 to 2013, there was an increase in the number of demolitions: 32 million tonnes in 2009 and a record of 58 million tonnes in 2012 compared to an average of 6 million tonnes from 2005 to 2008 (Danish Ship Finance, 2014). This phenomenon is not observed in the IWT market (see Figure 4.7 – dry cargo – and Figure 4.8 – tank barges). This means that the scrap market is only used to scrap old vessels and not vessels that are not needed in the market. That is the reason why there is a dotted line in Figure 4.11 from the freight market to the demolition market. Getting rid of excess capacity via the demolition market is not observed other than by demolishing old vessels, which are mostly small ones (<86 m).

The fifth market is the export market. In this market, vessels are sold to another region that is not connected to the European IWT market. So when a vessel is exported to, for example, Nigeria, the vessel disappears from the European IWT market and the cash will move into the European sector. Another important element in Figure 4.11 is the central position of banks, which play a vital 'pumping' role in the newbuilding and second-hand markets. Without banks, the cash flow between the different markets would stop. Banks have played a vital role in renewing and modernizing the inland fleet. Also, when, in theory, in the freight market large profits would be obtained, it is necessary to increase the shipping capacity to reduce the transportation prices, which is of importance for the shippers and ultimately for the final consumer. Banks are granting loans to vessel owners but they need some form of guarantee to back-up the loans. The higher the level of guarantee, the lower the risk profile and the lower the interest rate will be for the vessel owner (Schaffers, 2011). The two main forms of guarantees are (1) the level of liability of the company buying the vessel and (2) government guarantees.

In The Netherlands, roughly 70 per cent of the inland vessels are financed via a VOF (LLP) and a one-person business construction, and 20 per cent via a BV (Ltd) construction. The remaining 10 per cent is divided between CVs (cooperative companies) (8 per cent) and other forms (2 per cent) (PLATINA, 2014). The first group, the VOF and one-person businesses, are 100 per cent liable for the debts in the company. This means that personal savings, a car, a house etc. are taken as collateral. This is in contrast to the seagoing sector where a large majority is financed via the limited liability system. This means that in case of a long period of low freight prices, due to a surplus of shipping capacity or a decrease of demand, vessel owners who are 100 per cent liable will try to survive much longer than vessel owners who are only liable to a limited extent. Companies that have actually already gone bankrupt are therefore continuing to operate for too long. The second form of guarantee is a government guarantee. The Dutch government has given guarantees in relation to the financing.[15] This scheme is not sector-specific and applies to all Dutch small and medium-sized enterprises,[16] which means that the IWT sector is not excluded. It is therefore possible that a portion of the loans that banks have provided to IWT companies are covered by the Dutch government. This system does not exist in the other IWT countries. This means that in times of optimistic forecasts for demand for IWT capacity, even more vessels will be added to the market due to the fact that the risk profile of the vessel owner is reduced (van Hassel, 2013).

Basically, when a vessel owner is not able to repay its loans, it is technically bankrupt. However, when the vessel owner is bankrupt, the bank will take the vessel as collateral, along with the remaining savings and possessions of the vessel owner when it is 100 per cent liable. The bank is not a shipping company, so it will try to recover as much cash from the vessel as possible either by selling it on the second-hand market or by scrapping it. The book values of the vessel owners that are facing bankruptcies are quite high because these are the vessel owners who bought their large new vessel in the period from 2006 onwards (van Hassel, 2013). So, scrapping is not an option for the bank. Therefore, banks have no interest in declaring bankruptcy for these companies. If an IWT entrepreneur goes bankrupt, he will disappear from the sector, but the vessel will remain. It will go into the hands of the bank, which will attempt to sell it. This will take place at a lower price than the price for which it was financed. The bank has to bear this loss, if the guarantees are not compensating the low second-hand price. There is no decline in the supply of vessels: after all, IWT vessels give many years of service, meaning that cargo prices cannot recover and the malaise on the IWT market persists. If this process is nevertheless set in motion, this is referred to as the 'cold restructuring' of the inland waterway sector (Luman, 2013).

So, due to these above reasons, excess capacity will remain in the freight market. This can also be observed in Figures 4.2 and 4.4, where no decline of capacity is observed. There is also no history of market-based reduction of capacity because in the past, governments have intervened with demolition and old-for-new actions to restructure the sector. It can therefore be concluded that IWT is not operating in a perfectly competitive market. There is no mechanism of reducing access to capacity because if not all criteria of the perfectly competitive market are fulfilled, then this sector cannot be seen as a perfectly competitive market. Rather, other elements explain the low freight rates. Consequently, a large part of the vessel owners are making a loss, especially the owners with relatively large new vessels. As a result, cost reductions on crewing and maintenance are used to overcome the reduced revenue. There are two consequences of these actions:

1   increase in stress levels for the vessel owners / barge captains
2   reduced maintenance of the vessels.

Both actions could lead to an increase in the number of dangerous situations, and as a result an increase in the probability of spills and accidents. This firstly means that there will be an increase in the number of external accident costs. Secondly, also the value of the vessel could be reduced due to the postponed maintenance. This is on its own a bad situation, because lower second-hand prices are also not in the interest of the bank, who owns the vessel after a vessel owner has gone bankrupt. On the other hand, there is the position of the shipper. In this buyers' market, the main benefits are there for the shippers. They can obtain low freight price and can transport their cargo in a cheaper way. This also has a positive impact on the end-consumer. The question arises what is better for society as a whole: low freight prices (and low transportation cost), which benefit the end-consumer, or the potential increase in the number of accidents (and the related cost)? Now that the complexity of the IWT market is clear, and also the reasons why specific capacity-reducing measures are not functioning, the next section takes a deeper look into lessons we can take from past government-initiated measures so as to be able to set up a policy anyway.

4.5   Which government actions were taken in the past?

This section deals with how the overcapacity problem was dealt with in the past from a government viewpoint. Two actions will be discussed, namely scrapping and old-for-new actions. Finally, lessons learned will be drawn from what works under which conditions.

4.5.1   *Interventions in the market before the old-for-new and demolition rules*

A crisis in the IWT sector is not new. Already in the 1930s, a major crisis hit the sector, which consisted traditionally of numerous self-employed bargemen who represented the larger share of cargo space, together with a number of small and large shipping companies. This strong fragmentation was especially manifest in the dry cargo segment, and a lot less in the tanker segment, where the shipping companies had a more important share. The behaviour of these bargemen is surprisingly similar to what happens today. The way out of that crisis was the creation of the regulated markets in the different IWT countries and for the different IWT sub-markets (freighting in rotation, *Festfrachten, tour-de-rôle* etc.). The Rhine was always excluded due to the Act of Mannheim, and was therefore a free market (Beelen, 2011).

In this partly regulated market, minimum prices were guaranteed but there was still no way of controlling capacity. Already in the 1970s, the EC concluded that at a European level, a capacity-controlling system had to be developed and implemented so that supply (capacity) could better match demand. On top of that, several national demolition actions were implemented, with the one in Western Germany having had the biggest success. Also in Belgium, after the big strike actions in 1975, and in France and The Netherlands, similar demolition actions were implemented. Some tonnage was removed from the market, but overcapacity still existed due to three main reasons:

1   the measures were only temporary;
2   the actions were not coordinated between the different countries;
3   there was no stop of newbuildings on the market.

Therefore, the notion grew that only a coordinated plan of actions between the different countries could help the sector. After many years of difficult negotiations between the sector representatives of the vessel owners and the representatives of the EC and the Rhine Committee (CCR) in 1989, two main actions were developed:

•   demolition actions (EEG/1101/89) to demolish old vessels (to modernize the fleet) and to create 'acceptable terms' for skippers to leave the sector (reduction of capacity);
•   old-for-new actions (EEG/1102/89) to allow new capacity only under certain conditions to control the capacity of the IWT fleet.

The financing of these actions was a large problem. The IWT problems were concentrated in only four countries (Belgium, France, (Western) Germany and The Netherlands), while the other countries in Europe were not willing to contribute financially to solving the IWT problems. Only when it was concluded that the sector itself also had to contribute to the financing of the proposed actions was a definitive agreement signed. Via an annexed protocol of the Act of Mannheim, Switzerland also joined in the demolition and old-for-new actions.

4.5.2   Scrapping actions

The scrapping action (EEG/1101/89) was planned to last for ten years. Each involved country needed to set up a demolition fund for the dry cargo sector and one for the tank barge sector. The financing of the funds was done by the sector itself. At a later stage, the EC (1994 and 1996) and the involved countries also contributed with funds. Vessel owners who wanted to keep their vessel in the market needed to pay a yearly contribution based on the tonnage and type of vessel for the upcoming ten years. In practice, the countries pre-financed the demolition fund via a zero interest loan. The premiums paid by the sector were used to pay back this loan. The EC launched three main demolition actions. The first one was in 1990, the second between 1993 and 1995 and the last one between 1996 and 1998. During these periods, vessel owners who wanted to demolish their vessel were entitled to a demolition premium. Vessel owners had to specify which percentage of the demolition price they requested from the funds. The system worked via a tender system in which the vessel owners with the smallest request for funds were granted their request first. The percentage that was requested was in the first two demolition actions in the range of 70 to 100 per cent, but in the latest action (1998), this was increased to the range of 80 to 120 per cent to increase the attractiveness of the measure. Since the beginning of the demolition action in 1990, 2,889,115 tonnes of loading capacity were taken away from the market (EC, 1999). In nine years, the dry cargo IWT sector (push barges and motor vessels) was reduced by 2,278,696 tonnes (3,344 units) and the tank barge sector was reduced by 610,419 tonnes (610 units). In total, 10 per cent of the dry cargo capacity and 15 per cent of the tank barge sector was taken away from the market in 1990. With this restructuring programme, also the productivity of the vessels increased: average capacity per vessel increased from 839 tonnes to 983 tonnes for dry cargo vessels and from 1,088 tonnes to 1,334 tonnes for tank barges. A lot of financial means were required to finance the mentioned actions. In total, 338,000,000 ECU (or €360,000,000)[17] (EC, 1999) were required. From this amount, 62 per cent was spent on the latest action from 1996 to 1998. Approximately 65 per cent of the total €360 million was spent on the dry cargo sector and 35 per cent on the tank barge sector. The total amount was financed in the following order: 7 per cent by the EC, 46 per cent by the member states and 46 per cent by the sector via the contributions to the demolition funds and via the old-for-new actions.

4.5.3   Old-for-new

The main principle of the old-for-new action (EEG/1102/89) was that new capacity was only allowed to the market if:

- the same amount of tonnage was taken away from the market without intervention via the demolition funds;
- a penalty was paid which was collected by the demolition funds;
- or a combination of demolition and penalty applied if the demolished tonnage was smaller than the added capacity.

The demolition-to-newbuilding ratio[18] was adjusted from 1990 to 2003 based on the business cycle. In the first period (1989–1994), this ratio was 1:1. The ratio was also differentiated between dry cargo and tank barge sector and push barges. In the second period (1994–1999), the ratio became more strict at 1.5:1. The reason for this adjustment was that besides the unification of Germany (1990) and the entry of Austria to the European Union, Eastern European skippers also entered the Western European waterways after the fall of Communism. In order not to undermine the demolition actions undertaken from 1990–1999, the old-for-new regulations were prolonged with another four years (until 2003), while the demolition-to-newbuilding ratio was reduced each year from 1.5:1 in 1999 to 0:1 in 2003. From 2003, this system was set 'on hold' to be reinstalled in case of a *severe offset* in market, possibly in combination with other actions. Per sector segment (dry cargo, tank barge or push barges), the reserve funds will be maintained and will be reinforced with the reserves from the demolition funds (EEG/1101/89). These new old-for-new rules were established on 29 April 1999 (EEG/718/1999 and EEG/805/1999) and are applicable to the following countries: Belgium, The Netherlands, Luxembourg, Germany, France, Austria and Switzerland. The old-for-new regulations had a very positive impact on the sector. In the dry cargo sector, 650,906 tonnes of newbuildings were added to the market in the period 1990–1999, while at the same time also 600,509 tonnes of capacity were demolished. For non-compensated demolitions, a total of €9,000,000 of penalties were collected. In the same period, 240,364 tonnes of tank barge capacity were added while 131,018 tonnes of capacity were demolished.

4.5.4 Lessons learnt from history

The lessons learnt from history tell us that the present-day problems are not really new. Almost 85 years back, more or less the same problems were observed and the behaviour of the individually operating vessel owners is still the same. A form of regulation was applied, interventions at country level were made to reduce access capacity and even large-scale European intervention was implemented which took ten years and €360,000,000 to reduce ± 15 per cent of the loading capacity of the tank barge sector and 10 per cent of the dry cargo sector. And now, *L'histoire se répète!* The IWT sector is back to a similar situation as in the 1930s.

The main lesson is that there is something wrong in the inland navigation sector. An explanation can be found in the market structure of the sector, namely a strong fragmentation. Knowledge of this structure is relevant because it influences the behaviour of the carriers operating under it (Sys, 2010). This behaviour in turn affects the bargemen's performance: price setting, profits, efficiency etc. As long as all the bargemen are operating on a standalone basis, every short-run intervention (demolition rules, old-for-new etc.)

will eventually, when the restrictions are taken away, lead to the same situation: excess capacity and low freight rates and a sector in despair! This part was overlooked by previous actions taken to deal with overcapacity in IWT.

4.6   The way forward: how to control capacity?

The previous sections learned that knowledge of and insight into the IWT market functioning are crucial when trying to put in place solutions. Such knowledge is crucial, as it determines actor behaviour. The problem is that insufficient insights are available into IWT operators, with a consequently unadapted reaction pattern. This in turn leads to overcapacity, putting strong pressure on freight rates. The inland navigation sector has the problem of being unable to reduce capacity, in operational terms as well as in permanent terms, in times of decreased demand. That problem is crucial, as it implies the death or survival of the sector. To overcome this problem, there are basically two main strategies:

1   the free market strategy
2   the regulated market strategy.

In the former strategy, the free market mechanism applies. In this approach, no government intervention is applied and the sector has to manage itself to overcome the problem of adapting supply to demand. For this type of approach, a solution could be to form large cooperations (pools) in the IWT sector. These pools should control and manage the operational aspects of the vessels to manage the operational adjustments or to lay up a vessel (van Hassel, 2013). The main problem is that there is no real history of cooperation between large vessels (>86 m) and their operators, while these vessels are now making up the largest part of the IWT fleet (for dry cargo, 52 per cent of the total loading capacity is larger than 86 m, and for tankers, it is even 77 per cent). For the smaller vessels, there are cooperatives such as MSG, DTG (both Germany), NPRC, PTC, CBV, all in The Netherlands. Most of these cooperatives were founded in crisis years (De Middelaer, 2014). An incentive for more cooperation between the larger ships can be found in Figure 4.12. In this figure, the ratio between the different cost elements as a function of the ship size is given. If the ship size increases, a larger part of the average cost will be determined by the fixed cost (40 per cent for the largest ships). For highly capital-intensive assets (i.e. large IWT vessels), fixed costs are better managed by a central management that can deploy these vessels much better. This is much more difficult for a single captain-owner.

With respect to the surplus capacity that cannot be controlled via operational management of the fleet (laying up vessels within a pool or cooperation), a market mechanism must be introduced. That means that the vessel has to be demolished without the intervention of a government. This process can take, as described above, a very long time.

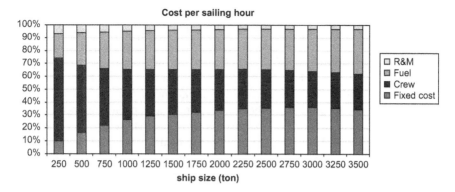

Figure 4.12 Ratio of cost elements in the IWT sector

For the second strategy, a large-scale government intervention could be proposed and the sector will remain very fragmented as it is today. History has shown that in the long run, the IWT market will eventually lead to a situation of overcapacity, and the period in which there is overcapacity will remain very long. A potential solution is to install a European *tour-de-rôle* system in which the available cargo is distributed equally between the different vessel owners. This seems not in the spirit of the liberalization that the EC is striving for, but can be considered a form of regulation in a market that is not working perfectly (i.e. lack of bankruptcies and market-induced reduction of capacity). On top of that, a permanent old-for-new rule can be installed. In this old-for-new rule, also the ratio between newbuilding and scrapping can be adjusted based on the business cycle. By applying a permanent old-for-new rule, the problem of creating overcapacity is tackled. With the money collected from the old-for-new regulation, also demolition actions can be financed. However, setting up these rules is difficult. Not only due to the fact that all the European IWT countries must be thinking and acting along the same lines, but also due to the fact that designing and controlling the rules is quite difficult. Therefore, if this path is to be followed, the past experience of the previous old-for-new regulations has to be used.

Choosing which of the above strategies to follow comes down to the following dilemma: can a free market mechanism be used if the market itself is not a perfectly competitive market? If one thinks that a free market mechanism can be used, the first approach seems the best solution. Otherwise, a set of regulations at a European level might work better. If the market system does work but only lacks at the point of exit of existing capacity, conditions could be created by some level of government intervention, so that a combination of strategy 1 and strategy 2 can be applied. It is not clear yet which direction of solution is best, but one thing can be concluded: a very fragmented IWT market without any form of regulation has no future! The proposed measures are in line with the broader actions proposed by Sys and Vanelslander (2010), mainly through their action points on 'introducing and/or keeping efficient regulation', 'proposing harmonisation across countries', and on 'enabling financing of IWT, suggesting professionalisation and transparency'. Equally, there is a sufficient level of political awareness. The Netherlands, for instance, called together the so-called '*Crisisberaad*'. IWT barge operators, banks, governments, freighters and sector associations were called together. One of the concrete measures proposed by this '*Crisisberaad*', the installation of a 'capacity alliance', which would group 85 per cent of IWT barge operators, was rejected, however, by the Dutch Competition Authority. Eventually, the measure was transformed into a voluntary lay-up system against payment, but even this was rejected by the Competition Authority. A good next step was the setup of an Inland Navigation Ambassador, and of Transition Committee Inland Navigation. The latter created the sector association Binnenvaart Branche Unie, which in 2014 joined the wider association Binnenvaart Logistiek Nederland. Furthermore, a sector initiative was the creation of the Dry Cargo Committee. Already in 2009, The Netherlands had tried to make a 'crisis announcement' to the EC, but the latter considered the situation to be conjunctural and not structural (De Middelaer, 2014). In Belgium, the Federal Minister of Mobility in 2013 had a broad meeting with the IWT sector, and with representatives of the Belgian regions. An official 'crisis announcement' was made with the EC, with a very-well-motivated file. European Directive 96/75/EC was referred to, that allows dealing with structural market disturbances. Structurally, this can be done by putting in place anti-dumping measures, modernizing the fleet with special attention to smaller vessels, installing a permanent market observation system and the creation of a harmonized technical, social and fiscal framework. Temporarily, this can materialize through capacity reduction and supporting cooperation. European Law EEG/169/2009 allows for cooperation agreements up to 500,000 tonnes to get exemption from competition rules. With respect to anti-dumping measures, in Belgium, a Royal Decree was passed on 28 November 2013, according to which it is no longer allowed to offer IWT services below the cost of the service. This newly established law is likely to make the accurate cost calculations more relevant for all the captain-owners. The main problem with the Royal Decree is that it is only valid for Belgium. For IWT transport passing by or with an origin or destination outside Belgium, this law is not valid. In any case, there seem to be ways to get out of the overcapacity situation, which require further in-depth analysis. Such analysis should in a structural way involve a permanent monitoring exercise, checking the balance between demand and supply and measuring the level of overcapacity. Moreover, one should not abandon the strategy of acting also on the demand side: a growth in market demand should be aimed for, in line with the consecutive EU White Papers. This can be reached through incentives for shippers – real ones, not just promotional campaigns – and/or internalizing external transport costs. Linked to this, sufficient data on capacity, tariffs and cargo flows should become available to monitor the sector and to identify potential future problems.

4.7 Conclusions

The analysis in this chapter has shown that IWT, even though being a favoured mode of transport because of its environmentally sustainable character, suffers from a number of inefficiencies, which make it evolve into an economically unsustainable mode of transport. Overcapacity is a huge issue, apparently not being able to be solved in the present-day working of the IWT market. This may create a huge challenge for the sustainability of transport and logistics in a wider sense, and for the EC 2011 White Paper targets in particular, which exactly aim at a strongly increased use of less-polluting modes of transport like IWT. The two main IWT segments are both affected, namely liquid and dry bulk shipping. Controlling capacity in any case is a necessity for those segments, in order to stabilize prices and keep them at economically viable levels. Two options seem possible. The first is government intervention, with the introduction of a *tour-de-rôle* system, as existed in the past, but which was abandoned because of the liberalization move. If this were to be re-introduced, it should of course be subject to strong regulation, so as to avoid market abuses. The second solution would consist of a voluntary, market-induced, move of IWT companies towards a self-organized pool cooperation system, whereby capacity would be controlled and managed. It seems that Europe, as its Directives indicate, could agree with such solutions under conditions. Europe itself takes infrastructural measures, but prefers not to initiate operational measures itself, unless markets indicate a need to do so. Important is that the initiative is taken by the involved countries, in a coordinated way, so as to avoid dispersed communication, signals and requests. IWT is borderless, and so should be policies guiding it.

Notes

1 The Netherlands, Belgium, Luxembourg, Germany, France, Austria and Switzerland.
2 The dry cargo fleet is defined as all dry cargo ships plus push barges pushed by a motor ship. Push barges pushed by a push element are not included due to a lack of data.
3 Based on EUROSTAT (2014), total inland waterway transport performed by *dry cargo motor barges* (ton.km performed by push barges are not included).
4 The last year that profits were obtained was 2008 (Van Dijk *et al.*, 2012). So, in those years supply and demand were more or less in balance. After that, losses were reported, especially for large ships (>86 m).
5 The navigability of the Rhine in Germany is measured by the 'Pegelstand'. Pegelstand is related to actual water depth. There are several locations along the Rhine where the Pegelstand is measured. KAUB is one of them.
6 The mode (the most frequently occurring KAUB level) is 1.64 m. There is therefore a difference between the most frequently occurring value and the median (the middle value in the data set).
7 The following rule is used to calculate the draught: the official draught equals the target depth (*1.90 m*) + (KAUB level – OLR [agreed low river level] water level (*0.80 m*)) – safety margin (*0.40 m*) (EICB, 2014). In practice, vessels are loaded to 1 m KAUB. It is evident from this that margins have been stretched.

8 Single hull versus double hull data from EBIS database obtained via Frank van de Ven on 4 June 2014.
9 Contango is a period in which the expected prices are higher than current commodity prices (i.e. increasing oil price).
10 Backwardation is the opposite of contango (i.e. decreasing oil prices).
11 For an overview of the proposed pool concept: see van Hassel (2013).
12 The demolition data of the tank barges are split in three vessel size categories. However in order to make the graph more readable, the data of the exports are presented as a summation of the three different ship sizes (<55 m, <86 m and >86 m). This is done because most exported vessels are larger than 86 m.
13 *Verna* (building year 2004) exported to Panama in 2012, *Meissen* (now Oxana) (building year 2004) exported to Estonia in 2009.
14 This overview is still work in progress and at this stage 88 per cent of the tank barge fleet capacity is covered by the freight brokers.
15 Government-guaranteed scheme for loans to small and medium-sized enterprises.
16 Despite the fact that this scheme is not sector-specific, the following companies/ professions are excluded: (1) doctors, (2) regulated markets such as the legal and notarial professions, (3) companies that generate more than 50 per cent of their turnover from: agriculture and horticulture, cattle breeding or aquaculture, banking or insurance and (4) the exploitation of immovable property.
17 1 ECU = 1.067 EUR.
18 The ratio of demolition tonnage to newbuilding tonnage.

Bibliography

Beelen, M., 2011, *Structuring and modelling decision making in the inland navigation sector*, Antwerp: University of Antwerp.
CCR, 2012, Marktobservatie N 15, Vraag- en aanbodsituatie in 2011 en analyse van de conjunctuur medio 2012.
CCR, 2013, KAUB water levels obtained via N. Kriedel.
CCR, 2014, Marktobservatie N 18, De binnenvaartmarkt in 2013 en vooruitzichten voor 2014/2015.
Danish Ship Finance, 2014, Shipping market review, may 2014, www.shipfinance. dk/Shipping-Research/~/media/PUBLIKATIONER/Shipping-Market-Review/ Shipping-Market-Review-May-2014.ashx (accessed June 2014).
De Middelaer, N., 2014, Kritische bespreking van potentiele samenwerkingsvormen voor de binnenvaart, Master's thesis, University of Antwerp.
Dullaert, W., Meersman, H., Moglia, F., van de Voorde, E., 1998, Regulation and deregulation in inland navigation, in *8th WCTR proceedings*, pp. 321–334.
EC, 1999, Zestiende rapport-eindevaluatie-over de gemeenschappelijke sloopactie in de binnenvaart.
EICB, 2014, http://informatie.binnenvaart.nl/algemeen/veiligheid/97-afladen-op-waterstand (accessed June 2014).
EUROSTAT, 2014, http://epp.eurostat.ec.europa.eu/portal/page/portal/transport/ data/database (accessed June 2014).
Haralambides, H., 2003, *The economics of bulk shipping pools*, Rotterdam: Center for Maritime Economics and Logistics (MEL), Erasmus University.

Hekkenberg, R., 2012, Inland ships for efficient transport chains, Thesis, TU Delft.

ING Economisch Bureau, 2015, Binnentankvaart verliest koers met aanhoudende overcapaciteit maakt ondernemerschap echt verschil.

IVR, 2013, Western European tank fleet (April 2013).

Jonkeren, O., Rietveld, P. and van Ommeren, J., 2007, Climate change and inland waterway transport: welfare effects of low water levels on the river Rhine, *Journal of Transport Economics and Policy* 41(3), pp. 387–411.

Luman, R., 2013, Herstel binnenvaart uit zicht wacht de drogeladingvloot een warme of koude sanering, ING Economische Bureau.

NEA, 2003, Onderzoek kosten per uur in de binnenvaart, specificatie van de kosten per reisfase voor verschillende scheepstype, Rijswijk, April 2003.

NEA, 2010, Kostenontwikkeling binnenvaart 2009 en raming 2010.

PLATINA, 2014, Market & Awareness, D1.5 Analysis of possibilities to enhance market transparency and synergistic actions – first draft, September 2014.

Quispel, M., 2014, Versterking van de binnenvaartsector 'Het roer van de toekomst in eigen hand?!', STC-Nestra.

Schaffers, H., 2011, Financing inland navigation, in *Future challenges for inland navigation: a scientific appraisal of the consequences of possible strategic and economic developments up to 2030*, ed. Sys, Christa and Vanelslander, Thierry, Antwerp: University Press Antwerp, pp. 189–202.

Schuttevaer, 2010, Waarom de NMA nee zei tegen de oplegregeling in de binnenvaart.

Stopford, M., 2010 [1997], *Maritime Economics*, 3th edition, London and New York: Routledge.

Sys, C., 2010, Inside the box: assessing the competitive conditions, the concentration and the market structure of the container liner shipping industry, Thesis, University of Antwerp.

Sys, C. and Vanelslander, T. 2010, Scenarios and strategies for the inland navigation sector, in *Future challenges for inland navigation – a scientific appraisal of the consequences of possible strategic and economic developments up to 2030*, ed. Sys, Christa and Vanelslander, Thierry, Antwerp: University Press Antwerp, pp. 217–234.

TON (Tankvaart Overleg Nederland), 1997, *Toekomst voor de binnentankvaart, naar grotere zelfredzaamheid van de binnentankvaart in West-Europa*, Rotterdam.

Van Dijk, G., van Bekkum, O. and van den Boogaard, K., 2012, Marktwerking en samenwerking in de binnenvaart: Een rapportage in opdracht van het transitiecomité binnenvaart, The Netherlands Institute for Cooperative Entrepreneurship.

van Hassel, E., 2011, Decreased supply on the small inland waterway network: causes and consequences, in *Future challenges for inland navigation: a scientific appraisal of the consequences of possible strategic and economic developments up to 2030*, ed. Sys, Christa and Vanelslander, Thierry, Antwerp: University Press Antwerp, pp. 101–132.

van Hassel, E., 2013, Structuurverandering in het segment van de grote drogeladingbinnenvaartschepen, Research paper 2013-025, University of Antwerp, Faculty of Applied Economics.

van Hassel, E., 2014, (Over)capaciteitsontwikkeling in de binnenvaarttankermarkt en mogelijke toekomstscenario's, Research paper 2015-005, University of Antwerp, Faculty of Applied Economics.

Van Reeven, P., Nijdam, M., Kuijpers, B. and Karamychev, V., 2010, Economische gevolgen crisisregeling binnenvaart, Erasmus University, Rotterdam.

Verberk, A., 2010, Advies binnenvaartambassadeur, Policy Research Corporation, for Ministry of Transport and Ministry of Economic Affairs.

Vereniging 'De Binnenvaart', 2014, http://debinnenvaart.nl/ (accessed June 2014).

Vlaamse Havencommissie, 2014, De Vlaamse havens – Feiten, statistieken en indicatoren 2013.

5 Existing waterway infrastructures and future needs

Cornelis van Dorsser

5.1 Introduction

Inland waterway systems serve many functions of which fresh water supply, safety against flooding and inland waterway transport (IWT) are generally considered the most important. This chapter concerns the use of the waterways for IWT. Section 5.2 starts with a discussion on the main characteristics of various IWT systems around the world; Section 5.3 addresses the historical development and present state of the West European IWT network, that despite its long history of normalisation and canalisation is now confronted with several new challenges; Section 5.4 provides insights into a few trends that are relevant when developing or upgrading an IWT network; and Section 5.5 concludes with some policy recommendations for the development of future-proof IWT infrastructures.

5.2 Inland waterway characteristics

Inland waters can be defined as areas of water not categorised as 'sea'. They include canals, tidal and non-tidal rivers, lakes, and some estuarial waters (an arm of sea that extends inland to meet the mouth of a river).[1] Vessels that sail on inland waters are not designed for the adverse wave and wind conditions that are encountered at sea. They operate in relatively sheltered waters with severe restrictions to the length, beam, draught and air draught of the vessels. IWT conditions vary considerable with respect to the natural shape of the rivers, the extent to which rivers have been normalised, the extent to which canals have been constructed, and the interaction with other infrastructures such as bridges for road and rail transport and dams for hydropower. Important characteristics of an IWT system are, among others:

- the available depth and draught on the waterways
- the available and allowed length and beam of the inland vessels
- the constraining bridge heights along the waterways
- the operational regime of the IWT infrastructure
- the wave and wind conditions that are encountered

- the strength of the currents that are encountered
- the occurrence and frequency of river ice events
- other specific conditions that affect inland shipping.

These characteristics are important because they constrain the competitiveness of the IWT system. To compete with other modes of transport an inland vessel should be able to obtain sufficient economies of scale as larger vessels have a lower per unit cost than small vessels. In addition the operational regime is also quite important. It makes substantial difference if vessels can be operated 24 hours per day instead of only a few hours during daytime (e.g. because of limited opening times for locks and bridges). It is therefore worth addressing the various waterway characteristics in further detail.

5.2.1   *Maximum available water depth and allowed draught for inland vessels*

For bulk cargoes the water depth is extremely important because deeper draughted vessels offer a higher loading capacity at only marginally higher costs than shallow draught vessels. Deeper draughted vessels are therefore also better able to compete with other modes of transport.

Natural deep water conditions are found in: lower parts of major river basins, such as in the lower part of the Yangtze and Congo; on lakes, such as lake Nasser; and in estuary parts of rivers such as on the Thames or the Gambia. In many inland waterway areas the availability of sufficient water depth is less obvious. Challenging conditions for the development of IWT are, for instance, encountered on rivers with a relatively small discharge volume, and on high discharge rivers with a wide unstable meandering flow bed, such as on the Niger. In these cases human intervention is necessary to obtain a sufficient deep fairway for inland shipping.

The water depth can be permanently increased by normalising the river and constructing dams and river training works as well as temporarily by means of dredging. Efforts to improve the navigability on the Rhine have been conducted since the normalisation and canalisation of the upper Rhine in the early nineteenth century (see Figure 5.1). Over the past two centuries the Rhine has developed into a high quality waterway with a guaranteed water depth of 2.80 m in the lower section and 1.90 m in the middle section (water levels guaranteed for 95 per cent of the time). The navigability of an inland waterway therefore depends not only on its natural conditions, but also on historical efforts to improve the fairway.

5.2.2   *Allowable length and beam for inland vessels*

When sufficient cargo is available longer and wider vessels will enhance scale effects and make IWT operations more cost-effective. The allowable length and beam of inland vessels on a certain waterway stretch is generally

Figure 5.1 The relatively deep normalised Rhine (Source: https://beeldbank.rws.nl, Rijkswaterstaat)

restricted by the available dimensions of locks and bridges (minus a safety margin) as well as by measures to improve the navigational safety in curved river sections. In addition measures are sometimes taken to avoid vessels from getting grinded at both sides of the river in case of distress. This is the main reason why indivisible vessels over 135 m length are not allowed on the Rhine upstream of the Dutch city of Gorinchem, while coupled units are still allowed up to 280 m.

Bulk vessels tend to be optimised at their maximum available draught, which implies that the overall capacity of a vessel combination scales with the product of its length and beam. For large bulk shipments a push barge combination can be very effective. Such combinations were first developed on the Mississippi in the 1850s. It took up to 1957 before the first push barge combination came into service on the Rhine. Figure 5.2 shows an example of a push barge operation.

On the Mississippi up to 40 barges (of 60 × 10.7 × 2.75 m) are shipped in a single flotilla.[2] Large push barge combinations are also encountered on the Orinoco in Venezuela and on the Paraguay-Paraná (Hydrovia waterway) where an entire new fleet of tugboats and dumb barges (of 61 × 15 × 4.27 m) came into service in 2014. These relatively wide and deep barges are able to sail in convoys of 4 × 4 units transporting some 40,000 tonnes at once. Push barge operations are smaller in Europe where depending on the actual water level shipments up to four or six barges (of 76.5 × 11.40 × 3.5 m) are allowed

Figure 5.2 Push barge operation on the Oder (Source: personal archive of author)

on the Rhine and up to nine barges on the Danube between Constanta and Belgrade.

For container transport (see Figures 5.3a and 5.3b) the beam of the vessel is often more important than the length as an increased beam also increases the stability against capsizing, which allows the vessel to stack its containers higher. A rule of thumb is that full containers cannot be loaded higher than they can be stacked wide.[3] For example, a vessel that is able to load four containers wide can carry up to four containers high.

5.2.3   Height constraints for inland vessels

Challenging for the development of inland container barge transport is the fact that many bridges have been constructed across the waterways, of which the historical bridges and the rail bridges causes bottlenecks that are the hardest to solve.

Historical bridges are often considered cultural heritage which make it hard to adjust them – and rail bridges are hard to raise because the railway track can only make a small incline, which implies that the run up to the bridge has to be raised over a long distance. A good example of a crucial waterway section where effective container transport is hard to develop due to the existence of historical bridges can be found in Cairo where the bridges over the Nile prohibit sailing with more than two layers of containers as well as the use of

Figure 5.3 The effect of the beam on the capacity of inland container vessels
(Source: a: Mercurius Shipping Group; b: Dutch Cargo)

larger cruise vessels with multiple decks. Other examples of low bridges are found in the historical cities of Europe such as in Paris.

5.2.4   *Different wind, wave and current conditions*

The design of vessels that sail on the inland waterways is affected by, among others, the wind and wave conditions in which they are operated (i.e. the sea state) and the strength of the currents that they encounter. Higher classification standards apply to vessels that are also intended to sail at sea. A higher sea state requires a stronger hull and a larger freeboard. This makes seagoing vessels heavier and more expensive than vessels that are only designed to sail on inland waters.

When it concerns seagoing vessels a general distinction is made between seagoing inland ships (or estuary vessels) and inland going sea ships (Müller, 2003). The first category concerns inland vessels for which the equipment, strength, stability and freeboard allows operations up to a certain sea state. The second category concerns sea ships (or coasters) for which the draught and air draught are kept low enough to sail upstream rivers.

In addition to the sea state the encountered currents also have an effect on the design of the vessel as stronger currents require a more powerful engine.

5.2.5   *Other specific conditions for inland waterway transport*

Other specific environmental conditions that affect the IWT system are, for instance, the occurrence of ice on rivers and the invasive growth of water plants. To give some examples: ice is an issue in Russia (see Figure 5.4a) and lake Victoria suffers from invasive growth of water hyacinths (see Figure 5.4b).

The quality of an IWT system is finally affected by a broad range of other aspects such as the available aids to navigation, the rules with respect to sailing at night, the available capacity and service level of locks and bridges on the waterway, the availability of sufficient mooring facilities, the extent to which producing and receiving companies have access to quays at the waterside, the institutional framework and legislation for vessel operations (e.g. rules for navigation, technical standards and crew requirements) and the availability of a cluster of maritime suppliers and shipyards.

5.3   West European IWT system

The previous section discussed how the characteristics of the inland waterway system determine the cost-effectiveness of IWT operations. Little attention was given to the role of the infrastructure provider in developing the system. This section concerns the effect of waterway infrastructure developments on the quality of the IWT system. It addresses how the West European IWT system was gradually developed over the past few centuries. This case highlights the large positive effect that infrastructure developments can have on the IWT

Figure 5.4 Frozen port of Moscow (a) and water hyacinths on Lake Victoria (b) (Source: a: www.photo-moscow.net; b: Henk Blaauw)

Figure 5.5 Rhine at Nijmegen (Braun, 1575) (Source: www.gebroedersvanlimburg.nl/
site/200)

system, but it also shows how historical decisions on the dimensions of the
waterways can have an inhibitory effect on the development of at least some
IWT flows.

5.3.1   History of the West European inland waterway system

The waterways used to be the main inland transport mode in Europe for
both freight and passenger transport, in particularly on the Rhine and in the
lower Rhine delta. The Romans already sailed along the Rhine with shallow
draught vessels to control their borders some 2,000 years ago.[4] From about
1100 Dutch fisherman sailed the Rhine upstream from Tiel, Utrecht and
Deventer to Koblenz using wind power (see Figure 5.5). In the seventeenth
and eighteenth centuries the Rhine was used to ship large shipments of wood
for the Dutch shipbuilding industry downstream to Dordrecht on enormous
rafts of up to 300 m long that were manned by about 500 sailors.

At a certain stage people started to dig canals that connected hinterland
areas to the natural river system.[5] Some early canals (small ditches) for the
transport of peat date back to the early thirteenth century, but the true development of canals started with the opening of the canal from Willebroek to
Brussels in 1561. This was the first canal on which transport of passengers
and goods took place by a so-called 'trekschuit', which is a vessel towed by

Figure 5.6 'Trekschuit', ca. 1850 (Source: Collection of Dutch Tiles Museum, inventory number 06192)

man or horse (see Figure 5.6). The 'trekschuit' remained the primary means of transport until the development of the railroads in the nineteenth century.

The first canals only provided a connection from the hinterland to the natural river system. But this changed with the opening of the Briare Canal in 1642 in France, which was the first canal to connect two different waterway basins by using locks. A more structured approach for the construction of canals flowed in the period from 1803 to 1810 when Napoleon aimed to develop his Grand Canal du Nord, that was intended to create a connection between the Scheldt, Meuse and Rhine. Though this canal was never completed, some parts of it were later integrated into other canal developments, such as the Zuid Willemsvaart in the Netherlands that became operational in 1826 (Filarski, 1995). At that time each canal still had its own dimensions for which the locks dictated the size of the vessels that could be accommodated.

The first major attempt to develop a more uniform system was undertaken in 1879 when the French minister of public works, Charles de Freycinet, launched legislation to upgrade and construct 9,000 km of canals. This legislation prescribed a standard vessel with dimensions of 38.5 × 5.05 m. As a result, the *péniche* vessel, with a cargo capacity of 300 tonnes, was designated as the standard vessel on the French canal network (Rijkswaterstaat, 2011). The dimensions of this waterway system were, however, smaller than the dimensions of the canals in the Campine area in Belgium and the Netherlands. In Germany the construction of the Dortmund-Ems Canal between 1886 and 1899 resulted in larger vessels with a length of 67 m and a beam of 8.2 m (for which the length was later increased to accommodate vessels up to 80 m). Subsequently, in 1914, the Rhine-Herne Canal opened which provided an important connection to Dortmund for vessels with a size of 80 × 9.5 meter (De Koter and De Koter, 1999). The allowed length of the barges on these canals has later been increased to 85 meters. Not much later even larger lock chambers of 185 × 23 m were constructed on the Upper Rhine to enable the development of hydropower, starting with the locks at Kembs in 1932. These locks set the beam of a standard Rhine vessel at 11.40 m (now allowed up to 11.45), allowing them to be served two-wide next to each other inside the lock chambers.

5.3.2   *Classification of inland waterways*

All these different waterway infrastructures created a desire for a more uniform European waterway classification system, but it took the Conférence Européenne des Ministres des Transports (CEMT) up to 1954 to agree on an international standard. This classification system divided the waterways into five classes, which were related to five commonly applied vessel types. The applicable waterway class was defined by the largest standard vessel that could be accommodated. The system also provided guidelines for the future dimensions of canals, bridges and ship locks. In addition CEMT recommended the Class IV vessels (those of the Rhine-Herne Canal type) to serve as the standard for waterways of European importance. This explains why this vessel is also often referred to as the 'Europa Vessel'.

When push barges were introduced on the Rhine in 1957 a swift transition from towing of vessels to pushing followed. The CEMT responded in 1961 by adding a Class VI to its classification, but after a while this classification turned out to be inadequate. PIANC, the World Association for Waterborne Transport Infrastructure, took the lead in revising the system. A working group that was specially set up for the purpose produced a report in 1990. A supplement to the report on Class Vb waterways followed later. This prompted the CEMT and the United Nations Economic Commission for Europe (ECE) to produce a uniform new classification, known as the CEMT-1992 classification after the year it was adopted. This new classification also took into account the East European waterways, which tend to have slightly smaller dimensions than in Western Europe. The classification system for the West European waterways (i.e. west of the Elbe) is shown in Table 5.1. A corresponding map that shows the European inland waterways according to their CEMT class is provided in Figure 5.7.

The original CEMT-1992 table contains a number of footnotes. Where two numbers are provided, the first number covers the current situation and the second number provides a guideline for the future. For container transport it was argued that the recommended waterway dimensions are sufficient for the transport of 8.5 ft (or 2.60 m) high containers under the condition that at least 50 per cent of the containers is loaded or that sufficient ballast is taken.

Table 5.1 CEMT-1992 classification for inland waterways west of the Elbe

Type of Inland waterways	Classes of navigable waterways	Motor vessels and barges (Type of vessel: générales characteristics)					Pushed convoys (Type of convoy - Générales characteristics)				Minimum height under bridges
		Designation	Length (m)	Beam (m)	Draught (m)	Tonnage (t)	Length (m)	Beam (m)	Draught (m)	Tonnage (t)	m
OF REGIONAL IMPORTANCE / D'INTERET REGIONAL	I	Péniche / Barge	38.50	5.05	1.80-2.20	250-400					4.00
	II	Kast-Caminois / Campine-Barge	50-55	6.60	2.50	4.00-650					4.00-5.00
	III	Gustav Koenings	67-80	8.20	2.50	650-1000					4.00-5.00
OF INTERNATIONAL IMPORTANCE / D'INTERET INTERNATIONAL	IV	Johan Welker	80-85	9.50	2.50	1000-1500	85	9.50	2.50-2.80	1250-1450	5.25/or 7.00
	Va	Grand bateaux Rhenands / Large Rhine Vessels	95-110	11.40	2.50-2.80	1500-3000	95-110	11.40	2.50-4.50	1600-3000	5.25/or 7.00/or
	Vb						172-185	11.40	2.50-4.50	3200-6000	9.10
	VIa						95-110	22.80	2.50-4.50	3200-6000	7.10/or 9.10
	VIb		140	15.00	3.90		185-195	22.80	2.50-4.50	6400-12000	7.10/or 9.10
	VIc						270-280 / 193-200	22.80 / 33.00-34.20	2.50-4.50 / 2.50-4.50	9600-18000	9.10
	VII						285 / 195	33.00 / 34.20	2.50-4.50	14500-27000	9.10

Source: Rijkswaterstaat (2006, p. 14), originally based on CEMT – Resolution No. 92/2

The reported minimum height underneath the bridges includes a safety margin of 30 cm between the highest point of the ship and the lower end of the bridge. The following minimum vertical clearances between the bottom of the bridge and the water surface were recommended:[6]

- 5.25 m for vessels with two layers of containers
- 7.00 m for vessels with three layers of containers
- 9.10 m for vessels with four layers of containers.

Class Vb is now recommended as the minimum standard for international European waterway connections, with a minimum headroom of 7.0 m for container transport. When existing waterways are upgraded or new ones are built, the CEMT stipulates that efforts should be made to achieve at least Class Va (Rijkswaterstaat, 2011).

5.3.3   *Issues with the present classification system*

The original CEMT-1992 classification is still officially applied but it no longer reflects the true characteristics of the present IWT fleet as the size of the barges has changed, and the cost effective transport of modern pallet-wide and high cube containers would require increased waterway dimensions. This section therefore addresses why a revision of the CEMT-1992 classification would be appropriate.

Roelse (2002) studied the dimensions of the West European fleet and concluded that many vessels have been lengthened. This implies that the average length and tonnage of the vessels has increased over time. In addition the vessels are now also loaded at a greater draught than in the past. Rijkswaterstaat (Dutch national authority responsible for IWT infrastructure) therefore developed the new RWS 2010 classification system that can be regarded as a refinement of the CEMT-1992 classification. The RWS 2010 classification system contains a larger number of categories and also includes the use of coupled units (in Dutch: *Koppelverband*). For a further discussion of the RWS 2010 classification system reference is made to the latest waterway guidelines of Rijkswaterstaat (2011), which are also available in English.

In addition to the use of longer and deeper vessels there are a few recent developments in the container sector that call for yet another major revision of the applied classification system (see also Brolsma, 2014). The standard container used to be 20 or 40 ft long, 8 ft wide, and 8.5 foot high, but nowadays so-called high cube containers of 9.5 ft height are gaining considerable market share. These containers, which are 30.48 cm higher than the standard ones, require more bridge height than accounted for by the CEMT-1992 and RWS 2010 classifications.

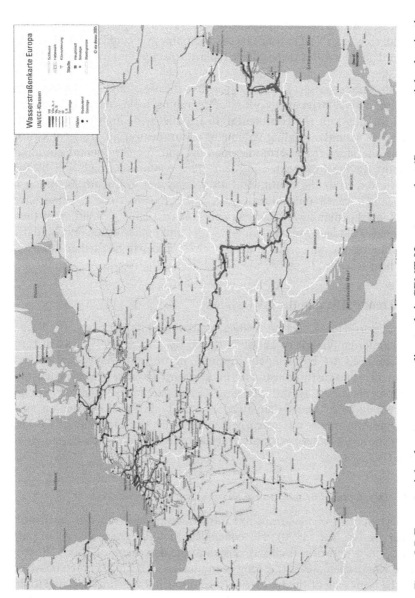

Figure 5.7 European inland waterways according to their CEMT-92 waterway class (Source: www.inlandnavigation.org)

The use of pallet-wide containers (having a width of 2.50, 2.56 or even 2.60 m instead of 2.44 m) is also becoming more common in Europe. These containers, which allow two standard 1.20 m wide European pallets to be loaded next to each other inside the container, do not fit (properly) into the holds of a standard 11.45 m (used to be 11.40 m) wide Class Va vessel.[7]

Solving this problem for the widest containers would ideally require the width of the locks to be increased. Alternatively one could develop asymmetrical vessels with a smaller gangway on one side. Though this option should be technically feasible it may not be very desirable as it could reduce the safety on board and decreases the available ballast capacity (requiring higher bridge heights).

Finally one can observe a strong growth in the use of high cube pallet-wide 45 ft containers. After many years of searching for a cost effective intermodal loading unit the continental 45 ft pallet-wide high cube container (that offers a similar loading volume as a European truck trailer) has now become the standard intermodal loading unit for continental container transport on the European continent. This container, which will be further referred to as the continental 45 ft container, is already booming in European short sea and rail transport, and is starting to be used more frequently on the inland waterways as well. The cost-effective loading of these containers will ideally require longer, wider and higher waterway standards depending on the concerned waterway class. This will be further discussed in the next section.

5.4   Trends affecting the IWT system

Hydraulic structures, such as bridges, weirs and ship locks typically have a technical design lifetime of about 75 to 100 years. New IWT infrastructures therefore need to be planned carefully in order to avoid suboptimal performance and costly adjustments in the future. To make new infrastructure developments robust against changing user requirements insight is required in very-long-term trends that affect the IWT system. Research on such very-long-term trends was recently conducted by Van Dorsser (2015). This section addresses some important trends that effect the long-term development of the IWT system.

5.4.1   Development of new transport infrastructure networks

The development of new transport infrastructure networks was extensively studied by Grübler (1990). He concluded that the rise and fall of new infrastructure networks is closely related to the movement of about 50 years lasting Kondratieff waves (i.e. long economic cycles), which can be observed since the beginning of the Industrial Revolution and are closely related to the fundamental long-term drivers of the world economy. Grübler found that each subsequent wave gave birth to a new transport infrastructure network

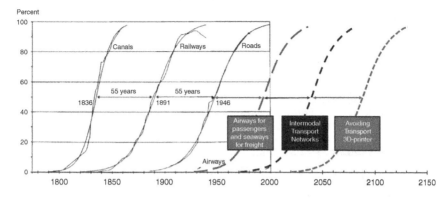

Figure 5.8 Historical and expected development of new transport infrastructure networks (Source: Van Dorsser, 2015, p. 230, based on Grübler 1990, p. 187)

and that the development of these networks took place over a period of about
two Kondratieff waves.

Figure 5.8 shows the historical development of new transport infrastructure networks. The s-curves for the development of the canals, railways and
roads were taken from Grübler (1990). They show the overall length of
the transport networks in the US as a percentage of their ultimate length.[8]
Interesting is that Grübler also found the size of each new transport infrastructure network to be an order of magnitude larger than its predecessor.
The logic behind this empirical 'law' is that in order to overcome the issues
with the old system a new solution is required that performs substantially
better. In this respect it is interesting to observe that the networks that follow
the road network (i.e. the airways and modern seaways) only make use of
ports and no longer require the construction of physical lanes. It is unlikely
that new transport infrastructure networks would have been developed if they
would have required the construction of physical lanes that are an order of
magnitude larger than the road network.

When Grübler published his work it was still unclear what infrastructure
network would be next. Van Dorsser (2015) concluded that a new transport
infrastructure network is now developing around the concept of intermodal
transport, for which he argues that this time it is the number of transport options
that increase by an order of magnitude. Following the rise of the intermodal
transport network he foresees a final transport network to be developed around
the principle of avoiding transport, for instance by means of 3D-printing techniques in combination with recyclable or locally produced bio-based materials.
The impact of 3D-printing on the overall transport volume is, however, expected
to remain rather small throughout the first half of the twenty-first century. For
the next 50 years the most important changes in the transport system are likely
to relate to the ongoing growth of the intermodal transport network.

An interesting feature of the intermodal transport network is that it does not replace the former networks, but combines them in an as smart as possible way. Older networks such as the IWT and rail network are no longer gradually phasing out, as they were the second half of the twentieth century, but instead have become a vital part of the modern intermodal transport chain. This gives a new impulse to the former IWT and rail networks and even requires the road network to be upgraded in order to allow for the use of larger and heavier trucks on pre- and end-haulage trips.

5.4.2   *Development of continental container transport*

The full development of the intermodal transport network can be thought of as going through certain stages. When considering the development of intermodal container barge transport in Western Europe one can distinguish between three subsequent stages. The first stage concerns the development of inland container terminals at quite some distance from the seaports. This stage, that roughly lasted from 1970 to 1995, gave birth to the hinterland container services on the Rhine between the Dutch and Belgium seaports and the German Hinterland. In the second stage container terminals were developed close to each other and close to the seaports. Towards the end of this stage, that is now reaching completion, a dense network of inland terminals exists that connects many logistical areas to the waterfront. The availability of this network is a necessary precondition for the development of continental container lines (i.e. between two inland terminals) in the third stage, which may now start to develop.[9]

The development of intermodal continental container barge transport is far more complicated than the development of hinterland container lines to/from the deepsea terminals, because the bundling of cargo in time and space is harder to accomplish for continental containers than for deepsea containers; an additional pre- and end-haulage trip and terminal handling are required;[10] and because continental 45 ft containers require more space on board the vessels than their deepsea counterparts. In addition continental 45 ft containers do not fit well into the holds of the vessels as pallet-wide and high cube container dimensions have not yet been taken into account in the CEMT-1992 classification.

Table 5.2 clearly illustrates the incompatibility between the space required for loading continental 45 ft containers and the available vessel dimensions for the five smallest waterway classes. On the basis of this table it can be concluded that Class I to V vessels are only able to utilise some 35 to 58 per cent of their overall loading volume when they sail with continental 45 ft containers.[11]

The European Commission (2011) aims to shift 30 per cent of all long haulage road freight over 300 km to intermodal transport by 2030 and 50 per cent by 2050. This policy can be enhanced by upgrading the existing waterways to improve the conditions for continental container barge transport. Possible measures would be to increase the length of the vessels on Class II waterways up to about 58–60 m in order to enable four continental 45 ft containers to be loaded in front of each other; to increase the allowable beam of

Table 5.2 Evaluation of loading efficiency for continental 45 ft containers

Item \ Waterway	Class I	Class II	Class III	Class IV	Class V
Maximum dimensions					
– Length	38.5 m	55.0 m	80.0 m	85.0 m	110.0 m
– Beam	5.05 m	6.60 m	8.20 m	9.50 m	11.45 m*
– Height	4.00 m	5.00 m	5.00 m	7.00 m	9.10 m
Hold dimensions					
– Length**	23.00 m	39.00 m	56.00 m	61.00 m	86.00 m
– Width***	3.70 m	5.25 m	6.85 m	8.15 m	10.10 m
Theoretical capacity					
– 45 ft cont. in length	1.66 box	2.81 box	4.04 box	4.40 box	6.20 box
– 45 ft cont. in width	1.42 box	2.01 box	2.62 box	3.12 box	3.87 box
– 45 ft cont. in height	1 layer	2 layers	2 layers	3 layers	4 layers
Total Capacity	2.36 box	11.30 box	21.17 box	41.21 box	95.98 box
Guaranteed capacity					
– 45 ft cont. in length	1	2	4	4	6
– 45 ft cont. in width	1	2	2	3	3
– 45 ft cont. in height	1	1	1	2	3
Actual capacity	1	4	8	24	54
Loading efficiency	*42%*	*35%*	*38%*	*58%*	*56%*

Note: *Based on actual dimensions; **Based on existing vessels; ***Based on beam minus 1.35 m

Source: Adopted from Van Dorsser (2015, p. 236) with slight modifications

the vessels on Class V waterways to about 11.6–12.0 m in order to support the effective loading of four 2.50–2.60 m wide containers next to each other;[12] and to increase the headroom underneath the bridges according to the heights proposed in Table 5.3.[13]

Adjusting the bridge heights will be a major challenge as the CEMT-92 standard still recommends a much lower headroom of just 7.0 m for Class IV waterways and 9.1 m for Class V waterways. Upgrading the width on Class V waterways may be less complicated as the PIANC (1990) guidelines already foresee the use of vessels of 11.5 and 11.6 m width, for which they advised an increase in the width of new locks from 12.0 m to 12.5 m. Knowing that vessels of 11.4 m are able to sail through locks of 12.0 m wide, the newly constructed 12.5 m wide locks should already be able to accommodate vessels up to some 11.9 m, in particular when it concerns container vessels that tend to have a relatively shallow draught compared to vessels sailing with bulk cargoes.

5.4.3 Other important trends that affect the IWT system

Other important trends that affect the IWT system can be related to the development of the type and size of the vessels and their relative competitiveness compared to other modes of transport.

Table 5.3 Calculation of required headroom

Item \ Waterway	Classes II–III	Class IV	Class V
Applied vessel dimensions	63 × 7.2 m	85 × 9.5 m	110 × 11.45 m
Capacity for continental high cube pallet-wide 45 ft containers*	3L × 2W × 2H 12 containers	4L × 3W × 3H 36 containers	6L × 4W × 4H 96 containers
Cargo weight in adverse loading condition**	40 tonnes	120 tonnes	320 tonnes
Average draught in case of vessel without extra ballast capacity in side wing tanks***	1.0 m	1.0 m	1.1 m
Required minimum draught at aft ship to keep propeller submerged	1.3 m	1.4 m	1.5 m
Draught at fore ship when vessel is trimmed to keep propeller submerged	0.7 m	0.6 m	0.7 m
Assumed height of double bottom	0.5 m	0.5 m	0.5 m
Height of container layers	2 × 2.9 m	3 × 2.9 m	4 × 2.9 m
Recommended headroom clearance	0.3 m	0.3 m	0.3 m
Required headroom for vessel without extra ballast capacity in side wing tanks	5.9 m	8.9 m	11.7 m
Additional ballast required to avoid trim and obtain even keel loaded ballast condition	110 tonnes	280 tonnes	380 tonnes
Required headroom for vessel with sufficient ballast capacity in side wing tanks to obtain even keel loaded ballast condition	5.3 m	8.1 m	10.9 m

Note: *Assuming four containers to be loaded next to each other in Class V vessels; **Assuming 80 per cent of the vessel to be loaded with empty 45 ft containers of 4.2 tonnes each; ***Based on tonnage certificates of real ships

Looking back over a period of about 100 years one can observe the road system to have become much more cost-effective due to the construction of motorways and the development of larger trucks with more powerful engines. As a result the smallest vessels face great difficulty to compete with road transport and have lost a great part of their market share. Hardly any Class I to III vessels have been constructed since the 1960s, which implies that almost the entire small vessel fleet is now over 55 years old (Van Dorsser, 2015). Newbuilding of small vessels does not take place because new vessels cannot compete with the old and fairly depreciated fleet and also have difficulty to compete with modern road transport.

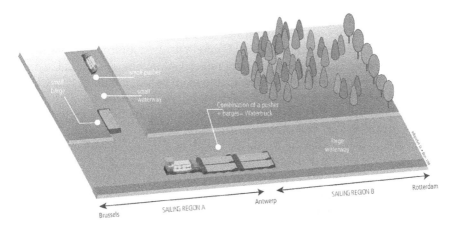

Figure 5.9 Illustration of watertruck concept (Source: Watertruck Brochure, www. watertruck.eu)

The utilisation of the smallest Class I to III waterways has entered into a negative spiral since the end of the Second World War. Inland vessel operations have been gradually phasing out on the smaller waterways because logistical companies turned their operations towards the road side, which is more flexible, requires less storage and is also more cost-effective in case of small transport volumes. This caused parts of the system to fall into disrepair, which is most obvious for the smallest Class I waterways. Despite an increased political interest in the revitalisation of the smaller waterways and the preservation of waterfront business areas[14] it is very well possible that IWT will gradually phase out on the smallest waterways, unless these waterways are upgraded to support larger vessels.

Some new Class I to III vessels may once again be constructed after the existing ones are discarded. If this happens newbuilding is most likely for bulk cargoes as the loading capacity of bulk vessels is not as much affected by the small beam as for containers. Assuming that some new vessels will be constructed (which is uncertain) one can anticipate an increased share of coupled units as these units are more cost effective than a single unit. How many old vessels will eventually be replaced is hard to say as competition with road transport remains challenging and staffing is increasingly becoming an issue, in particular for the smallest vessels that only provide small accommodation.

New business concepts are proposed to safeguard IWT on the smaller waterways, but these concepts are still on the drawing board or in the early stage of a subsidised pilot. Blaauw (2010) proposed a 'Barge Truck' concept with small barges that are coupled into a push barge combination on the larger waterways and use their bow thrusters to sail on their own on the smaller waterways. Van Hassel (2011) suggested a similar system in which the barges are equipped with stern thrusters that allow them to sail independently over a larger distance. The Watertruck project (www.watertruck.eu) subsequently proposed to use a small pusher on the smaller waterways and a large pusher on the larger waterways (see Figure 5.9). In addition it also aims to solve the staffing issue by adopting a completely different operational regime. It no longer works with a fixed crew that lives on board, but allows the boatsmen to drive home at the end of their shift. It is still too early to tell if one of these new concepts will be successful. The continuation of IWT on the smallest Class I to III waterways is therefore still uncertain.

For container cargoes the width and height of the waterways is much more important than for bulk cargoes, because the vessel capacity scales with the square of the beam (see Figure 5.3). Small Class II and III container vessels with a capacity of 24 to 32 TEU have an almost two times higher per container cost level than Class IV vessels with a capacity of 90 TEU.[15] Class IV vessels are presently the smallest size for which investments in new container vessels seem to be financially feasible. The performance of existing Class III vessels is sometimes improved by increasing their length up to 85 m (this recently happened with two vessels of the Mercurius Shipping Group) or by modifying them into a coupled unit.

Possible trends regarding the development of IWT on the larger inland waterways can be identified by looking at the characteristics of inland vessels. Hekkenberg (2013) studied the optimal size of an indivisible unit on the lower Rhine up to Koblenz for which he systematically varied the length (from 40 to 185 m) and the beam (from 5 to 25 m). He concluded that on international stretches from Rotterdam to Duisburg and Koblenz vessels with a length of 135 to 160 m tend to be optimal.[16] Raising the length from 160 to 185 m makes them relatively heavy and less cost effective. The maximum allowable length of 135 m is therefore quite sufficient. With respect to the beam he concluded that the widest vessels up to 25 m tend to be the most cost-effective. A further increase in the beam of inland vessels up to the maximum allowable width of 22.9 m is therefore to be expected.

The optimal barge sizes according to Hekkenberg also indicate a rationale for the development of larger dumb barges. An early study on the economic effects of push barge combinations with four larger barges of 90 × 14.0 × 3.5 m was conducted in the 1980s on behalf of Rijkswaterstaat (EBW, 1981). This study confirmed that larger barges can be operated at lower costs. A later study initiated by ThyssenKrupp Veerhaven BV paved the way for the introduction of larger dumb barges of 110 × 12.5 × 4.0 m (Hoogwout *et al.*, 2004). Following this study the CCNR was willing to accept these barges, but they were never constructed due to compatibility issues with old barges during the transition stage. Wider barges can also be very interesting for container transport because an increase in the beam from 11.45 m to about 14.5 m allows for an additional row and layer of containers, which potentially increases the loading capacity by about 56 per cent assuming that sufficient headroom is available.

5.5 Developing future-proof infrastructures

Based on the discussion in this chapter a few policy recommendations can be made for the development of future-proof IWT infrastructures.

5.5.1 There is no universal design standard for IWT systems

The properties of the IWT system vary considerable with respect to the natural depth of the waterways, the allowable length and beam of the vessels, the height constraints along the route, the encountered sea states and some other specific waterway conditions such as ice and uncontrolled growth of water plants. For each waterway system the optimal dimensions and service levels depend on the expected transport volumes and the required investments to create and/or maintain the system. It is not sensible to develop a single waterway classification system that can be applied on a universal basis. At best one can obtain a regional standard for a larger set of interconnected waterways. When developing or upgrading an IWT system in an area where IWT plays only a very moderate roll it is not advisable to base the proposed waterway dimensions on an existing standard for another IWT system because the conditions on these waterways are not likely to correspond with the actual situation in the area where the IWT system is to be developed and the applied classification system itself may no longer be optimal.

5.5.2 Create sufficient economies of scale

The large investments that are required to develop a navigable waterway make it hard to develop the IWT system in areas where IWT plays only a moderate role, in particular when the expected transport volumes are rather small such as in many African countries. An additional challenge compared to the heydays of IWT in the nineteenth century is that the IWT system has to compete directly with existing rail and road transport. This implies that new IWT infrastructure investments will only be successful if the vessels that use the infrastructure are large enough to create sufficient economies of scale. The chicken-and-egg problem in this respect is that governments are not willing to invest in the IWT system if there are no users, and vessel operators are reluctant to invest in vessels if the government lacks a sound track record in maintaining the water depth. In the Hydrovia project this issue was solved by a concession in which the construction and maintenance of the waterway is executed by a renowned dredging company that is entitled to charge a fee for the use of the waterway. Another important reason for the success of the Hydrovia waterway is, however, the fact that the channel is also used by seagoing vessels which makes the income flow for the concession holder less dependent on the relatively small contributions from inland vessels.

5.5.3 *Be aware of complications when upgrading the system*

Once in place the width of the waterway is the hardest to adjust. Hydraulic structures such as locks and bridges have a typical technical lifetime of about 75 to 100 years. This implies that the width between bridge piers or inside lock chambers is set for a very long period of time after construction. It is sensible to take some additional width margin into account when developing the system. The same holds for the height of the floor in the locks, as one can very well develop a waterway by gradually increasing the water depth as long as the floor of the locks does not become a bottleneck. With respect to the headroom underneath bridges policy makers are advised to base new rail bridges on the ideal height for future operations. This is less important for road bridges as these can be raised easier than rail bridges, as rail bridges only allow for a small incline of the access by 1 or 2 per cent while for road bridges an incline of the access up to 10 per cent may still be acceptable. The length of the locks is less an issue as ship locks can still be lengthened at a later stage if sufficient space is reserved. However, in case of a single lock chamber the waterway will be blocked for a long period during construction which is presumably not acceptable.

5.5.4 *Take different characteristics of bulk and container cargoes into account*

IWT infrastructures developers must be aware of the different characteristics of bulk and container vessels. For bulk vessels the draught is more important than the air draught. A marginal increase in the allowable length, beam or draught of a bulk vessel results in a marginal increase of its capacity. It is therefore sensible to expect bulk vessels to follow the dimensions of the available waterway infrastructure and focus primarily on maintaining and/or improving the depth of the waterways.

For container transport the stability against capsizing (i.e. a function of the beam) and the air draught are often more important than the draught. The nature of container transport is such that an increase in the capacity of the vessels takes place in discrete steps. If the dimensions of the waterway are only a few centimetres too small this can have a huge effect on the utilisation of the vessel. One can therefore not simply argue that the vessel size should be set according to the dimensions of the waterways. To enable cost-effective container barge transport one has to provide the infrastructure accordingly.

5.5.5 *Compatibility of high cube, pallet-wide, and 45 ft containers*

The dimensions of the high cube container were not yet taken into account in the CEMT-92 classification standard as their numbers were still relatively small, but the high cube container (that is 2.90 m instead of 2.60 m high) is now gaining a large share in the overall container fleet. This implies that inland vessels require more headroom to sail with the same number of containers. For European cargoes the pallet-wide container enables the effective loading of two Euro-pallets (of 1.20 m width) next to each other inside the container. Because these containers are 2.50 to 2.60 m instead of 2.44 m wide they no longer fit (properly) into the holds of a large Rhine vessel (Class V). In addition European short-sea transport uses longer 45 ft containers. These higher, wider and longer containers have eventually resulted in the development of the continental high cube, pallet-wide, 45 ft container that has a similar loading capacity as a standard European lorry truck. This continental container is now frequently used in European short-sea and rail transport and is also slowly finding its way onto the inland waterways.

5.5.6 Be prepared for continental container transport

The European Union aims at a shift of 30 per cent of all long haulage road transport over 300 km to intermodal transport by the 2030 and a 50 per cent modal shift by 2050. In areas where IWT is available it has the potential to offer a high quality intermodal transport solution, but in order to do so it needs to be cost-effective. This is complicated by, among others, the fact that the European IWT infrastructure is not fully compatible with the characteristics of the continental 45 ft container. To enable the cost-effective transport of continental 45 ft containers the following upgrades are suggested:

- Class II waterways: increase allowable length to 58–60 m
- Class II waterways: increase headroom to 5.3–5.9 m
- Class III waterways: increase headroom to 5.3–5.9 m
- Class IV waterways: increase headroom to 8.1–8.9 m
- Class V waterways: increase headroom to 10.9–11.7 m
- Class V waterways: increase allowable beam to 11.6–12.0 m.

The proposed upgrades provide an indication of the ideal waterway dimensions from the perspective of the vessel operator (i.e. allowing for an optimal utilisation of the vessels under all circumstances). For each adjustment two numbers are indicated. The lower number concerns the dimension for which transport of empty continental 45 ft containers of just 2.50 m width is possible if certain adjustments to the vessel are made at costs of a higher fuel consumption (i.e. by applying a shorter, less optimal hull shape and using a considerable amount of ballast capacity). The higher values indicate the ideal waterway dimensions for which transport of all kinds of empty continental 45 ft containers of up to 2.60 m width is possible in a more fuel effective way (i.e. using a smooth hull shape and no need for unnecessary ballast).

5.5.7 Anticipate changing user requirements on small inland waterways

The future use of the smaller Class I to III European waterways is uncertain. Hardly any new Class I to III vessels have been constructed since the 1960s, and the size of the fleet is now steadily decreasing. It is possible that IWT operations will not be continued on the smallest waterways at some stage in the future. In particular the smallest Class I waterways may require an upgrade in order to remain competitive *vis-à-vis* road transport. When IWT operations are continued one can expect an increased share of coupled units, for which the operational costs per tonne are smaller than for a single unit. In addition it is possible that small waterway operations will shift to the use of small push barge combinations, for which a number of new business concepts were recently proposed. Such changes are expected to have an effect on the functional requirements of the IWT system as they require longer locks, longer quays and sufficient facilities for mooring of dumb barges and coupling or decoupling of small push barge combinations.

5.5.8   *Anticipate the development of wider vessels on the Rhine*

A recent study on the optimal dimensions for inland vessels on the Rhine indicates that the maximum allowable length of 135 m for an indivisible vessel is quite sufficient, but that further cost reductions can be obtained by increasing the beam of the vessels up to or even beyond the maximum allowed beam of 22.9 m. The development of wider vessels therefore seems to be just a matter of time.

Notes

1 www.gov.uk/guidance/inland-waterways-and-categorisation-of-waters (accessed 18 November 2015).
2 The dimensions of the barges mentioned in this section are intended to give an indication of the size of the operations. In reality a few different barge sizes are used.
3 This is only a rule of thumb. For heavy containers the stability of a four-container wide vessel is often limited to three layers, while empty containers can often be loaded as an extra layer on top of the loaded containers without having much effect on the stability of the vessel.
4 The discussion in this section is based on Genealogisch en Historisch Genootschap Redichem (2009).
5 The discussion on the development of the early canals is based on, among others, Wikipedia and other internet sources.
6 When taking into account the required safety margin of 30 cm the maximum height of the vessel above the waterline is limited to 4.95 m, 6.70 m and 8.80 m.
7 Some 11.45 m wide vessels (with a hold of 10.10 m wide) manage to load four of the slimmest 2.50 m wide pallet wide containers next to each other (having 2 cm margin between each container). The loading of these containers is, however, problematic as hardly any heeling of the vessel is allowed during the loading process, the containers cannot be bulging and damages occur more frequently. The present width of 11.45 m is therefore too slim to load four pallet-wide containers properly next to each other.
8 The development of transport infrastructure networks took place more or less simultaneously in Europe except for the development of the canals that took place over a much longer period of time.
9 Reference is made to the transport of continental 45 ft containers between the Dutch inland terminals in Cuijk and Veghel and the shortsea terminals in Rotterdam that commenced in 2013 and the continental container service on the Rhine that was launched by the Danser Group in 2015.

10 Deepsea terminals generally charge a fixed terminal handling fee, regardless of the mode of transport on which the container enters or leaves the terminal, which is included in the freight rate of the deepsea transport leg.
11 The theoretical capacity of the vessels is based on the rule of thumb that containers can be loaded as high as they are loaded wide. For normal pallet-wide containers the width goes down to 2.50 m, but for special containers such as reefers or containers with curtains a wider frame of 2.56 m (or even 2.60 m) is used. Table 5.2 is based on a vessel loaded with empty continental 45 ft containers of 2.56 m width and full ballast in the side wing tanks.
12 Proper loading requires at least 5 cm free space at each side of the containers. When assuming 2.50 m wide containers, the required width of the hold becomes 10.25 m. This is 15 cm wider than the hold of a standard 11.45 m vessel, which implies that the width for a continental vessel should at least be set at 11.6 m to support the loading of four 2.50 m wide containers. For the loading of four 2.56 m wide containers the corresponding width is 11.84 m; in the case of 2.60 m wide containers the required width becomes 12.0 m.
13 Or possibly by a smaller amount when assuming a certain load factor in both directions, but unlike shipments to/from the deepsea terminals this does not necessarily have to be the case for continental cargoes.
14 This trend can be clearly observed in Belgium where the government is actively supporting the construction of new private quay walls, but it is also visible in the Netherlands where the province of Zuid-Holland has, for instance, adopted an active policy to preserve waterborne business areas.
15 To give an idea, the costs of a Class IV vessel is roughly one-and-a-half times the costs of a Class III vessel, which implies that the costs per container are almost two times as high for a Class III vessel than for a Class IV vessel.
16 Hekkenberg made designs for indivisible vessels of various lengths of which the longest ones are 135, 160 and 185 m. The vessels of 135 and 160 m turned out to outperform the vessels of 185 m which implies that there is an optimum after which it is no longer useful to further lengthen the vessel.

References

Blaauw, H. (2010) Barge Truck Overall Report, presentation at 6th EWIN Conference 2010, Baja, Hungary.
Brolsma, J.U. (2014) Rapportage containerhoogtemetingen, DVS Rijkswaterstaat.
De Koter, M. and R. de Koter (1999) *Binnenvaart wat vaart waar*, de Alk, Alkmaar.
EBW (1981) Enkele economische aspecten van duwvaart met 4 Europa III-bakken en 6 Europa IIA-bakken, Economisch bureau voor het weg- en watervervoer, Rijswijk.
European Commission (2011) *White Paper on transport: Roadmap to a single European transport area – towards a competitive and resource-efficient transport system*, Office for Official Publications of the European Communities, Luxembourg.
Filarski, R. (1995) *Kanalen van de koning koopman: Goederenvervoer, binnescheepvaart en kanalenbouw in Nederland en Belgie in de eerste helft van de 19ᵉ eeuw*, NEHA, Amsterdam.
Genealigisch en Historisch Genootschap Redichem (2009) *Echo's van zes dorpen*, No. 1, pp. 7–10.
Grübler, A. (1990) *The rise and fall of infrastructures: dynamics of evolution and technological change in transport*, Physica-Verlag, Heidelberg.
Hekkenberg, R.G. (2013) Inland ships for efficient transport chains, Thesis, TUDelft.

Hoogwout, P., B. Boneschansker, F. Quadvlieg and H. Blaauw (2004) Met 18.000 ton de Rijn op, *Schip en werf de zee*, May, pp. 26–29.

Müller, E. (2003) Innovative transport vehicles – Rhine, Working Paper for project: European Strategies to Promote Inland Navigation, WG3 Intermodality & Interoperability.

PIANC (1990) Standardization of Inland Waterways' Dimensions, Report of Working Group 9 of the Permanent Technical Committee I, Supplement to Bulletin No. 71, General Secretariat of PIANC, Brussels.

Rijkswaterstaat (2006) *Richtlijnen Vaarwegen*, 2nd edition, Ministerie van Verkeer en Waterstaat, Rijkswaterstaat Adviesdienst Verkeer en Vervoer, Rotterdam.

Rijkswaterstaat (2011) *Waterway Guidelines 2011*, ed. J.U. Brolsma and K. Roelse, English translation of Dutch Version, Rijkswaterstaat, Centre for Transport and Navigation.

Roelse, K. (2002) *Classificatie en kenmerken van de Europese vloot en de actieve vloot in Nederland*, Rijkswaterstaat, Adviesdienst Verkeer en Vervoer, Rotterdam.

Van Dorsser, C. (2015) Very long term development of the Dutch inland waterway transport system: policy analysis, transport projections, shipping scenarios, and a new perspective on economic growth and future discounting, TRAIL Thesis Series, TU Delft.

Van Hassel, E. (2011) Developing a small barge convoy system to reactivate the use of the small inland waterway network, Thesis, University of Antwerp.

6 Inland river ports

Brian Slack and Claude Comtois

Inland river ports represent a subset of ports that receive relatively little attention outside their own limited milieus. Academic focus in particular has been on deep-sea ports, and there is a large literature that has developed on port morphologies, traffic evolution, economic impacts, port-urban relationships, governance etc. (Notteboom, 2013; Rodrigue *et al.* 2009). We suggest that the principal reason for this is that deep-sea ports are particularly involved in container handling, and that as a relatively new activity container handling has generated significant impacts that are transforming port economics and operations, the shipping industry itself and global networks. Inland ports, in comparison, remain dominated by bulk commodities, activities that are perceived to be less complex and less dynamic. It is interesting to note that the bulk business of deep-sea ports too remains under-researched in the academic literature.

Yet inland ports represent very important nodes in transport chains. Their traffic contributes greatly to regional economic activity, and volumes often exceed that of the coastal ports. As inland water transport is seen as a green solution to road congestion its performance and ability to offer an alternative to other modes depends considerably on the efficiency and capacities of inland ports. This chapter examines the functions and importance of inland ports, including the actors involved in shipping and cargo handling, the governance and network structures, and their external links. It draws examples from four major river systems: the Rhine, the Yangtze, the St Lawrence-Great Lakes and the Mississippi. The analysis provides insights not only into the potentials and constraints of inland port development but also contributes to the growing academic enquiry into the how inland networks evolve and models of port regionalisation.

6.1 Defining inland ports

There is a great deal of imprecision in defining inland ports (Rodrigue *et al.* 2010). The term is frequently applied to inland terminals that are linked to ports by rail (Monios and Wang 2013; Rodrigue *et al.* 2010), facilities that are sometimes referred to as dry ports (Roso *et al.* 2009). When applied, to inland navigation terminals only the designation is loosely applied, so that detailed comparisons are difficult, and sometimes confusing. For example, are 'up-stream' ports such as Hamburg and Antwerp inland ports (Baird 1996)? It is evident that they and other ports such as New Orleans are located on rivers and may be hundreds of kilometres from the open ocean. Functionally and competitively they are comparable to ports more directly adjacent to seas that are usually referred to as gateway ports. Channel restrictions are usually associated with inland ports but this too is an imperfect differentiating characteristic, since many coastal ports too suffer from shallow access channels. Is distance from the ocean a criterion? On the St Lawrence the tidal reach extends over 1,000 km from the open ocean. A channel depth yardstick would be equally difficult to apply even though many inland navigation systems such as the Rhine are characterised by water depths only of a few metres. On the other hand, the St Lawrence-Great Lakes system offers access to vessels drawing up to 8 m, allowing many ocean-going ships to sail 2,600 km inland from the Atlantic. A functional definition would be imperfect because the cargo profiles of many river ports differ little from many small and medium-sized ports at ocean locations. Equally, a definition based on traffic volumes would be difficult to apply, since many inland ports exceed the cargo throughputs of coastal ports.

Given the difficulty in selecting appropriate criteria, here we apply a somewhat arbitrary classification. For each river system we assign the largest multifunctional port complex located closest to the ocean as the ocean gateway, and all the ports upstream, including public and private facilities, are defined as inland. This simple taxonomy works well for three of the four river systems: Shanghai for the Yangtze, Rotterdam/Antwerp for the Rhine and New Orleans for the Mississippi. The St Lawrence is more complicated because of its unique configuration. The largest port is Sept Iles, a few hundred kilometres from the Atlantic, but this is not a true multifunctional port. That status would apply to Montreal, 1,600 km inland. Unlike two of the other defined gateway ports, Shanghai and New Orleans, which also suffer from some water depth constraints, Montreal is non-tidal.

6.2   Inland ports, the role of bulk cargoes

Despite having proposed a working definition of an inland port, it is inordinately difficult to identify the actual number of ports in a given river-inland navigation system. The count of port infrastructures is very large because there are a large number of sites developed by and for manufacturing establishments and are largely independent of public oversight. For example, on the Rhine and its tributaries 334 facilities have been recorded, on the Mississippi the US Corps of Army Engineers (USACE) inventories 971 infrastructures, on the Yangtze official agencies record 220 fluvial ports, and on the St Lawrence-Great Lakes 105 ports are recognised. Many of these are insignificant, however.

Table 6.1 identifies the ten largest inland ports in each river system and provides an indication of the scale and importance of river ports that are comparable to many deep-sea equivalents. Functionally, the inland ports are dominated by bulk cargo shipments. With a few exceptions, discussed more fully below, bulk cargoes account for the entire traffic of inland ports. Even where other cargoes such as containers are handled they account for less than 10 per cent of the total traffic. Inland ports play a particularly important role in the shipment of agricultural products such as cereals, industrial raw materials such as coal and ores, construction materials such as sand and cement, liquid bulk such as petroleum and chemicals, and semi-finished manufactured goods such as steel products. These are goods that are shipped in large quantities and are not as time sensitive on the whole as compared to other goods, such as finished manufactured goods. Inland shipping provides a means of transport that is well suited to the demand. A further feature of the bulk trade of the rivers, with the exception of the Rhine, is that the majority of traffic movements are between ports within the systems themselves, whereas on the Rhine the flows are dominated by movements to and from Rotterdam and Antwerp. From a historical perspective these bulk products for the most part are the residual trades left to inland shipping after competition from other modes, road transport in particular, that have captured high value goods. Thus, inland ports have been seen, mistakenly by some, as residual transport fixtures because of their dependence on bulk goods and in many cases lacking dynamism in attracting new traffic.

What is overlooked is that inland ports remain important components of industrial supply chains. Terminals are at the beginning or end points in transport chains (Kreutzberger and Konings 2013) and have been established in proximity to mines where iron ore, coal, limestone and other industrial raw materials are produced such as Duisburg, Two Harbors and Stoneport, or where agricultural goods are assembled such as Thunder Bay. Road and rail connections are employed to link the ports to more distant supply and demand points. Other inland ports such as Ludwigshafen and Detroit are located adjacent to factories that use the raw materials produced elsewhere, including primary goods imported from overseas via the gateway ports. It is easy to undervalue the role of inland ports in handling aggregates such as sand and gravel for construction. This low-value commodity nevertheless is an essential requirement for road and building construction and most ports are involved in varying degrees, with the Yangtze ports handling large quantities, such as 28 million tons at Nanjing.

The historic industrial nature of inland ports directly affects their morphology and operations. With the exception of the St Lawrence-Great Lakes system, the capacities of inland craft are much smaller than deep-sea ships because of river and canal channel depth limitations. As a result inland ports have to provide a relatively large number of berths compared to the volume

Table 6.1 Largest ports on the four river systems, 2013 (traffic in millions of tons)

Rhine	traffic	Mississippi	traffic	Yangtze	traffic	St Lawrence-Great Lakes	traffic
Duisburg	49.4	S. Louisiana	252.1	Zhangjiagang	243.2	Duluth	34.7
Cologne	11.7	Baton Rouge	59.9	Nanjing	207.0	Detroit	25.3
Mannheim	8.7	Plaquemines	58.3	Nantong	185.2	Chicago	17.1
Strasbourg	8.0	Huntingdon	52.9	Jiangyin	132.5	Two Harbors	16.2
Ludwigshafen	7.6	Pittsburgh	35.2	Taizhou	132.1	Indiana Harbor	13.1
Neuss	7.6	St Louis	35.0	Chongqing	128.0	Cleveland	11.3
Basle	6.8	Memphis	13.6	Taicang	123.4	Hamilton	10.0
Karlsruhe	6.4	Cincinnati	11.1	Yangzhou	88.2	Toledo	9.6
Kehl	*	Louisville	6.1	Wuhan	76.3	Gary	8.8
Krefeld	*	St Paul	5.0	Changshu	64.1	Thunder Bay	7.5

Note: * the traffic of Dutch inland ports is not reported in Central Commission for Navigation on the Rhine (2014)

Source: various statistical agencies

of cargoes handled. In consequence long quay walls arranged along relatively narrow basins are typical of inland ports (see Figure 6.1). However, the industrial supply chains may require the maintenance of inventories, necessitating the provision of space for stockpiling dry and liquid bulk goods, and in many cases the manufacturing plants themselves may be adjacent to the docks. As a result the land take of many inland ports is significant. The port of Mannheim covers 1,100 ha for example.

The nature of inland bulk supply chains has resulted in relatively few actors playing a determining role. The flows are dominated by corporations such as Arcelor-Mittal, Bunge Grain, Shell, Union Carbide and Chinese State-owned industries such as Baosteel. These corporations not only dominate the production of the raw materials and their processing, but exert their control over the intermediate chains. They often own and operate their own facilities in inland ports, and in many cases they own their own fleet of vessels, or engage independent ship owners in long-term contracts. These features confer a very distinct character to inland ports. First, is the corporate presence which determines all the activities in the terminals: the volumes handled, the scheduling of throughput and vessel arrivals, and the kind of equipment to be used. There is little uncertainty of the kind found in most major ports where goods arrive and depart on the multiple schedules of a range of cargo owners and intermediaries. Second, the ownership of terminal operations along with control over cargo flows also confers a stability and predictability of business over periods of time. Because initial investments in mines and heavy industries are so large their life expectancies range over decades, so that inland bulk ports change very slowly. They appear stable and conservative, a feature that helps convey the image of a somewhat stagnant industry.

A further dimension of the corporate domination of bulk traffic at inland ports is the relationship with public agencies. Even on the Rhine, where for each riparian country there is a strong tradition of state and local government involvement in planning and control of land, the decisions and investments made by the corporations in inland ports are crucial for bulk shipping. In the United States port administration is under the control of states, and only in a few cases is this wielded with any authority. In many inland port complexes there is fragmentation of public jurisdictions. For example in St Louis there are six separate port authorities, three on the Missouri side of the river, three on the Illinois, each with very small administrations. As de Langen and Visser (2005) have indicated, the governance structure of the giant bulk port of South Louisiana is feeble. Port authorities have limited powers because it is the corporations that invest in, sometimes own, and operate the terminals. In the US the functions of inland port authorities are largely financial because of their capacity to raise capital by issuing bonds. Most of the capital investments tend not to be in port-related activities but in other manufacturing, tourism and real estate projects. The public agencies that play a major role are those that have jurisdiction over navigation and security. The USACE wields

Mannheim Port Infrastructures

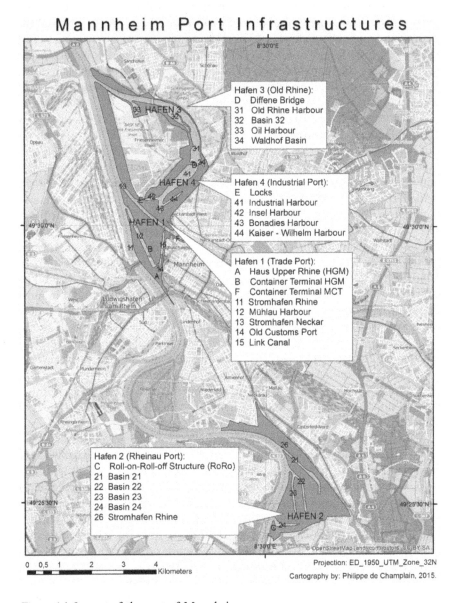

Figure 6.1 Layout of the port of Mannheim

enormous power, because it is mandated to carry out dredging and channel maintenance, as well as lock maintenance and operation.

In comparison with seaports where there is a large corpus of research on port–city relationships, in particular the planning of waterfront lands, inland ports are rarely mentioned. A search of the literature on waterfront redevelopment reveals the preponderance of cases that are major seaports (Merk 2013; Hoyle *et al.* 1988). The only significant exception is the case of Toronto, which was one of the pioneers in redevelopment (Desfor and Laidley 2011). Certainly, inland ports occupy extensive sites and river front locations, and many of the same land use conflicts found in seaports are evident there too. One possible explanation for the lack of attention given to port-urban development issues is the industrial nature of inland port traffic and its long established port districts under the control of large corporations. Over the years the surrounding cities have adjusted spatially to the port districts. The case of Toronto is instructive, because its conversion of port land came about because of a significant decline in port traffic, liberating large amounts of land adjacent to the city centre. As recent changes in port bulk traffic are taking place in some inland ports (see below), conversions to new port activities are taking place on the Rhine, and urban waterfront conversions are occurring in examples such as Cologne, Mannheim, Cincinnati and Duluth, but there is a lack of comparative analysis at present.

6.3 Inland ports, new traffic

While bulk shipments typify the activities of inland ports, several new trades have been developed over the last three decades. Here the focus is on three examples: heavy lift goods, roll-on roll-off and containers. It is the last of these that has gained particular prominence in two of the four inland waterways discussed in the chapter.

6.3.1 *Heavy lift goods and roll-on roll-off (roro)*

Heavy-lift is a traffic type that has existed for many years in ports, but which has acquired recently a new importance. Oversize contract cargo, as it is sometimes referred to, includes items that cannot be transported on road or rail because of weight or dimension restrictions. Transformers, generators, oil rigs, container gantry cranes are examples. The spread of the use of wind turbines has greatly enlarged and widened this business as has the growth in the sales and delivery of large recreational boats. This is a niche market, but inland ports such as Cleveland and Moerdijk are exploiting the commercial possibilities. Roro traffic is where road vehicles are loaded directly on specially designed ships for transit. On most major rivers this has existed for a long time as ferry services. In recent years roro has developed on a larger scale along the Yangtze in response to the establishment of vehicle assembly plants at sites such as Wuhan and Chongqing. On the Rhine there are a few companies such as Interrijn Autotransport operating specialised vessels capable of transporting assembled vehicles between plants and markets. The company cited moves 200,000 vehicles per year between Cologne, Duisburg and Rotterdam.

6.3.2   *Containers: the Rhine*

Container handling has had a far more significant effect. The impact of containers on global shipping has been profound. In the 50 years since the container made its international appearance seaports have been revamped with new superstructures and infrastructures, and because the shipping lines have achieved impressive scale economies the new terminals have to be extensive, representing a significant land take, as well as located adjacent to deep water. The growth of the container trade has put pressure on the distribution of the containers between the gateway ports and their hinterlands. Shippers place an emphasis on speed and reliability in landward distribution. The result is that for most deep-sea container ports road transport has captured the largest market share of hinterland traffic because of its flexibility in serving customers over a wide area with high service reliability (Notteboom and Rodrigue 2005).

Over time the costs of land distribution of containers has become a major issue. The cost per tonne-km may be many times higher for moving a container between an inland market and a port than that of transporting the box half-way round the world by ship. At the same time road congestion at port access points has led to concerns in the trucking industry because of costly delays, in commuters who are inconvenienced by traffic congestion, and in citizens in general who oppose increased road transport because of externalities such as noise and air pollution.

In the Netherlands and Belgium, home to two of Europe's gateway ports (Rotterdam and Antwerp, both located on Rhine delta distributaries), the response to growing concerns of the dominance of road transport has been a concerted effort to bring about a modal shift. National and local governments, port authorities, terminal operators, barge companies and shipping lines have been involved in promoting inland navigation as a means of reducing dependence on road transport. By 2014 inland shipping accounted for more than 35 per cent of hinterland container traffic of both Rotterdam and Antwerp, the highest proportion of any gateway ports in the world.

Inland ports are important to assure success in container shipping on the Rhine and its tributaries. Dedicated container terminals with appropriate handling gear have to be provided to ensure rapid turnarounds. Inland barge services have to compete with road transport, and thus both rapid and efficient handling in the inland terminals is essential. At the same time inland ports must be able to generate sufficient traffic to justify calls by barges, because if traffic is insufficient the transport providers would have to make more port calls to cover shipping costs, and this would reduce overall transit times. Konings and Priemus (2008) suggest that 30,000 TEUs per year is the break-even point of profitability for a port. This volume has to be generated by customers within a short distance of the terminal, because transferring containers by road beyond a certain radius would make water transport uncompetitive with all-road deliveries. For ports closest to Rotterdam, where competition from road transport is fiercest, the radius is a mere 15 km

(Konings and Priemus 2008), while further inland radii of between 60 and 75 km have been suggested (Kreutzberger and Konings 2013). Volumes are important also because they can help justify daily or even more frequent services by barges, thereby replicating one of the advantages of road transport.

Barge operators play a central role in the development of container transport on the Rhine. It is noteworthy that inland barges have been a feature of Rhine navigation for centuries. Unlike elsewhere, barging regained its market importance on the lower Rhine in the 1890s even after the development of railroads in the early part of the nineteenth century (Klemann and Schenk 2013). The Dutch government has long supported the barge industry as a means of exploiting the commercial opportunities of the Rhine corridor. With the introduction of containers, the old multifunctional barges, mainly owned and operated by family firms, were pressed into service, but their capacity was limited. Newly built dedicated vessels were more economic, and there was a conversion to dedicated container barges as the traffic increased. The capital requirements for this conversion led to the increasing dominance of companies operating container barge fleets. By the late 1980s competition between barge carriers led to vertical integration between the forwarders organising the trade and barge operators, and the container trade came increasingly under the control of three company groups, Wincanton (1990), Rhenus (1995) and Danser Container Line which controlled 70 per cent of the market in 2004 (Fremont and Franc 2010).

There are presently 33 inland ports in the Netherlands, 45 in Germany and 12 in Belgium (Konings and Priemus 2008). The numbers in the Netherlands and Belgium indicate the success of barge transport for even relatively short distances from the gateway port. Table 6.2 provides the figures for 2013 traffic of the largest German, French and Swiss inland container ports, from the Central Commission for Navigation of the Rhine (2014). These exclude the Dutch ports, but reveal that the performance of all top ten ports exceed the viability threshold by considerable margins. It is noteworthy that one port, Duisburg, has emerged as a hub. However, Duisburg is really a multimodal hub with road, rail and container shipments, and barge traffic there represents less than one-quarter of the total container throughput. Neuss and Strasbourg also are container centres where barge transport represents a minority of the traffic (25 per cent and 31 per cent respectively). On the other hand, Wörth and Basel are wholly dependent on inland shipping, and in the case of Mannheim barges represents 71 per cent of the traffic.

Up until the present, container traffic on the Rhine system has been dependent upon the exchanges with the ports of Rotterdam and Antwerp. Line and direct service configurations link the inland ports with these gateways (Kreutzberger and Konings 2013). Recently, services between Rhine river ports and those on tributaries such as the Moselle have been established, which because of their river draughts and market size, are served by smaller barges transhipping containers from Rhine ports. Konings and Priemus (2008) refer to these as trunk-feeder services. There is a difference

Table 6.2 Container traffic at the ten largest Rhine ports, 2013 (excluding Dutch and Belgian ports)

Duisburg	409,293
Mannheim	138,138
Wörth am Rhein	125,351
Germersheim	125,345
Strasbourg	118,359
Mainz	110,815
Emmerich	106,855
Basel	105,000
Cologne	102,390
Neuss	99,884

Source: Central Commission for Navigation on the Rhine (2014)

between the Rhine ports and those in the delta tributaries in the Netherlands. In the former typically three port calls are made beyond Rotterdam on each service string, but in the latter case, ports are served directly from Rotterdam. The difference is explained by distance from the ocean terminals. The Dutch inland ports are competing with road transport, and transit time is more critical there than for the more distant German, French and Swiss ports (Kreutzberger and Konings 2013). The growth of container traffic on the Rhine waterways and the role of inland ports in this trade has generated a growing amount of academic research in recent years. An important thread of this effort has been directed at understanding how and why this happened, and the role of the actors who brought about the transformation (Rodrigue *et al.* 2010; Fremont and Franc 2010). Framed by the model of port regionalisation (Notteboom and Rodrigue 2005) evidence has been assembled for the roles of port actors in particular. Examples include the Rotterdam Port Authority's actions to establish cooperation partnerships with several delta ports such as Moerdijk and Dordrecht, including infrastructure investments; ECT, one of the major Rotterdam port terminal operators, has invested in terminals at Venlo and Duisburg through their extended gate concept; Maersk, a major ocean shipping line, has invested in Neuss inland terminal; and, as noted above, barge companies operate a large number of the Rhine river ports.

Two recent papers have sought to position these coordination actions with theories of cooperation. Both papers are based on general hinterland coordination actions, including all modes. Franc and van de Horst (2010) examine inland chain coordination involving container shipping lines and terminal operators in the context of Transaction Cost Economics (TCE) with Resource-based View (RBV), a theory developed in the field of Resource Management. RBV focuses on the firm, while TCE is broader, involving all actors, public and private. In comparing the two approaches it is concluded that each theory 'makes a valuable contribution' (Franc and van der Horst 2010, p. 565), but neither fully accounted for regional differences in the application of coordination arrangements, and that the origins and internal culture of the firms is largely uncounted for. Van der Horst and van de Lugt (2011) take a unique set of coordination agreements and analyse them through the lens of TCE. What their data show is that while inter-firm alliances are the most common type of coordination agreements overall, the barging sector employed this solution to a higher degree than rail or road modes. This is explained by the complexity of the inland shipping chain, and by the required minimum load requirements in order to be competitive. Wilmsmeier *et al.* (2011) refer to the broader issue of intermodal penetration of hinterlands as one of two spatial processes: outside-in, where the penetration comes from the seaport and external actors, and inside-out, where the developments originate within transport corridors. In a subsequent paper (Monios and Wilmsmeier 2013), where case studies are examined, that of Venlo is cited as an example of outside-in. Nevertheless, the actual situation is more nuanced. Kreutzberger and Konings (2013) refer to the role of local governments promoting container terminal development, and inland port authorities themselves, such as Duisburg and Strasbourg have been involved in certain terminals. Duisburg has even invested in the port of Antwerp. The port-city impacts of inland container terminals have been examined by Witte *et al.* (2014). Sampling a number of inland port cities in the Netherlands a complex picture of relationships is revealed. Issues relating to the conflicting uses of water between port, residential and recreation activities are very prevalent, while in ports such as Venlo, Moerdijk and Dordrecht port terminal and city land use and spatial planning are in reasonable accord among the different agencies. In other ports there are issues arising out of the local governments' lack of awareness of the needs of the terminals, with a resultant potential for conflicts. For example, in the case of Nijmegen the port is hardly considered in city strategic policy-making.

6.3.3   Containers: the Yangtze

The Yangtze has become a major corridor for container shipments (Rimmer and Comtois 2009). The Chinese port of Shanghai is the world's largest container port, handling 32.6 million TEUs in 2013. This compares to its traffic of 14.0 million TEUs ten years previously. In the early years of Shanghai's container trade boxes were transported to markets predominantly by truck, since most of the economic growth was taking place in the regions immediately adjacent to the city. While road transport is still a very important mode even for markets distant from the port, largely because of the poor freight performance of the railway, the development of river traffic has expanded considerably. In 2013 the total river traffic had grown to 10.3 million TEUs from 3.1 million TEUs in 2006. Approximately three-quarters of this

Table 6.3 Container traffic at major Yangtze
River ports, 2013 (ordered by increasing
distance from Shanghai)

Total throughput	Containers (TEU)
Taicang Port	4,014,600
Nantong Port	504,300
Zhangjiagang	1,502 400
Jiangyin Port	1,153,800
Yangzhou Port	410,000
Zhenjiang Port	375,000
Nanjing Port	2,300,000
Wuhan Port	765,000
Chongqing	796,000

traffic is Shanghai port generated, the remainder representing traffic from several river ports on the lower Yangtze, such as Nanjing, Zhangjiagang and Taicang, that are operating short sea services to ports such as Busan as well as other coastal ports. Nevertheless, a river feeder trade of over 7 million TEUs is exceptional (see Table 6.3). A factor in the recent growth of the traffic of inland ports on the Yangtze is the port of Shanghai's development of its Yang Shan terminals, on islands in the East China Sea. Although the site is linked by a 30 km long bridge which begins 30 km south of the city, the terminal's relative isolation and road transport costs have favoured services by vessels from the Yangtze river ports.

Although municipalities can obtain central government financial assistance in developing facilities and many ports are municipally owned, the most important facilities have been developed by other agencies, including the Shanghai International Port Group (port of Shanghai authority), COSCO shipping line and several other groups such as Modern Terminals, China Infrastructure Group (Hong Kong), PYI (Singapore) and MIIF (Australia) (Notteboom 2007; Veenstra and Notteboom 2011). Veenstra and Notteboom (2011) have undertaken a quantitative analysis of the spatial patterns of inland port development along the Yangtze and relate it to theoretical models of seaport development such as those of Taaffe *et al.* (1963) and Hayuth (1981). They note intrinsic differences between the Yangtze river port system and coastal ports because of the river's tree like structure, with increasingly shallower depths up stream, and no inter-river basin connections. These constraints limit port differentiation based on physical advantages of one port over another. The results reveal bounded development, whereby a major urban centre such as Chongqing can never attain the importance of a port in a lower river section. The results reveal a clustering of ports, which in fact compares to the recognised divisions of the river into upper, middle and lower sections, each focused on a major port.

6.3.4 Containers: Mississippi and St Lawrence-Great Lakes

In contrast to the other river systems, there are no hinterland services by water transport from the gateway ports on these two corridors. The difference with the Rhine and Yangtze is striking, given the extent of the North American waterways and the size of populations in the catchment areas. There are multiple explanations for the differences, some of which apply to both river systems, others to specific cases. The most important factor is modal competition. Unlike Europe and China where the railways handle both passengers and freight, in North America the railroads are privately owned and are exclusively freight-oriented. Deregulated at the time of the development of containerisation, they exploited the market opportunities afforded by import and export traffic at seaports, and over time increased their line haul traffic because of the conversion of domestic inter-regional traffic through domestic containerisation (Slack 1994). They operate a well-established system of rail hubs that serve regional markets by truck within a market radius of between 250 and 400 km. In this way the railroads have assured the cooperation of the trucking industry, which in former times was a bitter rival of rail (Slack 1990). Today these rail hubs have become centres of logistics and distribution companies. In Europe and China the railroads have relatively poor service reputations and, despite deregulation in Europe, are facing difficulties in assuring operational efficiency (Slack and Vogt 2007).

In North America the railroads in many cases have sought to oppose initiatives to develop inland water transport. On the Mississippi, a container barge service linking Houston, Baton Rouge and Memphis faced predatory pricing from the railroads, which brought about its demise. The innovative programme of the Port of New York and New Jersey to offer barge services to a number of points, including Albany, came to nought after the subsidies ended. More recently, a slightly different case was the effort to ship aluminium semi-finished products from the smelter at Port Cartier to the port of Trois Rivieres instead of the previous use of trucking. Within a couple of years CN Rail offered a lower rate from the smelter, even though it meant trucking the aluminium to a rail ferry at Baie Comeau and crossing the St Lawrence to Matane, which is the regional rail terminal of CN. For the St Lawrence-Great Lakes a major constraint is the closure of the Seaway for 10–12 weeks each year because of winter ice. For bulk traffic this is less disruptive, since goods are stockpiled, but a container service would have to switch to the railroads or trucking, which would greatly increase costs to shippers and be an incentive to switch permanently to the alternate mode. With the exception of New Orleans and Montreal (and a partial exception of New York) no North American gateway ports are accessible by river and canal to hinterland markets. All of the West Coast ports, and those on the East Coast such as Norfolk, Charleston and Savannah are not located on navigable waterways, thus precluding any inland shipping. A further difference with Europe and China is the limited intervention of national and state governments in inland shipping. While ports are nominally under the control of the states most have small and weak administrations. In addition, states have little interest outside their own boundaries to promote transport chain improvements, especially those that involve water transport, since their bureaucracies are almost exclusively oriented to road transport.

6.4   Conclusions

Although this chapter has applied a working definition to the term 'inland port' it is evident that there is a need to clarify terminology. In much of the recent literature the term is applied to any intermodal facility in port hinterlands. While there may be some functional similarities between such terminals located on waterways and those established at rail hubs, the former have very different locational and spatial characteristics, and carry out other functions such as bulk handling. In this chapter it is demonstrated that even though the intermodal traffic is growing at inland ports on waterways, bulk remains the dominant activity, a feature ignored when academic researchers consider inland ports to be either rail or waterway-based container facilities.

Inland ports in all four inland waterway systems studied are nodes in industrial supply chains. Corporate actions determine the types and volumes of goods handled, terminals may be owned and operated by private or state-owned corporations that also maintain their own vessels or charter others on multi-year contracts. It is a sector that has existed below the radar of most academic research, and there are large gaps in our understanding of the organisation of the trade flows, the local and regional port impacts, and the challenges and opportunities that bulk traffic presents at inland ports. This lack of attention has reinforced a perception that bulk trades are not important, and public authorities have little or no knowledge of what is going on in the ports. It is only when a mine or factory linked to an inland port closes that its former importance is recognised. By then it is too late.

Regarding the container trade at inland ports, there is a striking contrast between North American waterways and the Rhine and Yangtze systems. On the St Lawrence-Great Lakes and Mississippi inland ports have been unable to develop container handling, while in the latter two port business is burgeoning. The success of inland ports on the Rhine and Yangtze is due in part to the search by many actors to improve access to inland markets, and present an alternative to road transport. The combined actions of these actors have been shown to be critical to the success. It is unlikely that the success will be repeated in North America because the railways have established an inland distribution network based on regional hubs that make it difficult for inland ports to compete, in addition to the other constraints they face.

The growth of container traffic at Rhine and Yangtze ports has been a commercial and environmental success. The process has been accompanied by a diffusion of ports along the waterways, with sites closest to the mouths of the rivers being most dense, despite the most severe competition from road traffic. However, the density of barge ports in the Rhine delta could be a matter of concern, since many have grown because of subsidies or considerations by public bodies and because their local market areas are so constrained. Any changes in the economics of these services, upscaling in barge sizes or improved gate access for trucks for example, could affect the viability of some terminals in the way (admittedly in very different circumstances) the very dense network of rail piggyback facilities in the US was transformed by rail load centres (Slack 1990).

One of the challenges for Rhine barge services linking inland ports outside the delta arises from the number of calls (usually three, but up to eight are possible) that have to be made at different deep-sea terminals in the port of Rotterdam, each one a potential constraint on transit times. Several solutions are being considered to address this problem (Konings *et al.* 2013). Some of the ports on the lower sections of the Yangtze have been able to broaden their functions by providing services for short sea shipping to sea ports other than Shanghai, Ningbo in particular. This is an option for Rhine ports that has been debated for some time.

Inland ports present a paradox: on the one hand their dominant but largely stable trade activity remains under-researched with little public attention, and on the other hand their container business is growing in some waterways and is relatively well analysed and receives more attention from policy-makers. The difference between the two could be breached by a challenge that is just beginning to be recognised by public authorities and by the ports themselves, even in North America where public policy has historically neglected inland ports. This is the issue of climate change and water depths. Predictions of more variability of precipitation and less snow have the potential to impact river transport in particular, because draughts are limited anyway. For example, a recent report for the Great Lakes Council predicts direct costs of $1.92 billion for Great Lakes ports and shipping due to low water and that to divert cargoes to other modes would cost $2.65 billion (Mowat Centre 2014). Low water could be the issue that provokes a better understanding of inland ports and shipping.

References

Baird, A. J. (1996). Containerization and the decline of the upstream urban port in Europe. *Maritime Policy and Management*. 23(2), 145–156.

Central Commission for Navigation of the Rhine (2014). Inland Navigation in Europe: Market Observation Report No. 18. Strasburg.

De Langen, P. and Visser, E.-J. (2005). Collective action regimes in seaport clusters: the case of the Lower Mississippi port cluster. *Journal of Transport Geography*. 13, 173–186.

Desfor, G. and Laidley, J. (eds) (2011). *Reshaping Toronto's Waterfront*. University of Toronto Press: Toronto.

Franc, P. and van de Horst, M. (2010). Understanding hinterland service integration by shipping lines and terminal operators: a theoretical and empirical analysis. *Journal of Transport Geography*. 18, 557–566.

Fremont, A. and Franc, P. (2010). Hinterland transportation in Europe: combined transport versus road transport. *Journal of Transport Geography.* 18, 548–566.

Hayuth, Y. (1981). Containerisation and the load centre concept. *Economic Geography.* 57, 160–176.

Hoyle, B.S., Pinder, D. and Husain, M.S. (1988). *Revitalising The Waterfront: International Dimensions of Dockland Redevelopment.* Belhaven Press: London.

Klemann, H. and Schenk, J. (2013). Competition in the Rhine delta: waterways, railways and ports, 1870–1913. *Economic History Review.* 66, 826–847.

Konings, R., Kreutzberger, H. and Maras, V. (2013). Major considerations in developing a hub-and-spoke network to improve the cost performance of container barge transport in the hinterland: the case of the port of Rotterdam. *Journal of Transport Geography.* 29, 63–73.

Konings, R and Priemus, H. (2008). Terminals and competitiveness of container barge transport. *Transportation Research Record.* 2062, 39–49.

Kreutzberger, E. and Konings, R. (2013). The role of inland terminals in intermodal transport development. In J.P. Rodrigue, T. Notteboom and J. Shaw (eds). *Sage Handbook of Transport Studies,* Sage: London. 179–207.

Merk, O. (2013). *The Competitiveness of Global Port-Cities: Synthesis Report* (No. 2013/13). OECD Publishing.

Monios, J. and Wang, Y. (2013). Spatial and institutional characteristics of inland port development in China. *GeoJournal.* 78, 897–913.

Monios, J. and Wilmsmeier, G. (2013). Giving a direction to port regionalisation. *Transportation Research. Part A.* 46, 1551–1561.

Mowat Centre (2014). *Low Water Blues.* Council of the Great Lakes Region.

Notteboom, T. (2007). Container river services and gateway ports: similarities between the Yangtze River and the Rhine River. *Asia Pacific Viewpoint.* 48(3), 330–343.

Notteboom, T. (2013). Maritime Transportation and Seaports. In J.P. Rodrigue, T. Notteboom and J. Shaw (eds). *Sage Handbook of Transport Studies,* Sage: London. 83–100.

Notteboom, T.E. and Rodrigue, J.P. (2005). Port regionalization: towards a new phase in port development. *Maritime Policy & Management.* 32 (3), 297–313.

Rimmer, P.J. and Comtois, C. (2009). China's container-related dynamics, 1990–2005. *GeoJournal.* 74(1), 35–50.

Rodrigue, J.P, Comtois, C. and Slack, B. (2009). *The Geography of Transport Systems,* Second Edition. Routledge: London.

Rodrigue, J.P., Debrie, J., Fremont, A. and Gouvernal, E. (2010). Functions and actors of inland ports: European and North American dynamics. *Journal of Transport Geography.* 18(4), 519–529.

Roso, V., Woxenius, J. and Lumsden, K. (2009). The dry port concept: connecting container seaports with the hinterland. *Journal of Transport Geography.* 17(5), 338–345.

Slack, B. (1990). Intermodal transportation in North America and the development of inland load centers. *Professional Geographer.* 42, 236–243.

Slack, B. (1994). Domestic containerisation and the load centre concept. *Maritime Policy and Management.* 21, 229–236.

Slack, B. and Vogt, A. (2007). Challenges confronting new traction providers of rail freight in Germany. *Transport Reviews.* 14, 399–409.

Taaffe, E.J., Morrill, R.L. and Gould, P.R. (1963). Transport expansion in under-developed countries: a comparative analysis. *Geographical Review*. 53, 503–529.

Van der Horst, M. and van der Lugt, L. (2011). Coordination mechanisms in improving hinterland accessibility: empirical analysis in the port of Rotterdam. *Maritime Policy & Management*. 38, 415–435.

Veenstra, A. and Notteboom, T. (2011). The development of the Yangtze River container port system. *Journal of Transport Geography*. 19, 772–781.

Wilmsmeier, G., Monios, J. and Lambert, B. (2011). The directional development of intermodal freight corridors in relation to inland terminals. *Journal of Transport Geography*. 19, 1379–1386.

Witte, P., Wiegmans, B., van Oort, F. and Spit, T. (2014). Governing inland ports: a multi-dimensional approach to addressing inland port–city challenges in European transport corridors. *Journal of Transport Geography*. 36, 42–52.

7 Developments in inland waterway vessels

Robert Hekkenberg and Jialun Liu

7.1 Inland vessels around the world

The term inland vessel covers a wide variety of floating units that operate on inland waterways, lakes and canals across the globe. At one end of the spectrum, we find many very small vessels operating on the waterways of emerging economies. Such vessels may have a capacity of only a few tons and can be powered by small outboard motors. At the other end of the spectrum we find the large pushtows operating on the Mississippi, Paraná and Yangtze, consisting of dozens of barges and having a cargo-carrying capacity of tens of thousands of tons. Between these extremities, a large variety of vessels exist. In this chapter, the more prevalent types of inland vessel are discussed, followed by a discussion of the main reasons for innovation in inland vessel technology. The chapter concludes with an overview of the most important developments and innovations in the field of inland vessel design and technology. The focus of this chapter will be on European IWT due to the availability of relevant data. The main characteristics of the inland fleets in other regions are discussed briefly to demonstrate their main differences and similarities. For a detailed discussion of inland vessels in the USA, refer to Fischer and Shearer (2004).

7.1.1 Inland vessel fleets per region

The main type of vessel that is used to transport goods over inland waterways differs by region. On large rivers like the Yangtze, Danube and Mississippi, the majority of vessels are large pushtows. On a river like the Rhine, with its many smaller tributaries and canals, the inland fleet is composed of pushtows as well as self-propelled vessels, as shown in Table 7.1. The table also shows a large number of (often small) self-propelled vessels in China. For other regions with significant amounts of inland waterway transport, like Russia and Brazil, only limited data is publicly available in Dutch or English. Kormyshov (2005) mentions 15,000 units in Russia, with an average deadweight of 847 tons. Dazert (2014) states there are around 200 pushers and 2,500 barges of typically 1,500 tons in Paraguay. For Brazil he mentions a figure of 1,546 self-propelled cargo vessels.

Table 7.1 Fleet statistics

	W-Europe (CCNR, 2012)	Europe-Danube (CCNR, 2012)	USA[a] (USACE, 2013)	China (Song, 2010)
Self-propelled				
Dry cargo				
#	6,753	373	635[b]	
Avg. DWT	1,025 T	1,037 T	≈600 T	
Tank				
#	1,992	37	2	
Avg. DWT	1,790 T	912 T	14,594 T	
Total #	8,745	410	637	132,000
Push barges				
Dry cargo				
#	3,117	2,559	23,418	
Avg. DWT	1,307 T	679 T	1,642 T	
Tank				
#	155	233	3,220	
Avg. DWT	1,517 T	1,022 T	2,601T	
Total #	3,272	2,792	26,638	33,000
Pushers				
#	1,039	422	3,442	
Total				
#				165,000
Avg. DWT				364

Notes:
[a] Data for the US, except for the number of self-propelled dry cargo ships, only include vessels sailing on the Mississippi River System and Gulf Intracoastal Waterway. Data for Great Lakes System and coasts are excluded from the table since they include a significant but unknown number of seagoing ships and barges.
[b] Number is equal to the number of shallow draught dry cargo ships operating throughout the US.

Not only the type of vessel that is used differs from region to region. The organizational structure of inland waterway transport (IWT) also differs strongly. Since the organization of the sector influences the development and implementation of technical innovations, this will briefly be discussed here. A review of fleet statistics from various sources reveals that the largest five operators in the USA, Ingram Barge Company, American Commercial Line, American River Transportation, Kirby Inland Marine and AEP Memco, together operate over 12,500 barges and 600 towboats, nearly half of the total fleet. In contrast, the European inland waterway transport sector features many small businesses consisting of a captain-owner that operates a single vessel together with his wife and as few employees as possible. The vast majority of European vessel owners operate one to three vessels and/or barges, while only very few companies operate more than 20 vessels (Quispel *et al.*, 2015). Among the largest operators in Europe are Imperial Reederei (around 10 pushers, 75 barges, 70 self-propelled vessels and another 500 vessels under contract with private owners), CFT (approx. 35 pushers, 127 barges and 23 self-propelled vessels), ThyssenKrupp Veerhaven (8 pushers, 100 barges), Reederei Jaegers Group (170+ vessels) and Interstream Barging (30 vessels owned, 109 chartered from private owners). None of these European operators approaches the size of the large American companies. In China, there are about 80,000 individuals and 4,000 companies that operate inland vessels, while about 20 per cent of the tonnage is owned by the public sector. About 48 per cent of the tons and 29 per cent of the ton-kms of transport on Chinese waterways are carried out by owner-operators. The largest operator operates roughly 1,700 vessels with a combined capacity of 2.5 million tons (Amos *et al.*, 2009).

7.1.2   Aspects that drive the choice for a type of vessel

In China and along the Rhine, a large portion of the fleet consists of self-propelled vessels (see Figure 7.2), while along the Danube, in the US and in Paraguay the majority of vessels are pushtows (see Figure 7.1). The choice for a certain vessel type can be explained by the characteristics of that vessel type. Self-propelled vessels are the more straightforward of the two

Figure 7.1 A six-barge pushtow operating on the Rhine (picture courtesy of ThyssenKrupp Veerhaven)

Figure 7.2 A self-propelled dry cargo ship (Source: own image)

types: they are 'easy' to construct, sturdy, streamlined and can be operated by a small crew. Each of these aspects gives them an advantage over pushtows. Pushtows require separate construction of a powered unit (a pusher or towboat) and a cargo unit (barge), which increases the cost of construction. Since an essential feature of pushtows is that the barges may be detached from the pusher, the barges and pusher are connected by temporary connections, usually steel wire ropes. This makes them less sturdy, which may be a problem in exposed areas with significant waves. Connecting and disconnecting the barges from the pusher and each other is a labour-intensive activity, which increases the required number of crewmembers and thereby increases crew costs. In Europe, this higher number of crew members is prescribed by law (CCNR, 2013). Furthermore, since the draught of the barges will be different from that of the pusher, their hulls do not form a streamlined whole, which makes the resistance and fuel consumption of pushtows larger than that of typical self-propelled vessels with the same cargo-carrying capacity. The pushtow's disadvantage of having higher resistance can, however, at least partly be compensated by larger, more efficient propellers. The reason for this is that the pusher itself does not carry any cargo. As a result, its draught is constant. This in turn allows pushboat designers to adapt the pusher's stern form in such a way that propellers with a diameter that exceeds the vessel's draught can be fitted.

Despite the abovementioned initial drawbacks, pushtows do have some major advantages over self-propelled vessels. The most important of these relates to the loads on the vessel. As vessels get larger, the forces on the hull also become larger and the vessel gets heavier. This makes it more expensive to build and reduces its cargo-carrying capacity when water levels are low. Using several barges instead of one large vessel will lead to lower bending moments and, therefore, to lighter, cheaper vessel structures. This explains why the largest units sailing on inland waterways are all pushtows composed of many barges. These large units can achieve economies of scale that lead to lower costs and lower fuel consumption per transported ton than can be achieved by self-propelled vessels. Another important advantage of pushtows is their modularity. A pusher can be detached from the barges while they are loaded or unloaded. It can then be coupled to other barges that are already ready for departure. This way, its crew and main machinery, the most expensive fixed cost components in the operation of an inland vessel, are more productive. Additionally, the barges can be used as floating storage units. In contrast, during the loading and unloading of self-propelled vessels, the entire vessel has to wait until all port operations are completed. Especially on shorter hauls, this means that the vessel will spend a significant amount of its time tied up along a quay instead of being productive.

The choice to use pushtows instead of self-propelled vessels may also be driven by regulations. For example, on the Rhine, the Central Commission for Navigation on the Rhine (CCNR) does not allow the use of 'indivisible vessels' longer than 135 m. If a vessel owner wants to lengthen his vessel beyond 135 m, e.g. in order to increase its cargo-carrying capacity and achieve larger economies of scale, he will need to add a barge to it or exchange it for a pushtow. In their quest for economies of scale inland waterway transport operators in Europe are increasingly using large coupled units (see Figure 7.3) with lengths up to 200 m that have a flush connection between the vessel and the barge. This allows them to combine the best aspects of both vessel types: the scale advantage, low bending moments and part of the flexibility of a pushtow and the low resistance of a self-propelled vessel.

7.1.3   *Types of transported cargo*

Inland waterway transport is a slow mode of transport that needs economies of scale to compete with road and rail transport. This makes it most suitable for the transport of bulk goods. In all major IWT regions around the world, the majority of inland cargo vessels are used to transport dry bulk. The other major commodity group transported by inland vessel is liquid bulk. The cargoes are mainly oil, oil products and chemicals transported in tank barges

Figure 7.3 A coupled unit (Source: own image)

Figure 7.3 (continued)

Figure 7.4 A tank ship (picture courtesy of Mercurius Shipping Group)

and tank vessels (Figure 7.4). Depending on the properties of the product to be transported, tank vessels can have steel tanks with various types of coating or stainless steel tanks, which may be integrated into the hull or separated from the main load-bearing structure of the vessel.

Since the 1980s there has been a large increase in the transport of containers on the inland waterways in the western part of Europe, especially from and to the main seaports that are connected to the Rhine. The vessels that are used to transport containers are often dry bulk vessels with hold dimensions that are suitable for the efficient stowage of containers (see Figure 7.5). Only a few vessels are dedicated container vessels with cell guides. On the Yangtze and Pearl rivers in China, there is also considerable container transport (Amos *et al.*, 2009, p. 18). On other waterway systems the use of inland vessels for the transport of containers appears to be much less developed.

There are also several vessel designs dedicated to the transport of niche cargoes like cars (see Figure 7.6), trucks, powders and gases, but these do not form a significant portion of the market anywhere.

7.2   Innovation characteristics and innovation adoption in inland vessel design

In the previous sections, we discussed the general nature of inland vessels. The properties of these vessels are, however, not constant. Over time designs change, new designs are created and obsolete vessels leave the market. In Section 7.2.1, we will discuss the conditions and impediments for successful innovation in

Figure 7.5 Container ships (pictures courtesy of Mercurius Shipping Group)

Figure 7.5 (continued)

Figure 7.6 A ship adapted for the transport of cars (Source: own picture)

IWT, while in Section 7.2.2 we discuss the goals that operators typically want to achieve through technical innovations. In Section 7.3 the nature of design changes and the most important recent innovations in inland vessel design are elaborated in more detail.

7.2.1 Conditions and impediments for successful innovation in IWT

Changes in the design of both seagoing and inland vessels are typically incremental rather than radical: vessel design often consists of the improvement of an existing design instead of a redesign 'from scratch' (Wijnolst, 1995). If they do occur, radical deviations from existing designs are often initiated by the vessel owner rather than by a shipyard because a shipyard normally strives to minimize risks during production while a vessel owner will strive to reduce life cycle cost. According to Wijnolst:

> In the ideal design environment for achieving innovation and creating a competitive advantage in shipping, the owner has a minimum in-company expertise and analytical skills for the monitoring of markets and operations, as well as a liaison with the specialist consultants and builders of vessels.
>
> (Wijnolst, 1995, pp. 21–22)

Inland vessels are expensive pieces of equipment that typically cost several million euros. Despite that, in practice IWT is a business that can be entered quite easily by individual entrepreneurs with an education that is primarily aimed at sailing the vessel. As a result, many of the operators are very small businesses that are able to successfully run the day-to-day operation of a vessel but lack the skills and expertise to monitor markets and analyse them in depth. Neither do many operators fully grasp the physics underlying the technology that makes the vessel function. As a result, it is difficult for such operators to initiate successful innovations. The low amount of capital and close link between the finances of the company and the income of the owner further hampers innovation by the owner-operators. Still, even some of the smallest companies do innovate. Often these innovations are new applications of existing technologies, design changes based on 'common sense' or the owner's own ideas. Innovations that are the result of extensive dedicated research projects are rarer and even hydrodynamic analysis or hullform optimization through Computational Fluid Dynamics (CFD) or model tests are often not executed during the design stage of inland vessels. In contrast, for seagoing ships, this is common practice. The reasons behind this are not only the gaps in the owner's expertise and lack of financial leeway, but also include the low building cost and fuel consumption of inland vessels compared to seagoing ships. This implies that the potential gain from innovations is often not large enough to justify large investments in research. Notable exceptions include the crashworthy Y-shaped side structure (Ludolphy, 2001), air lubrication of the hull to reduce resistance (Foeth, 2008) and bio-inspired propulsion (Berg, 1996; O-foil, 2015). These innovations are all preceded by extensive research.

7.2.2   *The goals of technical innovation in inland vessels*

Despite the abovementioned inhibitors, there is continuous innovation in the sector. There are many ways to categorize the innovations that occur, e.g. on the scale of incremental to radical innovation, whether it takes place at component, system or vessel level or whether it is initiated by the user or developer of the technology. However, in this case we believe the clearest, most insightful subdivision is by the goal they are meant to achieve. Based on our own observations, we identify the following primary goals that operators in the IWT sector have strived to achieve through innovation and development:

1   cost reduction
2   improving environmental performance
3   accessing niche markets
4   complying with new regulations
5   adaptation to climate change.

Each of these goals is discussed briefly in a separate paragraph below, while a more elaborate quantitative analysis is presented in Section 7.3.

Cost reduction is the goal of many of the innovations and developments in the sector in recent years. Transport cost is an important factor in the decision making of shippers that ship commodities that are suitable for inland waterway transport. Furthermore, especially the many small operators in the sector have few other options to increase their competitiveness than to reduce their costs (Hekkenberg, 2013). The majority of recent technological improvements, innovations and inventions in IWT are aimed at reducing fuel costs, which is one of the three main components of the vessel's operational cost. The other two main components are capital costs and crew cost, the latter of which is governed more by regulations than by technology. A large part of the capital cost of inland vessels is related to the (steel) structure of the vessel and its propulsion system, for which no major alternatives with the same or better performance but lower capital costs have been implemented commercially in the last decades. The most widespread and effective cost reducing change to inland vessels, however, is scale enlargement of the vessel. By making the vessel bigger, the capital cost, fuel cost and crew cost per ton of cargo-carrying capacity will go down, as is quantified by, for example, Hekkenberg (2013).

Improving environmental performance of inland vessels has received considerable attention since the early 2000s. Until the 1990s there was little discussion about the superiority of (inland) shipping over other modes in terms of emissions of CO_2, particulate matter (PM) and NO_x. With the advent of more stringent emissions regulations for road transport, especially PM and NO_x emissions of this mode have fallen to levels that are much lower than those of inland vessels. This has triggered the introduction of various exhaust gas treatment techniques as well as pilot projects to investigate the use of hydrogen or LNG as alternative, cleaner fuels. Since the environmental performance of inland vessels impacts their immediate surroundings as well as the global environment, there are several examples of governments or private parties like ports offering financial incentives for the improvement of the environmental performance of vessels. These incentives can for instance be a reduction in port fees for clean vessels (e.g. Green Award) or subsidies for investments in emission-reducing technology (e.g. the Dutch 'VERS regeling'). Since such incentives are not intended to pay for the entire investment, owners still have to invest themselves. This in turn implies that innovations need to have the potential to save more money than they cost in order to be attractive to the owner. This potential currently does not exist for, for example, typical after-treatment techniques like filters or catalysts. This makes it doubtful if they will be applied on a large scale as long as regulations do not prescribe their use or more customers start demanding that the transport of their goods is 'green'.

Accessing niche markets in some cases requires the development of dedicated vessels. As long as niche markets remain just that, they will not lead to major changes to the inland cargo fleet as a whole. They have, however, led to some interesting new vessel designs and applications of new techniques. The vast majority of inland vessels are either dry bulk/container vessels or tank vessels for liquid cargoes. These vessels are limited in the type of cargo they can carry and the locations where they can load or unload them. The most eye-catching examples of vessels designed for niche markets are developed either to handle different types of cargo or to handle cargo in a way that other vessels can not.

Complying with new regulations is a reason for the initiation of design changes and innovations when it is no longer possible to adhere to these new regulations with existing designs and/or technologies. Typical examples in the IWT sector are increased safety standards for the transport of dangerous cargoes and increasing emission standards for vessel engines. Increased safety standards are, among others, leading to a phasing out of single-hulled tank vessels by 2019 in Europe (Economic Commission for Europe, Committee on Inland Transport, 2015, section 1.6.7.4) and by 2015 in the USA (Fisher and Shearer, 2004, P39–23), which in turn has led to a newbuilding wave of new double hull tankers. The introduction of CCNR I and II emission standards by the Central Commission for Navigation on the Rhine (CCNR) has triggered the introduction of cleaner engines for inland vessels in Europe. Once CCNR III emission standards are introduced, this will undoubtedly trigger the development of the after-treatment techniques that are required to meet this standard. Despite the fact that the exact standards and introduction date of CCNR III regulations are as yet unknown, parallels in American EPA tier 4 regulations for marine diesel engines and EURO VI regulation for European trucks, make it highly likely that the CCNR III limits will only be achievable with such after-treatment techniques or alternative fuels like LNG or hydrogen.

Adaptation to climate change is something that is often perceived as a cause for changes in vessel design. This cause does, however, not appear to exist in practice. The idea is that climate change will change the patterns of rainfall and snowmelt, leading to more extreme water depths, i.e. longer periods of high and low water, in free-flowing waterways. The logical action to take from the vessel owner's point of view would be the development of lightweight, shallow draught inland vessels. However, the KLIWAS project concludes that until at least 2050, no major climate change effects on the discharge of the Rhine are to be expected (Nilson *et al.*, 2011). The ECCONET project comes to the same conclusion (Schweighofer *et al.*, 2012). There also appear to be no indications that there will be a dramatic climate-induced deterioration in navigation conditions any time soon for other waterway systems with significant amounts of inland waterway transport. What remains is the challenge of dealing with low water depths that already occur in many natural waterways, either periodically or permanently. This is, however, essentially a way of minimizing transport costs by adapting the vessel to the waterway on which it sails. For example, for the river Odra in Poland, low draught pushtows have been developed in the INBAT project (Guesnet, 2005), but these have not left the drawing board. Neither has the design of a lightweight self-propelled vessel made of composites (Lightweight Structures, 2015). Especially on the Rhine, there has been a large increase in scale in recent years, as a result of which the draught of new built vessels actually increased rather than decreased. The sector is aware that these new vessels lose their competitive edge over smaller vessels in periods of drought but this has not yet led to a discernible reduction in design draught.

7.3   The most influential innovations and developments of recent years

In the previous section, we identified four primary goals that the IWT sector has tried to achieve through development and innovation. In the following paragraphs, we examine the actual innovation and development activity behind these goals in more detail. Section 7.3.1 discusses cost reduction, Section 7.3.2 discusses environmental performance and Section 7.3.3 discusses dedicated vessels for niche markets. Because it is not always evident whether or not environmental performance-related improvements are voluntary or regulation-induced, the goal 'complying with regulations' is not discussed separately but included in the discussion in the section on environmental performance.

7.3.1   Cost reduction

In the quest for cost reduction, many new technologies and products have been developed. These include air lubrication of the hull to reduce resistance (Foeth, 2008), novel propeller designs, bio-inspired propulsion (Berg, 1996; O-foil, 2015) and new hull forms. For such major deviations from conventional vessel designs it is typically hard to penetrate the market, especially when dealing with the single vessel captain-owners that are prevalent in Europe. These operators' entire business revolves around a single vessel so applying an unproven, and often expensive, technique to that vessel entails large risks. At the same time, the potential savings are usually limited due to the low fuel consumption of inland vessels, making it hard to earn back any major investments. These are two important reasons why only a few of the developed improvements make it past the drawing-board stage. However, some radical changes do emerge from unexpected places. As an example, in 2012, the *Semper Fi*, a 110 m long container vessel owned by a small operator, entered service. The vessel is equipped with hybrid diesel-electric propulsion and counter rotating propellers. Also, in 2011 the first inland vessel to use LNG for propulsion, the tanker *Argonon*, was built for a company operating only five vessels. One of the few non-fuel-related approaches to cost reduction is the development of the Y-shaped side structure (Ludolphy, 2001), which has actually achieved a reasonable market penetration. This innovative vessel structure is intended to make tank vessels more crashworthy, which in turn allows the vessel to have fewer and larger cargo tanks, which leads to cost reductions. Despite such showcases of radical innovation, the vast majority of vessels still follow the well-trodden path of incremental improvements of existing designs using proven technology. This approach has, however, led to some significant improvements, mainly through scale enlargement. The underlying idea is that larger vessels lead to lower costs per transported unit of cargo without resorting to unproven technology.

Scale enlargement of individual vessels and barges mainly appears to be an issue on those waterways where many self-propelled vessels are used, i.e. Europe and China. China aims to increase the average size of vessels sailing on the Yangtze to 2,000 ton by 2020 (Song, 2010), while the average deadweight of China's inland vessels was around 364 tons, see Table 7.1. The average deadweight of European vessels has been increasing steadily for decades, while the maximum deadweight has grown rapidly in especially the last 15 to 20 years. Figure 7.7 shows the increase in average tonnage and maximum tonnage of European newbuild vessels over a period of 18 years, from 1996 to 2013, based on a data sample of 1,400 vessels from the database of *Vereniging de Binnenvaart*. Although this database does not contain data on all European

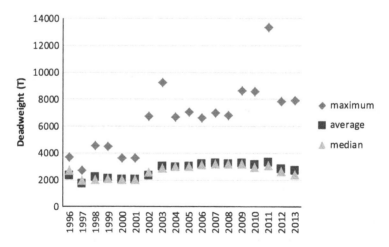

Figure 7.7 Maximum, average and median values of deadweight of newbuilt ships

newbuild vessels in this period, the number of included vessels is considered large enough to be representative. Figure 7.7 also shows a strong increase in the size of the largest vessels built each year and reveals a jump in the average size of newbuild vessels around 2003. Each year, the average deadweight of newbuild vessels, as presented in Figure 7.7, is larger than the European self-propelled fleet average of 1,220 tons in 2012 (CCNR, 2012).

Figure 7.7, however, does not specify the size of individual vessels. There is actually a clear rationale behind the choice of the main dimensions of European inland vessels, which can be deduced from Figure 7.8. The choice for certain main dimensions is often driven by infrastructural limitations and changes in regulations that are related to the length of ships.

Figure 7.8 shows that many vessels are built with a beam of 9.5 to 9.6 m or a beam of 11.4 to 11.45 m. These beams are the largest beams that still fit through the locks in canals that are classed IV and Va by the European Conference of Ministers of Transport (1992). For locks in these waterway classes, 85 m and 110 m respectively are common length limits. These dimensions are, therefore, very common in Figure 7.8. Other noteworthy lengths that show up in these figures are 70 and 86 m, the lengths at which more crew is prescribed in the regulations. Finally, the length of 135 m is the previously discussed maximum allowed length of indivisible vessels on the Rhine. Only the bunker tanker *VT Vorstenbosch* exceeds this length. It operates in and between the seaports of Amsterdam, Rotterdam and Antwerp.

To gain further insight into how often ships with given dimensions have been built, refer to Figure 7.9, which is a 3D representation of Figure 7.8. From the large spikes in Figure 7.9, it can be concluded that in Europe, the most frequently built vessel dimensions since 1996 equal the maximum

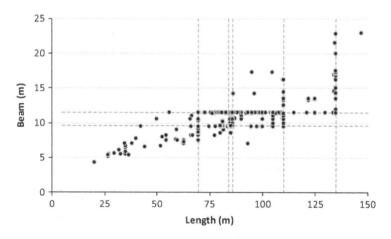

Figure 7.8 Numbers of newbuild ships vs length and beam

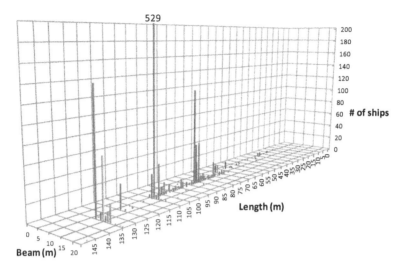

Figure 7.9 Top-down graph of Figure 7.8

dimensions of locks in class Va canals (i.e. 110 × 11.45 m) and that even the longer vessels have a beam that allows them to fit through such locks, in case the locks are long enough. From this, it is concluded that many vessel opera- tors strive to maximize the size of their vessels without limiting the number of waterways on which they can operate too much. There is also a significant number of ships that sacrifice economies of scale for the ability to penetrate smaller class IV waterways. These ships show up in Figure 7.9 as the cluster of spikes around a beam of 9.5 m length of 85–86 m length. Finally, there are also a significant number of operators that accept a more limited area of navi- gation in favour of maximization of economies of scale, as becomes apparent from the spikes at 135 m length.

The figures above are all based on individual self-propelled vessels or barges. Technically it is possible to further increase the size of these vessels beyond that of the largest of these vessels, but for the river Rhine, research has shown that the economic benefits of doing so are very limited (Hekkenberg, 2015a, 2015b). This negates the need to question the CCNR's regulatory length limit of 135 m. The figures above, however, do not include coupled units or pushtows. Such vessels are already allowed to have larger overall dimensions and may benefit from them because they have the ability to limit the amount of time the powered unit spends in port. As examples, coupled units *Camaro* and *Camaro II*, transporting containers, both consist of a vessel and three barges, with a total length of 183 m, a beam of 22.9 m and a deadweight of over 8,000 tons. *Ursa Montana*, consisting of a vessel and a barge is 193 m long, 17.35 m wide and has a deadweight of roughly 10,400 tons.

Even for 269.5 m long and 22.8 m wide six-barge pushtows, the largest units sailing on the Rhine, research has been conducted to determine if further scale enlargement was possible by using four larger barges of 4,500 tons rather than six standard *Europa II*-type barges of 2,800 tons. This enlargement would bring the total capacity of the pushtow to 18,000 tons (Hoogwout *et al.*, 2004). This has, however, not led to implementation in practice. With this scale enlargement, the capacity limits of the Rhine are just about reached. In stark contrast, pushtows on the much larger Mississippi river may feature upwards of 40 barges with a capacity of 1,500 tons each (Hilling, 1999).

Scale enlargement is not only seen as a solution to improve the competitiveness of inland waterway transport on large waterways. Especially in the Netherlands and Belgium, authorities and commercial parties alike have recognized that vessels with a capacity of 1,000 tons or less have difficulty competing with other modes of transport. Because of the low competitiveness of such vessels, a significant portion of the existing waterway network in these countries runs the risk of becoming obsolete. Therefore, initiatives to revitalize these waterways were started, leading to a number of projects that developed small pushtows featuring barges with a limited amount of propulsion power. The Belgian Inlanav project (Hassel, 2011) and the Dutch Barge Truck project developed similar concepts where barges sail independently on the small waterways. These waterways often also have speed restrictions and therefore the required amount of propulsion power in the barges is limited. Once they reach larger waterways, the barges can be coupled to a pusher with sufficient power to propel the entire convoy at higher speeds. This way economies of scale are maximized on those parts of the route where it is possible, without compromising the vessels' ability to enter the small waterways. A somewhat different concept was elaborated in the Q-barge project, which developed small self-propelled vessels with a length of 45 m and a beam of 5.8 m that can be coupled but do not require a separate pusher to reach the required speed on larger waterways. Thus far, none of these projects aimed at scale enlargement on small waterways have left the drawing board.

Summarizing, there have been, and continue to be, many developments and innovations that aim to reduce the cost of IWT through improvement of the vessel, but only a few of these have gained a significant foothold. Especially the more radical innovations face major difficulty in being implemented. Thus far, scale enlargement of vessels using proven technology has been the most common way to reduce the transport cost per ton of cargo.

7.3.2 *Improvement of environmental performance*

Traditionally, the IWT sector prides itself on its environmental performance and uses this as a marketing instrument. Until the last decade of the twentieth century, its claim of being cleaner than road or rail transport was largely unchallenged. Especially large vessels and pushtows have an energy

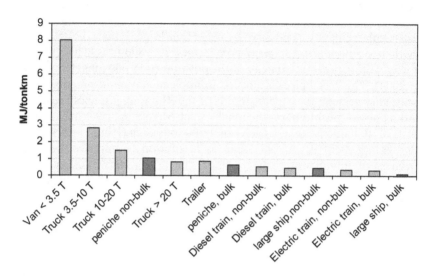

Figure 7.10 Energy consumption in MegaJoules per tkm of transport

consumption per ton-kilometre (tkm) of transport performance that is substantially lower than that of trucks, as is shown in Figure 7.10, adapted from CE Delft (2003). The figure, however, also shows that for smaller inland vessels like the old European 400 ton *Peniche*, specific energy consumption may actually be worse than that of common 27 ton trucks. More importantly, in the past decades emission legislation for road transport has been developed. It has drastically reduced the emission of harmful substances like nitrogen oxides (NO_x) and particulate matter (PM). CO_2 emissions are not addressed by these regulations. Legislation for the emissions of inland vessels is lagging behind, and as a result a typical inland vessel will have much higher emissions of these substances per kilowatt-hour (kWh) of consumed energy. While the latest European EURO norms (EURO VI) allows trucks to emit 0.4 grams of NO_x per kWh and 0.01 grams of PM per kWh, the current CCNR II regulations for European inland vessels allow 6 to 11 g/kWh of NO_x and 0.2 g/kWh of PM. This implies that vessels are allowed to emit 10 to 27.5 times as much of these pollutants as trucks. In the US, the environmental protection agency (EPA) uses regulations with somewhat different values, but the same general picture emerges. A simple calculation now reveals that unless vessels use at least ten times less fuel per tkm of transport, inland navigation emits more NOx and PM than road transport, endangering its reputation as a clean mode of transport. This poses a considerable challenge that only the largest vessels and pushtows may be able to meet. Which mode has the best overall environmental performance is not easily determined, among others because the external costs associated with each substance are different. For

PM, it is even related to the population density at the location of emission (CE Delft *et al.*, 2008). Specific conclusions about which mode has the best environmental performance should, therefore, only be drawn for specific cases where the details of the transport route as well as the specifications of the vessels are well-defined.

Emissions from vessels can, however, be lowered by various after-treatment techniques: NO_x can be removed from the exhaust gas almost completely by a catalyst while PM can be removed with a filter. In Europe, incentive pro-grammes have enticed several operators to install such equipment in their vessels. Furthermore, the sector's voluntary early switch to sulphur-free fuel has eliminated the technical problem that sulphur is harmful to particulate matter filters. However, as long as such devices are not made compulsory it is unlikely that they will be applied on a large scale. Both devices cost money in the form of the initial investment, maintenance and, in case of catalysts, consumed urea. Neither option is likely to earn these costs back because they have little to no potential to reduce fuel consumption or may even lead to an increase in fuel consumption.

Several research projects have investigated ways to assess and reduce the emissions of inland vessels through the use of alternative fuels, after-treatment techniques and different engines, including CREATING (2004–2007), exe-cuted within the EU's 6th framework program, and MoVe IT! (2011–2014), executed within the EU's 7th framework program (e.g. Schweighofer and Seiwerth 2007; Hekkenberg and Thill 2014). In both projects, researchers and vessel owners worked in close cooperation to identify the most promis-ing solutions. From this cooperation it became apparent that there are few solutions that are both beneficial to the environment and to the vessel own-er's business. The most promising solutions emerging from the projects are those that lead to a reduction of fuel consumption and/or fuel costs. This is in line with the ongoing developments in inland vessel designs as discussed in Section 7.3.1: over the years many innovative propulsors, hullforms, drive train configurations, resistance reduction techniques etc. have been devel-oped, all with the aim of reducing the amount of fuel that is required to sail the same distance at the same speed with the same amount of cargo. These improvements in some cases claim energy consumption reductions of well over 10 per cent, although in the majority of cases these optimistic claims are not supported by independent scientific proof (Hekkenberg, 2013, p. 217). However, these innovations reduce energy consumption but not the specific emissions per kWh. Therefore, their potential impact on the emission of NO_x and PM is substantially more limited than that of after-treatment techniques, which can almost entirely eliminate these emissions.

Apart from the previously discussed after-treatment techniques, changing fuel appears to be the most effective way to reduce these emissions. For a while, hydrogen promised to be a viable alternative fuel but due to the contin-ued high cost of fuel cells, the large required fuel tanks and the complications associated with handling hydrogen, studies to use hydrogen to propel inland cargo vessels have not gone beyond the drawing board. On a smaller scale, a few passenger boats are successfully sailing on hydrogen, including the *Nemo H2* sightseeing boat in the canals of Amsterdam and the *Alsterwasser* passenger boat in Hamburg. Their limited range and low power requirement make them more suitable for such applications than inland cargo vessels.

The switch to sulphur free gasoil has proven to be effective at eliminating SO_x emissions, but it does not solve the emission of NO_x and PM. In the last couple of years, however, the replacement of traditional gasoil by LNG seems promising. LNG has the potential to almost completely eliminate PM emissions, reduce NO_x emissions by 80–90 per cent and reduce CO_2 emissions by 20–25 per cent (Hoogvelt and de Vries, 2011), but also claims to be cheaper than diesel. There are, however, considerable challenges associated with the use of LNG as a fuel for inland vessels: investment costs for LNG equipment are high and price development of LNG is still highly uncertain. Furthermore, European regulations regarding the design of inland vessels need to be changed because they do not permit the use of fuels with a flame point below 55 degrees Celsius and a supply chain needs to be set up, since it is not yet possible to bunker (i.e. refuel) inland vessels with LNG. Nonetheless, in 2011, the first LNG-powered inland vessel, 110 m long chemical tanker *Argonon*, entered service. The vessel features dual-fuel engines, allowing it to sail both on LNG and traditional gasoil (diesel). Since then several other vessels with LNG propulsion have been built. Tankers *Greenstream* and *Green Rhine* have full LNG propulsion, coupled unit *Eiger-Nordwand* has been retrofitted with an LNG installation and several development studies for other LNG-powered inland vessels are on the drawing board. Authorities are working on the regulations to allow LNG as a fuel and these regulations are expected to enter into force in 2015. At the same time, a large consortium including vessel owners, vessel builders, ports, research institutes and classification societies is working on a three-year study (2013–2015) to develop an LNG masterplan for the Rhine-Main-Danube region, which will analyse the costs and benefits of LNG, transfer knowledge on LNG to inland navigation, facilitate the creation of a European regulatory framework, deliver technical concepts for new and existing vessels, elaborate the LNG supply chain, execute pilot projects with vessels and terminals, develop an LNG implementation roadmap and prepare for large-scale implementation. Despite all these developments and efforts, reducing the cost of LNG installations to a level that allows transport operators to earn back their investment remains a major hurdle to be taken before LNG can become a widespread fuel for inland vessels. If LNG fails to gain a strong position in the sector, a significant improvement of the environmental performance of IWT in terms of NO_x and PM emissions will probably have to be forced through more stringent regulations or through pressure from customers. The lack of payback potential of current emission reduction-related equipment makes it unlikely that many transport operators will implement them without such incentives.

7.3.3   Dedicated vessels for niche markets

Although the vast majority of inland vessels are 'standard' dry bulk vessels, containers vessels and tank vessels that transport dry bulk, containers, oil or oil products, there are examples of dedicated vessels that have been developed to serve niche markets and/or transport niche cargoes. The dedicated vessels that are actually built and have managed to find their way into the spotlights are discussed in this section: geared container vessels, vessels for the transport of unitized cargoes, a flour transport vessel, vessels for the transport of cars and vessels carrying aircraft parts.

7.3.3.1   Geared container vessels

The transport of containers by inland waterways traditionally requires dedicated terminals with container cranes or other equipment that can handle containers. Many companies that are located directly at the waterfront do not have such equipment, making it impossible for them to load containers directly on inland vessels. Instead, cargo is carried off by truck and taken to a port or directly to its destination, thereby increasing traffic on the road and leaving the waterway along which they are located unused. In 2005, the *Mercurius Amsterdam*, shown in Figure 7.11, was introduced to improve this situation. The vessel is a container vessel with its own crane. This enables it to load and unload containers at such sites, thereby tapping into an as yet inaccessible market for inland vessels and relieving local roads in congested areas around, among others, the ports of Amsterdam and Rotterdam. A second vessel, *Transferium*, was built in 2009.

7.3.3.2   Transport of palletized cargoes

In an attempt to move part of the distribution of fast moving consumer goods in the Netherlands from road to water, the Distrivaart project (2000–2004) developed a logistics concept for the waterborne transport of palletized goods (see Figure 7.12). A 62 m long, 7.2 m wide vessel was built to realize this concept. The vessel featured a covered hold and an automated system to load, store, retrieve and unload the pallets. Although the technical concept itself worked, the project was halted. One of the reasons stated in the media was that the transported volumes were insufficient to make the concept competitive at the time.

There have been several follow-up studies, but these have not led to a revival of the project on the same scale. On a much smaller scale, a dedicated 18.8 m long and 4.26 m wide electrically propelled vessel with a crane and a capacity of 40 roll containers ('the beer boat') is used to supply the bars and restaurants along the historic canals of the Dutch city of Utrecht, while a similar-sized vessel is used to collect waste in the historic centre of that same city. Since 2010, a vessel similar to the supply vessel in Utrecht operates in

Figure 7.11 The *Mercurius Amsterdam* (picture courtesy of Mercurius Shipping Group)

Figure 7.12 The *River Hopper*, the vessel developed for the Distrivaart project (picture
courtesy of Mercurius Shipping Group)

Amsterdam. The 20 m long and 4.25 m wide *City Supplier* supplies businesses along the city's canals.

7.3.3.3   *Transport of flour*

In cooperation with a flour producer, Mercurius Shipping Group built and operated a dedicated 1,450 ton flour vessel, the *Mercurial Latistar*, between 2002 and 2007. The vessel transported flour in the Netherlands, between the factory in Zaandam and the processing plant in Nijmegen. One of the remarkable features of the vessel was its vacuum cleaner-like loading and unloading system that enabled it to load and unload flour by itself. After the processing plant closed, the vessel was converted to a container vessel.

7.3.3.4   *Transport of aircraft segments*

Two 75 m long and 13.8 m wide vessels, *Breuil* and *Brion*, built in 2004, transport fuselages and wings of the Airbus A380 aircraft from Pauillac to Langon on the French river Garonne. Cargo is loaded over the stern as RoRo (Roll on – Roll off) cargo. The vessels are designed specifically to have low emissions, low noise and the ability to pass the Pont de Pierre historic bridge in the city of Bordeaux.

7.3.3.5   *Transport of vehicles*

These previously discussed vessels are all more or less unique. Vessels for the transport of cars and other vehicles do tap into niche markets but appear in slightly larger numbers. Car transport on the Rhine dates back to 1983 and there are now around 20 dedicated vessels and barges (WZ, 2008). The Interrhine group, for instance, operates five self-propelled vessels and four pushbarges to transport around 180,000 new cars per year between Germany, Belgium, Luxembourg and the Netherlands and operates two other vessels for larger Roll on-Roll off cargo. On the Danube, Willi Betz operates a regular service with four 114 m × 22.8 m vessels that transport loaded trailers.

7.4   Impacts of these developments on the competitiveness of IWT

In this chapter, we have discussed that innovations in IWT are mainly directed at reducing fuel consumption, maximization of scale or entering niche markets. The continuous increase in both the average and maximum size of inland vessels in Europe will on the one hand improve the average competitiveness of the sector with other modes. On the other hand, it threatens to lead to underutilization of smaller waterways and thereby to a narrowing of the market that is serviced by inland waterway transport. The size of inland vessels on the Rhine is reaching the capacity limits of the waterway, especially related to draught. Due to the fluctuating water levels, the largest vessels can not always be loaded to their design deadweight.

Reduction of fuel consumption is strongly related to the design improvements made to the vessel. In general, improvement of the performance of inland vessels is a gradual process, the summation of multiple small improvements. It is, therefore, not to be expected that there will be a sudden change in the competitiveness of IWT because of changes in vessel technology. Improving the environmental performance of IWT still remains a challenge, despite the fact that failure to improve this performance will seriously harm the sector's 'green' image. At the time of writing this chapter, LNG appears to be a promising contributor to the solution, but time will tell if the technology will manage to get a sufficiently firm foothold and if the high cost of LNG installations can be lowered to commercially viable levels. Niche markets are expected to remain just that, as a result of which their impact on IWT as a whole will be limited. Notwithstanding the above, there is still significant room for improvement of inland vessels. Thus far only few innovations are the result of extensive research. Especially the more complex aspects of the design of inland vessels are still poorly understood. These aspects include the complex shape of the aft part of the hull (see Figure 7.13), which is essential for achieving good performance of the propeller(s) while still keeping the vessel's resistance acceptable. The influence of water depth on the vessel's resistance and on the optimal shape of the vessel is also still largely unknown, even though it is known to be significant. For seagoing ships, this influence is known better, but the extremely low depth of inland waterways is outside the validity range of the existing prediction methods.

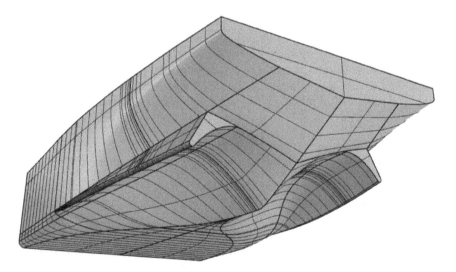

Figure 7.13 A typical aftship form of a self-propelled inland ship (Source: Rotteveel and Hekkenberg, 2015)

Due to a lack of data it is even unknown how often inland vessels encounter certain water depth, even if it is known when a vessel will sail on a particular waterway. This makes it impossible to properly optimize the hull design of the vessel. Recently the Top Ships and CoVadem projects were initiated. The first focuses on the optimization of the hullform through systematic Computational Fluid Dynamics (CFD) calculations of different hullforms at different water depths (Rotteveel and Hekkenberg, 2015). The second strives to continuously map the riverbed on part of the lower Rhine using the depth sounders of a large number of inland cargo vessels. With the data from both projects, it becomes possible to make a better assessment of the performance of a vessel design and to actually improve the design of future vessels. This still leaves the problem of a high cost-to-benefit ratio of researching the improvement of vessels. The authors believe that creating the proper incentives to improve the vessels is the best way to diminish this problem. This should be done through e.g. the development of energy and emission labels for inland vessels which will enable shippers to identify the most environmentally friendly vessel. This in turn makes it possible for them to hire these vessels and tell their customers that they are an environmentally responsible company. Once shippers start hiring the 'better' inland vessels, this will be an incentive for the improvement of new vessels, which should trigger new innovation and developments in the field of inland vessel technology. The development of such energy and emission labels as well as the development of the knowledge and calculation methods to develop them, however, still require significant research and development effort.

References

Amos, P., J. Dashan, N. Tao, S. Junyan and F. Weijun. 2009. Sustainable development of inland waterway transport in China. World Bank report 54962.

Berg, W. van den. 1996. The Whale Tail Wheel. ITTC 1996 Workshop on Unconventional Propulsion.

CCNR. 2012. *Market Observation 2012–1*. Strasbourg: Central Commission for Navigation on the Rhine.

CCNR. 2013. *Reglement betreffende het scheepvaartpersoneel op de rijn (RSP) 2010*, edition 2013. Strasbourg: Central Commission for Navigation on the Rhine.

CE Delft. 2003. To shift or not to shift, that's the question: the environmental performance of the principal modes of freight and passenger transport in the policy-making context. Report publication number: 03.4360.09. Delft.

CE Delft, INFRAS, University of Gdansk and Fraunhofer Gesellschaft. 2008. *Handbook on Estimation of External Costs in the Transport Sector: Produced within the Study Internalization Measures and Policies for All External Cost of Transport (IMPACT) – Version 1.1.* Delft.

Dazert, R. 2014. Verkenning binnenvaartmarkt Zuid-Amerika. HME Trade seminar. Ede, The Netherlands.

Economic Commission for Europe, Committee on Inland Transport. 2015. European Agreement concerning the International Carriage of Dangerous Goods by Inland Waterways (ADN), Volume I. ECE/TRANS/243 (Vol. I). United Nations. New York and Geneva.

166 Robert Hekkenberg and Jialun Liu

European Conference of Ministers of Transport. 1992. Resolution No. 92/2 on New Classification of Inland Waterways.

Fischer, J.P. and E.L. Shearer. 2004. Inland and lake vessels. In T. Lamb (ed.), *Ship Design and Construction*, Volume II. Jersey City, NJ: The Society of Naval Architects and Marine Engineers. Chapter 39.

Foeth, E.J. 2008. Decreasing frictional resistance by air lubrication. 20th International Hiswa Symposium on Yacht Design and Yacht Construction. Amsterdam.

Guesnet, T. 2005. Innovative barge trains for effective transport on shallow waters, final technical report. VBD Europäisches Entwicklungszentrum für Binnen- und Küstenschifffahrt.

Hassel, E. van. 2011. Developing a small barge convoy system to reactivate the use of the small inland waterway network. Thesis, University of Antwerp.

Hekkenberg, R.G. 2013. Inland ships for efficient transport chains. Thesis, TU Delft.

Hekkenberg, R.G. 2015a. Optimization of the dimensions of dry bulk ships: the case of the river Rhine. *Maritime Economics & Logistics*, online 22 January 2015. doi: 10.1057/mel.2014.36.

Hekkenberg, R.G. 2015b.Technological challenges and developments in European inland waterway transport. In C. Ocampo-Martinez and R.R. Negenborn (eds), *Transport of Water versus Transport over Water*. Dordrecht: Springer. pp. 297–314.

Hekkenberg, R.G. and C. Thill. 2014. Retrofit solutions for inland ships: the MoVe IT! approach. European Inland Waterway Navigation Conference. Budapest.

Hilling, D. 1999. Inland shipping and the maritime link. *Proceedings of the ICE: Water Maritime and Energy*, 136(4). doi: 10.1680/iwtme.1999.31982.

Hoogvelt, B. and B. de Vries. 2011. LNG als brandstof voor de binnenvaart. CMTI report CMTI.11.107.5.1A. Zoetermeer, the Netherlands.

Hoogwout, P., B. Boneschansker, F. Quadvlieg and H. Blaauw. 2004. Met 18000 ton op de Rijn. *Schip en Werf de Zee*, May, pp. 26–29.

Kormyshov, E. 2005. Russian market of inland water transport. ECMT/UNECE/CCNR/DC Workshop. Paris.

Lightweight Structures, www.lightweight-structures.com/compocanord-composite-barge-for-inland-shipping/index.html, accessed July 2015.

Ludolphy, H. 2001. The unsinkable ship: development of the Y-shape support web. 2nd International Conference on Collision and Grounding of Ships. Copenhagen.

Nilson, E., M. Carambia, P. Krahe, M. Larina, J.U. Belz and M. Promny. 2011. Generation and application of discharge scenarios for water management at the river Rhine. KLIWAS Second Status Conference. Berlin.

O-foil, www.ofoil.nl, accessed July 2015.

Quispel, M., W.A. van Putten and R.A. van Liere. 2015. Versterking van de marktstructuur in de binnenvaart: een inventarisatie van mogelijkheden voor commerciële samenwerkingsverbanden. STC-NESTRA.

Rotteveel, E. and R.G. Hekkenberg. 2015. The influence of shallow water and hull form variations on inland ship resistance. International Marine Design Conference. Tokyo.

Schweighofer, J. and P. Seiwerth. 2007. Environmental performance of inland navigation. European Inland Waterway Navigation Conference. Visegrád, Hungary.

Schweighofer, J., E. Nilson, B. Klein, I. Lingemann, P. Krahe, G. Balint, B. Gnandt, A. Horanyi and G. Szépszó. 2012. Impact of climate change on hydrological conditions of navigation. Consolidated workpackage report. ECCONET deliverable 1.5.

Song, D. 2010. Introduction to development of inland shipping on Yangtze River and other rivers in China PRC. 1st Rivers of the World Forum. Rotterdam.

USACE. 2013. Waterborne transportation lines of the United States, calendar year 2012, Volume 1 – National summaries. US Army Corps of Engineers Waterborne Commerce Statistics Center. New Orleans.

Wijnolst, N. 1995. *Design Innovation in Shipping: The Only Constant Is Change.* Delft: Delft University Press.

WZ. 2008. Trafiekprognose SSW. Document number 8101-519-125-02. Waterwegen en Zeekanaal NV, Afdeling Bovenschelde.

8 A new wave for the inland waterways

Palletized goods

Koen Mommens, Dries Meers, Tom van Lier and Cathy Macharis

Inland waterways are distinguishing characteristics in our landscape. Their waters often represent physical borders between regions while simultaneously connecting many of our cities. Moreover, their course determined the location of those historic cities, and where missing, canals between cities and regions were excavated by men. For centuries, inland waterways represented the main mode for freight transport on medium and long distance on the landside. As an example, one can think of the Hansa-network. The Hansa was a commercial confederation of European merchant guilds who dominated the – mainly Baltic – inter-city trade performed with vessels in the seventeenth century. As freight transport by rail and road gained interest in the nineteenth and twentieth centuries, the use of inland waterways decreased, especially in urban settings. Only uniform, large volumes of bulk remained to be transported by vessels. Bulk therefore constitutes the symbolic first wave of the modern inland waterway transport. Even nowadays, bulk goods still represent the largest share in the volumes transported via inland waterways. Evolutions within the transport market of bulk goods are thus by consequence of great importance for the inland waterway sector. However, for large, uniform volumes of both liquid and solid bulk requiring transport over relatively long distances, there is no transport mode able to really compete with vessel transport. During the last decades, this favourable market position of inland waterway transport increasingly shifted bulk volumes to vessels. In the future, different European inland waterway and port authorities expect even larger bulk volumes on their waterways, despite current dependency on the declining heavy industry in Europe.

The second wave for the inland waterways resulted from the simultaneous globalization and standardization in transport in the post-Second World War era. More specifically containers, which were introduced in the 1950s in maritime shipping, found their way to European inland waterways by the end of the 1960s. Transport volumes, however, only really started rising in Western Europe in the late 1980s and 1990s, connecting the sea ports of Antwerp and Rotterdam to important parts of their hinterland (Notteboom, 2007). The containerization also brought about innovation. Dedicated vessels were built

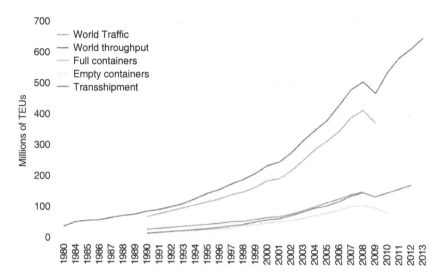

Figure 8.1   World container traffic and throughput (millions of TEU) (Source: Rodrigue *et al.*, 2013)

especially for container transport, and in several countries bridges and inland waterways were adapted to the new standards (Konings, 2009). Multiple inter-modal container terminals were developed. These effects are also illustrated by the evolution in number of containers transported on the inland water-ways. Except for a drop during the economic crisis of 2008/2009, worldwide volumes of containerized goods have grown constantly in the last two decades (see Figure 8.1). Policy-makers support this growth in container vessel trans-port as European governments – at all levels – promoted and still promote the use of inland waterway transport, mainly for its sustainable characteristics. Both the market potential of intermodal terminals and the impact of dif-ferent governmental aid programmes as well as potential internalizations on those market areas have been studied during the past decade (e.g. Macharis and Pekin, 2009; Macharis *et al.*, 2010).

The container transport market via inland waterways is still not saturated, and so remains an important growth market. Both policy-makers and port authorities still aim to increase the modal share of inland waterway transport (Vermeiren, 2013), acknowledging current and expected capacity constraints in road transport. And as freight volumes are expected to grow in the com-ing years/decades, it can be assumed that volumes transported on the inland waterways will also do so. Moreover, the European Commission is targeting to shift 30 per cent of its long distance freight traffic from road to rail and to inland waterways by 2030 (European Commission, 2011b). As such, inland waterway transport has an important role to play in future sustainable transport, and not only for bulk and containerized goods.

Although pallets are an older form of loading units than containers, it was not until the past decade before pallets were addressed to such an extent with regards to vessel transport that one could speak of a third wave of inland waterway transport (Verbeke *et al.*, 2007). Different private players – with adapted or newly built vessels – are already active in this rapidly evolving market. And there is quite some potential. Palletized goods represent, according to EUROSTAT[1] data, 11.4 per cent of total freight flows in volume (tons) and 17 per cent when expressed in ton-kms. The diversity among palletized goods is, however, huge and not all goods lend themselves to the same extent to a modal shift towards inland waterways. This chapter will focus on the modal shift of palletized goods. The concept, its history and its context will be discussed in the second section. That context is becoming increasingly urban. Some urban distribution concepts are already using the available inland waterways. As the European Commission aims to have CO_2-free cities by 2030 (European Commission, 2011b), one might even claim that city distribution by inland waterways is a potential upcoming fourth wave. Examples of current projects are Mokum Mariteam in Amsterdam, the Beerboat in Utrecht and Vert Chez Vous in Paris (Janjevic and Ndiaye, 2014). Some of those projects make use of pallet transport by inland waterway, like Vracht door de Gracht in Amsterdam or the Madagascar in Paris (Mommens *et al.*, 2014a). Other cases of the inland waterway transport of pallets are discussed in the third section of this chapter. Additionally, market evolutions will be addressed based on policy documents and interviews with some of the private actors executing inland waterway transport of pallets. The fourth section will be dedicated to the Location Analysis Model for Barge Transport Of Pallets (LAMBTOP). Its methodology and results for different cases will underpin the conclusions presented at the end of this chapter.

8.1   Pallets on the inland waterways?

Transport of palletized goods via the inland waterways is not something completely new, however past initiatives were small in scale. In 1964, palletized tiles were transported by vessels on Belgian inland waterways. Also the *Madagascar* vessel has been transporting palletized building materials in the Region of Paris since 1987. In the Dutch Distrivaart project, palletized drinks were transported with a sophisticated pallet-warehouse-vessel in the early 2000s (Groothedde *et al.*, 2005). Although the Distrivaart project was stopped after two years (Poppink, 2005), it meant the start of a feasibility study for the modal shift of palletized goods in Flanders, Belgium (VUB and COMiSOL, 2006). The results of this study indicated a large potential for a modal shift and pinpointed the construction sector as a pioneer sector for the concept. Several pilots were executed with different types of vessels and pontoons, different types of palletized construction materials and different types of transhipment techniques. Those pilots were a success as they both confirmed the potential and identified the problems and threats of the concept. Moreover, the pilots generated interest amongst all concerned actors, namely the construction sector, government and inland waterway carriers. The construction sector found opportunities to move their stock closer to their customers, as such enhancing reliability in their supply chain. From its side, the government, as an advocate of a modal shift, succeeded in reducing the environmental, social and economic impact of the transport of palletized goods (Mommens *et al.*, 2014b). Finally, the inland waterway carriers identified new business opportunities thanks to this market opening towards palletized goods. The fact that the different interests of all concerned actors are joined into a common goal has made Flanders the current world leader in applying the concept on a larger scale. To our knowledge, at least nine different origin-destination (OD) combinations of palletized goods are currently being connected via inland waterway transport in this region. The OD combinations are clustered in central Flanders (axis Brussels – Antwerp – Campine Canals – Leuven – West Flanders), but reach into the Netherlands and Wallonia (Belgium). One of the main reasons for this clustering within the Flemish region is the governmental aid issued by the regional government of Flanders. That aid consists of an operational part and investment support. The goal of the investment support is to stimulate innovations regarding transport and transhipment techniques. It is allocated according to an 80/20 partition. The government accounts for 80 per cent of the costs, with a maximum of €200,000 spread over three years. The operational part of the incentive is designed to cover initial financial deficits due to the modal shift, and covers 80 per cent of the transport-related deficit in the first year, decreasing to respectively 60 per cent and 40 per cent of the deficit for years two and three. The aid is only granted if both origin and destination are located within Flanders and if the operational incentive is not higher than 30 per cent of total transport costs. Both operational and investment incentives were simultaneously launched in two calls in 2012 and 2013. Applicants need to apply and they are evaluated in terms of volume, viability, efficiency and societal value. Moreover, they need to guarantee a certain modal shift over a five year period. Otherwise the aid has to be repaid (European Commission, 2011a; Mommens and Macharis, 2013; Waterwegen en Zeekanaal NV and NV De Scheepvaart, 2011). In addition to this financial support, inland waterway administrators are themselves investing in transhipment-infrastructure dedicated to palletized goods. Moreover, those administrators appointed – together with the enterprise unions – so-called transport experts who give free advice to interested companies.

Although the aid does not address a specific type of goods, it is important to highlight that – except for two projects with palletized drinks – all palletized goods currently transported are construction materials. There are several reasons for this. First, many producers and retailers of construction

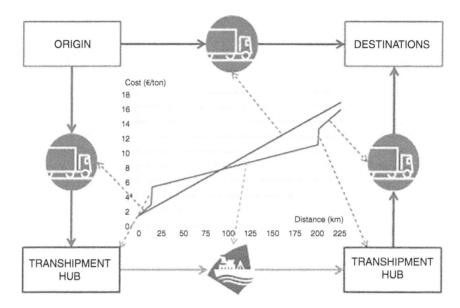

Figure 8.2 Intermodal and unimodal transport chain for palletized goods and the related cost structure

materials are for historic reasons located at or near an inland waterway. Therefore transhipment costs and costs for pre- and/or post-haulage can be limited or even avoided. The intermodal transport chain of palletized goods is typically characterized by pre-haulage via road between the origin and the transhipment hub if the origin is not at the waterside. From the transhipment hub onwards, a vessel transports pallets to the destination if it is located at the waterside. In case the destination is not located along an inland waterway, the vessel will navigate to another transhipment hub. The final leg between the transhipment hub and this non-water-bound destination is called the post-haulage, and is also performed via road. Both transhipment costs and pre- and post-haulage costs are important for the feasibility of the concept, as illustrated in Figure 8.2. The different steps in the intermodal- and unimodal transport chain and their related costs are shown.

A second reason why many construction materials are well suited for palletized transport is their relative low value density and large, uniform transport volumes. In addition, many of these goods are resistant to rain and cold. Based on the specific total logistics cost analysis for palletized goods by Lestiboudois and Macharis (2013), an analysis was performed in order to quantify the importance of different commodity characteristics and supply chain features on the potential for a modal shift. Changes in these characteristics will cause changes in total logistics costs, in break-even distance and consequently in the feasibility of a modal shift. Table 8.1 shows different

Table 8.1 Transport service and goods' characteristics and their variations

Characteristic	Standard	Variation 1	Variation 2	Variation 3	Variation 4
Value of goods (€/ pallet)	250	100	500	750	1,000
Depreciation (%)	2.5	1.0	5.0	20.0	50.0
Shelf-life (years)	2	5	10	25	100
Reliability of road transport – speed (60km/h) (% deviation of average transport speed)	0 (=60km/h)	–50 (=90km/h)	25 (=45km/h)	50 (=30km/h)	
Reliability of vessel transport – speed differs by vessel type (% deviation of average transport speed)	0	10	25		
Internalization of external costs (€/ pallet)	No	Internaliza- tion			
Working hours – hub (h)	8	24			
Working hours – vessel transport (h)	8	24			

Source: Mommens *et al.*, 2015

realistic variation values of different commodity and supply chain parameters that can be combined with one another to enable in-depth analyses. A selection for analysis would e.g. be a combination of pallets containing goods with a value of €500/pallet and a shelf-life of two years, transported at standard average speeds for road and vessel transport, using eight hour working days and including internalization of external costs. These values are based on scientific literature (Blauwens *et al.*, 2012; Maibach *et al.*, 2008) and contact with transport experts and carriers.

Table 8.2 illustrates conditions of commodity and supply chain characteristics that are favourable for a modal shift and also shows the relative importance of these different variations. This importance is given quantitatively by the relative change in the ratio Total Logistics Cost (TLC) intermodal / TLC unimodal for the overall analysed volume, in this case European transport data from EUROSTAT.[2] Positive values indicate increased opportunities for modal shift, compared to the standard situation; negative values indicate that a certain variation decreases the potential for modal shift.

The results indicate that the higher yearly demand and consequently average daily demand are, the more feasible a modal shift will be. This is due to

Table 8.2 Importance of commodity and supply chain characteristics for modal shift

Characteristic	Favourable	Importance			
TLC-model variables	Favourable	Variation 1	Variation 2	Variation 3	Variation 4
Value of the goods	Low	53.9%	−63.4%	−116.1%	−161.5%
Depreciation	Low	2.0%	−3.4%	−22.6%	−57.9%
Shelf-life	Long	43.7%	60.3%	71.9%	77.0%
Reliability of road transport	Low	−18.4%	13.6%	31.8%	
Reliability of vessel transport	High	−0.6%	−1.8%		
Internalization of external cost	Internalization	25.6%			
24h daily working hours – hub and vessel	24h	1.7%			

Source: Mommens *et al.*, 2015

the fact that a higher yearly/daily demand allows transporting larger volumes at once, which is obviously in favour of inland waterway transport. Moreover, economies of scale offered by inland waterway transport optimize stock rotation. The same is true for commodity shelf-life. The higher commodity value and depreciation rate, the less feasible a modal shift will be. These relations were expected, but to our knowledge unexplored and unquantified in the context of the modal shift of palletized goods. Moreover, those relations illustrate that the modal shift of palletized goods to inland waterways is not equally feasible for all types of palletized commodities. Large, uniform volumes of low-value commodities characterized by low depreciation rates and long shelf-life – like construction materials and palletized drinks – show the most potential, which explains why those commodities are 'pioneers' in the concept (Mommens *et al.*, 2015). According to current market players, however, other palletized commodities can be shifted too.

8.2   Market evolution

Due to the combination of the huge potential of transported palletized goods, increasing congestion and growing societal interest from governments, the market of inland waterway transport of palletized goods is evolving rapidly. Consequently, challenges and opportunities arise at a fast pace, as are market innovations. This section addresses those market evolutions mainly based on regular contacts with different market players and transport experts who are closely monitoring the inland waterway transport of pallets. Moreover, several market players were interviewed face-to-face for over one hour using a standardized survey. Their views and experiences, combined with the policy perspective and results from academic research are combined in a SWOT analyses. A SWOT analysis is a decision support tool that lists the strengths and weaknesses of a measure or project, along with the related opportunities and threats (Pahl and Richter, 2007). Each one of these four components (Strengths, Weaknesses, Opportunities and Threats) will be addressed separately in the next paragraphs.

However, first a quite remarkable fact on palletized goods transport via inland waterways is discussed to further explore ongoing projects. At the beginning of this concept, newly designed vessels for pallet transport were developed or existing vessels were adapted specifically for transporting pallets. Important investments were thus made from the early start. An example of such an adapted vessel is the *Madagascar* in Paris, which is a classic vessel equipped with a crane on the vessel itself (Figure 8.3), transporting between 1,500 and 2,000 tonnes of palletized construction materials a week for Point P – a retailer in construction materials (Sétra, 2008). A similar crane vessel is the *Fluviant* of Shipit (Figure 8.3), navigating between West-Flanders, Wallonia and Utrecht in the Netherlands. Both vessels target big volumes on large inland waterways. Many inland waterways are, however, limited in size. Yet, those smaller inland waterways can also connect supply and demand clusters of palletized goods. For those waterways, smaller vessels were adapted, for example the *Patmar Z* used by André Celis NV (Figure 8.3). In this particular case the cargo hold was optimized and sleepers were removed, increasing capacity from 442 pallets to 598 pallets, without impeding the accessibility of the vessel on inland waterways of CEMT class II. As transhipment speed is a very important cost parameter, transhipment is done by two forklifts, allowing an average transhipment speed of 120 pallets per hour. Nevertheless, loading or unloading of an entire vessel takes at least several hours, up to one day. Different techniques were already tested, including mobile cranes, lifts, forklifts and crane-vessels, with forklifts and crane-vessels turning out to be the best performing techniques. The transhipment speed of crane-vessels is lower, but one to two FTE can be saved, reducing staff costs.

A first example of a newly constructed vessel for palletized goods is the *Riverhopper* of the Distrivaart project, based on the idea of a floating warehouse. The concept – as mentioned before – failed, but lessons were learned. The Pallet Shuttle Barge, or PSB, applies another concept. The PSB can carry 300 tonnes or 198 pallets – stacked one high. It is thus a relatively small vessel in comparison to the previous ones, but also has additional distinct features The PSB is a catamaran equipped with its own crane (Figure 8.3). Logically, all the goods are stored on the upper-deck, thereby facilitating transhipment and enhancing security. Currently there are two PSBs, named *Zulu I* and *Zulu II*. The operating company – Blue Line Logistics – plans to build more PSBs in the near future. An entire fleet of PSBs will – among others vessels – benefit

Figure 8.3 From left to right: *Madagascar*, Pallet Shuttle Barge, *Fluviant* and *Patmar Z* (Sources: Sétra, 2008; received from Blue Line Logistics, 2014; Shipit, 2014; AB-Inbev, 2014)

from a network of transhipment hubs. Currently none such hubs exist. Most transports operate from a water-bound origin to a water-bound destination. Exceptions to this rule use the available quay-infrastructure, from which pre-and/or post-haulage is organized. However, as increasing palletized volumes are expected on inland waterways, inland waterway administrators are looking for optimal locations to develop such transhipment hubs. In the next section, a model is discussed that calculates optimal hub locations based on existing transport flows and total logistic costs. The model was used by the Port of Brussels, currently developing two transhipment hubs for its metropolitan region. Also other cities are rediscovering the abilities of inland waterway transport, so the development of new transhipment hubs for palletized goods in other cities can be expected as well. These transhipment hubs will be able to act as advanced storage or water-bound urban distribution centres. Such hubs need a critical mass to justify their development. VIM (2012) estimated that a minimal yearly volume of 20,000 pallets would be required to exploit a transhipment hub for pallets. Additional storage, however, also implies additional costs which should be justified in the supply chain. According to the current cost structure, those additional storage costs would kill the feasibility of the concept. Nevertheless, inland waterway administrators and private actors are investing in the concept, while debating on who should manage the upcoming transhipment hubs.

The investments made so far by certain market actors illustrate their belief that the concept of pallets on the inland waterways holds lots of strengths. Strengths, however, vary among the above mentioned projects as they differ from each other. Still, similarities can be detected. They all transport pallets on inland waterways and not via road like the classic transport chain of palletized goods. It is from that common perspective with respect to road transport that strengths, and later on weaknesses, opportunities and threats are discussed. The strengths are mainly derived from the arguments that inland waterway carriers of palletized goods use to convince potential clients. Their first main argument is by far price. According to the questioned market actors this is also the most convincing argument. The inland waterway transport of pallets is in various cases cheaper than road transport. Exact figures on the cost ratio depend on commodity and transport chain variables, and are by consequence very case-dependent. Table 8.2 gives an idea of the relative importance of those variables in relation to this cost ratio. More insights on the importance of those variables can be found in Mommens *et al.* (2015). The second argument is sustainability. Numerous studies (den Boer *et al.*, 2011; Gibson *et al.*, 2014) have demonstrated the ecological, economic and societal benefits of inland waterway transport (IWT) over road transport. A recent study for the IWT of palletized empty crates of beer illustrated a societal benefit – which includes decreases in air pollution, climate change, congestion, noise nuisance, accidents and infrastructure impact – of 36.6 per cent (Mommens *et al.*, 2014b). The third argument is reliability. Congestion has a large impact on the economy and urban life. Freight transport via road adds to the congestion problem, while simultaneously suffering from it. The resulting uncertainty of delivery time for the receiver at the end of the trans-port chain comes at a cost. IWT only suffers from congestion at certain locks and ports. Consequently, the receiver can have a better estimation of the arrival time in comparison with unimodal road transport and can plan activi-ties accordingly. Transhipment hubs acting as an advanced storage centre will even further enhance this reliability for the receiver. Reliability is one of the most important parameters in modal choice (Danielis *et al.*, 2005).

Pallets on the inland waterways have weaknesses too. First of all, the extra handling, especially in cases with pre- and post-haulage, brings extra costs and an increased damage risk. The second weakness is that the current IWT of pallets lacks retour-flows and therefore suffers from lots of empty hauls. High capacity transport modes – like IWT compared to road – do benefit from economies of scale. This is a strength as long as the loading degree is high. However, the current average loading factor is approximately 50 per cent, which has repercussions on economic feasibility. Current projects in Belgium are running break-even or make minor losses, even taking subsidies into con-sideration. However, as palletized volumes on inland waterways tend to grow, all actors are quite confident that profitable operations will follow in the near future. Although costs are generally considered a strength of the concept, as some OD combinations already confirm, some cost-related bottlenecks – like the current loading factor – still need to be addressed. In order to improve loading factors, operators will need to persuade other actors in the supply chain – mainly shippers – of the strengths of the concept. As mentioned above, one of those strengths is the sustainability of IWT in comparison with road transport. Although this argument in general still holds, road transport is closing the gap rapidly thanks to the progress made in reducing its impact on air pollution (den Boer *et al.*, 2011; Gibson *et al.*, 2014). If IWT wants to maintain sustainability as a strength rather than a weakness, investments in greening the fleet are required. Except for the Mokum Mariteam project in Amsterdam – where the vessels have an electric engine – all mentioned projects transporting palletized goods are using classic diesel propulsion. However, those private actors who are planning to build new vessels – for instance Blue Line Logistics – are considering new propulsion techniques including hydrogen.

The market of palletized goods on inland waterways is still emerging, which creates lots of opportunities. One of those opportunities is indeed the greening of the fleet as new vessels are and will be built. The investment in green and efficient technology and propulsion will enhance benefits for both society and the operator. The biggest opportunity is, however, the still enormous volume of palletized goods currently transported via road. The potential share of IWT for this volume is nevertheless hard to measure. In the Build-over-Water project – a feasibility analysis for the modal shift of palletized construction materials within Flanders – it was estimated to be 38 per cent of the captured volume based on interviews with main producers of palletized building materials in Belgium (Mommens and Macharis, 2014), while a feasibility analysis for the modal shift of palletized fast-moving consumer goods for the Brussels Metropolitan Region resulted in a potential of 55 per cent of captured volume (Mommens *et al.*, 2014a). Those percentages have not been reached yet. It should also be noted that those percentages are derived from a survey among interested shippers, and by consequence do not apply to the overall volume of transported palletized goods. Large portions of palletized goods have characteristics which do not match with current IWT services, such as temperature-sensitive and high-value goods, products with low shelf-life etc. Although some carriers already consider covered and conditioned vessels, this opportunity could be as much a weakness of the concept. Above mentioned percentages result from analyses with the model, which will be discussed in the next section and considers an optimal hub network. The perspective of development of such transhipment hubs in different urban areas will bring opportunities as well, enhancing visibility of the concept, enabling the consolidation of different flows, storage of large volumes and pre- and post-haulage optimization. Urban environments are ideal for such transhipment hubs of palletized goods, as they suffer from severe congestion problems, resulting in different policy measures and restrictions (for example low emission zones, time windows etc.). Both congestion and restrictive measures are expected to increase in the coming years as well as the related transport costs. Inland waterways are often offering an urban transport infrastructure with spare capacity. Recently, awareness of this potential started to increase and projects were successfully developed. In Utrecht in the Netherlands a so-called *Beerboat* is navigating along the canals of the city, supplying different bars and restaurants since 1996. Another project in the Netherlands is Mokum Mariteam, transporting different kinds of goods – including palletized ones – within Amsterdam. Also cities like Paris and London have IWT projects. The concept of the IWT of pallets fits well in this idea of urban freight distribution via the existing waterways. The current actors of IWT of pallets are well aware of that, as they have established contacts with interested cities. Additionally, emerging concepts like IWT of pallets lend themselves to function as launch-platforms for innovations, mainly because new investments are made and there is still some room for trial and error. As mutual benefits can be obtained, both inland waterway carriers of pallets and innovators find each other, with positive results. New transhipment techniques with lifts and crane-vessels are quite innovative. Blue Line Logistics also looked at labour conditions, changing the concept of the skipper living on the vessel to a skipper working in normal shifts and returning home on the mainland afterwards. As already mentioned, also new propulsion systems like LNG are being studied, but even more innovative ideas such as self-navigating vessels, reducing all staff on board, are being considered. On the supply chain organization, there are also lots of opportunities for innovation. A network of transhipment hubs for palletized goods is one of them. Synchromodality is another recent buzzword in contemporary logistics. Synchromodality adds additional features to the traditional concept of intermodal transport, such as real-time planning and coordination and the interchangeability between modes by means of a-modal booking (Verweij, 2011). Synchromodality therefore implies the use of advanced ICT tools that facilitate using transport modes at their best and at the same time to better fit the preferences of shippers. Currently, different synchromodal transport cases have been implemented, in particular for container transport in the Netherlands (Platform Synchromodaliteit, 2014). A barrier to the application of synchromodality for the transport of palletized goods, however, might be its current lack of flexibility.

Next to the opportunities, the threats of the concept of pallets on the inland waterways have to be considered. All identified threats are cost-related. As palletized volumes on the inland waterways are expected to grow, important investments are made. Those investments were only possible thanks to substantial governmental aid. This aid is, however, limited in time and subject to certain conditions. For further enhancement of the concept, subsidized actors will need to persuade new shippers of palletized goods of the merits of a modal shift and financial institutions to invest in them. Given the current economic context and the conservative attitude of the logistics sector, this is not the easiest task, so both can be threats to the success of the concept. Moreover, competition between inland waterway carriers for those investments and potential clients will increase. Until now, private players mainly profiled themselves with respect to road transport. Finally, investments are starting to be made in transhipment facilities and transhipment hubs, e.g. in Brussels. Those require critical volumes while their use comes with additional costs. The current market is not ready to pay those costs, so complementary aid or measures – like road pricing or governmental aid – will be necessary to encourage the use of transhipment hubs. Those hubs are otherwise forming a threat to the entire concept as no one will be willing to pay for them. The location of future transhipment hubs is therefore essential, as it will determine the market area of hubs and transport-related costs.

8.3 Location Analysis Model for Barge Transport Of Pallets

The Location Analysis Model for Barge Transport Of Pallets (LAMBTOP) was developed within the 'Research Centre Mobilo on commodity and passenger flows'. It is a GIS-based (Geographic Information System) model for Belgium, and has recently been enlarged to a European scale. The enlargement illustrates the transferability of its methodology. LAMBTOP uses three types of input data. The first input is an Origin-Destination-matrix (OD-matrix) including transported palletized volumes in tonnes between each origin-destination combination. Additional information concerning transported goods – for instance value, shelf-life, weather resistance, water-bound locations etc. – can be included and enhances the analysis. The OD-matrix is ideally obtained through a survey which enables taking into account the various parameters influencing the potential for a modal shift towards inland waterways. Nonetheless, such surveys are often not available or too expensive to carry out. OD-matrices provided by governmental or statistical agencies offer alternatives; however, usually only on a more aggregated level. Above-mentioned parameters are not included in these aggregated OD-matrices. Consequently, assumptions have to be made, which influences the results. This influence is rather large as is illustrated in the following paragraphs. GIS-layers are the second input. Three layers are required, namely: one for the road network, one for the inland waterway network and finally a GIS-layer representing origins and destinations of the obtained OD-matrix. The road network is used for unimodal road transport, as well as for pre- and post-haulage. In turn, the inland waterway network is used for IWT. The third and final input is a cost structure. Based on the work of Lestiboudois and Macharis (2013), a Total Logistics Costs analysis is performed. The values used for this TLC analysis are based on contacts with transport experts and concerned actors and on the results of several pilots. Additionally, integration of external costs into the TLC is incorporated as a scenario.

Based on those three inputs, LAMBTOP uses several steps to determine optimal locations for the transhipment hubs and TLC of both the unimodal transport of palletized goods via road, as of the intermodal alternative via IWT. The detailed description of the different steps can be found in Mommens and Macharis (2014) and will be explained only briefly in this paragraph. In a first step, a distribution analysis of the obtained volumes is performed. This enables detection of spatial concentration. The distribution is also used in the determination of the optimal locations of transhipment hubs. This location analysis is the second step. It is based on the *p*-hub median problem (Campbell 1996; ESRI 2014; O'Kelly 1987; O'Kelly and Miller, 1994), using a minimization of the costs of pre- and post-haulages of all volumes of which the origin and destination are located within a pre-defined distance of an inland waterway. The pre-defined distance is based on the limits determined by the TLC structure, and consequently also depends on the geographical scale on which the analysis is done. Thanks to the economies of scale of vessel transport, longer main-haulages are in favour of a modal shift. Consequently, higher scales, like the European one, allow longer main-haulages and so longer pre- and/or post-haulages by road. Transported volumes of which the origin and/or destination are located outside this area – and so do not show any potential for a modal shift according to the TLC structure – will be excluded from the location analysis of the transhipment hubs. Potential transhipment hub locations are defined as a continuous selection of points with a fixed distance interval between them – depending on the analysis scale used – along the inland waterway. The model runs a loop in which one hub is added in consequent iterations. This is done in order to determine the optimal number of transhipment hubs, which is determined by the volume caught within each network of transhipment hubs and the cost-efficiency of the modal shift obtained through that network. The calculation requires the construction of an intermodal network which combines the road and the inland waterway network. Both networks are connected through the determined transhipment hubs. The optimal routes within all networks are calculated according to the Dijkstra algorithm (1959), combining a minimization of the transport time for unimodal road transport and pre- and post-haulages and a minimization of the transport distance for the main-haulage by IWT. The model takes into account three types of vessels with their related cost-structures: Kempenaar (50 × 6.6 × 2.5 m), Rhine-Herne-Canal vessel (80 × 9.5 × 2.5 m) and Big Rhine vessel (95 × 11.4 × 2.7 m). The final step of LAMBTOP is a sensitivity analysis of the obtained results. This is done via scenarios with realistic variations related to commodity parameters (shelf-life, value, yearly demand etc.) or external parameters (road pricing, subsidy measures, storage in transhipment hub etc.).

LAMBTOP has proven its use throughout different projects. The model was initially developed to estimate the potential for a modal shift of palletized goods towards Belgian inland waterways. This estimation required a location analysis for future transhipment hubs. Due to a lack of disaggregated data, road transport data of palletized goods obtained from the Belgian national statistical agency (ADSEI) were used. In that set, data were aggregated on a municipal level. By consequence, the initial assumption was made that none of the origins and destinations were water-bound. This favoured the use of hypothetical, optimal located transhipment hubs. However, the related costs of transhipment and pre- and post-haulage influenced the potential for modal shift towards inland waterways to a large extent. Only 0.1 per cent of flows showed transport-related financial benefits. Assuming a water-bound location of those origins and destinations closely located to the inland waterways increased the potential modal shift up to 14 per cent. The water-bound location of origin and/or destination is therefore very important in the initial phase of the concept (Mommens and Macharis, 2013).

The LAMBTOP analysis for the Build-over-Water project – coordinated by VIM (Flemish Institute for Mobility) – came to similar conclusions. Within this project, different concerned actors from the private and public sectors cooperated to research the feasibility of a modal shift of palletized construction materials towards Belgian inland waterways. The analysis was based on data gathered via a survey among the largest producers of construction materials. As data were gathered on address level, it could be estimated if an origin and/or destination is water-bound. Transport-related costs could as such be allocated realistically, making the results more accurate. Those results are, with a potential modal shift of 38 per cent, far more promising. As such, the above statement about the importance of water-bound locations in the initial phase of the concept was confirmed. Moreover, both analyses came to another common conclusion. The optimal transhipment hub locations resulting from the location analysis of LAMBTOP are mainly situated near the largest cities, as illustrated in Figure 8.4. This result underpins the potential of transhipment hubs being used as advanced storage facilities from which a – sustainable – last mile distribution can be organized within the urban area (Mommens and Macharis, 2014).

A city well aware of this potential is Brussels, where the Port of Brussels investigated the potential for modal shift of palletized fast moving consumer goods towards inland waterways. Already convinced of the potential for a modal shift of palletized construction materials, the port authorities identified fast moving consumer goods as most promising when targeting new markets. A survey among large producers and retailers of palletized fast-moving consumer goods resulted in a captured volume of more than 2.9 million pallets. Based on those captured transport flows, LAMBTOP identified the optimal hub network. Through the implementation of this network, 55 per cent of captured volume can be shifted towards inland waterways, being served at a lower cost than the actual road transport cost (Mommens *et al.*, 2014a). The two transhipment hub locations situated within the administrative area of the Port of Brussels are currently being developed. Research also played an important role in implementation of the concept by private inland waterway carriers of palletized goods. Blue Line Logistics used the distribution analysis of LAMBTOP to persuade potential investors. In the conservative market of transporters and shippers – who often are unaware of the potential of inland waterway transport – and with reticent banks, each convincing argument can make the difference. André Celis NV in turn used the results of the external cost analysis performed for their pilot with palletized empty crates of beers. The results showed a societal benefit – impacting air pollution, climate change, congestion, noise nuisance, accidents and infrastructure – of 36.6 per cent in terms of costs in favour of the pilot (Mommens *et al.*, 2014b). This valorization of the concept is important. Therefore external costs can also be included in the TLC used in LAMBTOP. It can be concluded that the analyses performed

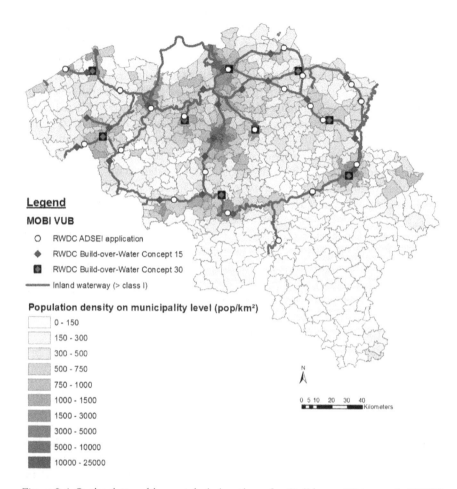

Figure 8.4 Optimal transhipment hub locations for Build-over-Water and ADSEI data, relative to the population density on the municipality level

with LAMBTOP calculated and as such demonstrated the potential of inland waterway transport of pallets. It stresses the societal and economic benefits of the concept, while pinpointing current limitations and threats. The analyses underpin thereby the results of the SWOT analysis of the previous paragraph.

8.4 Conclusion

Inland waterways are an important asset for our current supply chain. They offer a green and reliable alternative for common, congested road transport. IWT has as such its role to play, both for long distance transport and for urban freight distribution. Traditionally, bulk is considered ideal for IWT and container transport via inland waterways is a second large market, which is not saturated yet and remains an important growth market. But, in addition to bulk and containers other types of loading units show potential for a modal shift towards inland waterways. The enormous market of palletized goods has been addressed in this chapter. Although some isolated projects already existed, only recently the concept of a modal shift of palletized goods towards inland waterways found its way to the private market. Currently, over nine transports of palletized goods are operationally performed by IWT. Those are largely clustered within the Flemish territory, thanks to local authorities' support as well as initial and detailed feasibility studies which were performed for the region.

This chapter discussed the concept of IWT of pallets with a focus on current initiatives and innovations. Firstly, a SWOT analysis was presented based on both scientific research and experiences which were obtained via in-depth interviews with inland waterway carriers of palletized goods and via regular contacts with transport experts who are monitoring the concept. The SWOT indicated that the innovation that is currently taking place within this market is offering both strengths and opportunities. From a price perspective, the concept can compete with road transport. And regarding societal and sustainable aspects, vessel transport is on average still ahead of road transport. Moreover, new vessels and future developments might even increase current benefits. With regard to the road congestion problem, this concept can contribute to partially alleviate the burden, but more importantly, it gives a congestion free – and therefore more reliable – alternative to the transport market. Despite all that, threats in terms of current governmental aids dependency have to be taken into account. Moreover, transhipment hubs will induce additional costs which could kill the current market. The further development of the concept and associated increases in volumes – as can be expected from upcoming initiatives – will contribute to the need and affordability of transhipment hubs.

The outcome from the SWOT analysis and from analyses performed with LAMBTOP, the GIS-model described in the last part of this chapter, demonstrates that the inland waterway sector is currently penetrating the market of the transport of palletized goods. The potential is a reality, and different private actors are already making large investments. To have a return on investment and a proper and durable third wave for IWT, one main recommendation can be given: to exploit the favourable setting in Flanders – with the subsidy and the awareness of the main actors – to expand geographically to the neighbouring regions and countries. This will induce longer transport distances and new volumes, which will bring both larger profits and new investments.

Notes

1 Reporting countries: Austria, Belgium, Bulgaria, Croatia, Cyprus, Czech Republic, Estonia, Finland, France, Germany, Greece, Hungary, Latvia, Liechtenstein, Lithuania, Luxembourg, Netherlands, Norway, Poland, Portugal, Romania, Spain, Slovakia, Slovenia, Sweden, Switzerland.
2 See footnote 1.

Bibliography

AB-Inbev (2014). AB InBev en André Celis nv slaan de handen in elkaar met testproject voor ecologisch transport via waterwegen. Retrieved from: www.ab-inbev.be/nl_BE/press/release/111-ab-inbev-en-andr-celis-nv-slaan-de-handen-in-elkaar-met-test project-voor-ecologisch-transport-via-waterwegen.html (accessed 5 August 2015).

Blauwens, G., De Baere, P., and Van De Voorde, E. (2012). *Transport Economics.* Fifth Edition. Berchem, Belgium: De Boeck.

Campbell, J.F. (1996). Hub location and the p-hub median problem. *Operations Research*, 44(6), 923–935.

Danielis, R., Marcucci, E. and Rotaris, L. (2005). Logistics managers' stated preferences for freight service attributes. *Transportation Research Part E: Logistics and Transportation Review*, 41(3), 201–215.

den Boer, L.C., Otten, M. and van Essen, H. (2011). *STREAM International Freight 2011: Comparison of Various Transport Modes on a EU Scale with the STREAM Database.* Delft, the Netherlands: CE Delft.

ESRI (2014). Location-allocation analysis (In ArcGIS Desktop 10.1 Help ed.). Retrieved from: http://resources.arcgis.com/en/help/main/10.1/index.html#//004700 000050000000 (Accessed 30 January 2014).

European Commission (2011a). Steunmaatregel – Aid SA.30987 (N/2010) – België: Steunregeling van het Vlaams Gewest betreffende exploitatiesteun ten behoeve van het vervoer van palletgoederen via de waterwegen [Belgium: aid regulation of the Flemish Region concerning the exploitation aid in favour of the transport of pallets via the inland waterways] (N554/2010). Brussels, 08/08/2011. C(2011) 5801 def.

European Commission (2011b). WHITE PAPER – Roadmap to a Single European Transport Area: Towards a competitive and resource efficient transport system.

Gibson, G., Varma, A., Cox, V., Korzhenevych, A., Dehnen, N., Bröcker, J., Holtkamp, M. and Meier, H. (2014). *Update of the Handbook on External Costs of Transport.* Final Report for the European Commission – DG Mobility and Transport.

Groothedde, B., Ruijgrok, C. and Tavasszy, L. (2005). Towards collaborative, intermodal hub networks: a case study in the fast moving consumer goods market. *Transport Research Part E*, 41(6), 567–583.

Janjevic, M. and Ndiaye, A.B. (2014). Inland waterways transport for city logistics: a review of experiences and the role of local public authorities. In *Urban Transport XX*, C.A. Brebbia (ed.), Southampton, UK: WIT Press, 279–290.

Konings, J.W. (2009). Intermodal barge transport: network design, nodes and competitiveness. Thesis, TUD Technische Universiteit Delft.

Lestiboudois, S. and Macharis, C. (2013). Een Modal Choice Model voor Intermodaal Pallettransport op Basis van de Totale Logistieke Kost [A modal choice model for intermodal pallet transport based on total logistics costs]. Master's Thesis, Vrije Universiteit Brussel, Faculty of Economic, Social, Political Sciences and Solvay Business School, Brussels.

Macharis, C. and Pekin, E. (2009). Assessing policy measures for the stimulation of intermodal transport: a GIS-based policy analysis. *Journal of Transport Geography*, 17(6), 500–508.

Macharis, C., Van Hoeck, E., Pekin, E. and van Lier, T. (2010). A decision analysis framework for intermodal transport: comparing fuel price increases and the internalisation of external costs. *Transportation Research Part A: Policy and Practice*, 44(7), 550–561.

Maibach, M., Schreyer, C., Sutter, C., Van Essen, H., Boon, B., Smokers, R. and Bak, M. (2008). *Handbook on Estimation of External Cost in the Transport Sector. Internalisation Measures and Policies for All External Costs of Transport (IMPACT), Version 1.1.* European Commission, DG TREN. Delft: CE Delft.
Mommens, K. and Macharis, C. (2013). Pallets on the inland waterways. Policy paper, legal depot number: D/2012/11.528/13, Research Centre Mobilo on commodity and passenger flows.
Mommens, K. and Macharis, C. (2014). Location analysis for the modal shift of palletized building materials. *Journal of Transport Geography*, 34, 44–53.
Mommens, K., Lebeau, P. and Macharis, C. (2014a). A modal shift of palletized fast moving consumer goods to the inland waterways: a viable solution for the Brussels-Capital Region? In *Urban Transport XX*, C.A. Brebbia (ed.), Southampton, UK: WIT Press, 359–371.
Mommens, K., van Lier, T. and Macharis, C. (2014b). Together for better: cooperation in transport of palletized goods via the inland waterways. In *Vervoerslogistieke Werkdagen, November, 27–28, 2014, Breda (Netherlands)*, Zelzate: University Press, 340–353.
Mommens, K., Lestiboudois, S. and Macharis, C. (2015). Modal shift of palletized goods: a European feasibility and location analysis. [Manuscript submitted for publication].
Notteboom, T. (2007). Inland waterway transport of containerized cargo: from infancy to a fully-fledged transport mode. *Journal of Maritime Research*, 4(2), 63–80.
O'Kelly, M. (1987). A quadratic integer program for the location of interaction hub facilities. *European Journal of Operational Research*, 3, 393–404.
O'Kelly, M. and Miller, H. (1994). The hub network design problem: a review and synthesis. *Journal of Transport Geography*, 2(1), 31–40.
Pahl, N. and Richter, A. (2007). SWOT analysis: idea, methodology and a practical approach. Scholarly Research Paper, GRIN, Berlin.
Platform Synchromodaliteit (2014). Cases. Retrieved from: www.synchromodaliteit. nl/nl/cases/ (accessed 23 December 2014).
Poppink, P. (2005). Project roept vragen op: Distrivaart laat beperkingen modal shift zien [Project evokes some questions: Distrivaart shows the limits of the modal shift]. *Transport en Logistiek*, 4, 26–27.
Rodrigue, J.P., Comtois, C. and Slack, B. (2013). *The Geography of Transport Systems.* Third Edition. New York: Routledge.
Service d'études techniques des routes et autoroutes (Sétra) (2008). Le transport fluvial de palettes à Paris: une activité peu ordinaire [Barge transport of pallets in Paris: a rare activity]. Revue Transports, Ministère de l'écologie, du développement et de l'aménagement durables, May 2008, Nr. 5.
Shipit (2014). Bulk & Project Services. Retrieved from: www.shipit.be (accessed 5 August 2015).
Verbeke, F., Cornillie, I. and Macharis, C. (2007). De derde golf in de binnenvaart: palletvervoer succesvol getest in de praktijk [The third wave in barge-transport: pallet transport successfully tested in practice]. In *Vervoerslogistieke Werkdagen 2007*, Grobbendonk, Belgium: Nautilus Academic Books, 376–389.
Vermeiren, T. (2013). *Intermodal Transport: The Delta in the Delta.* Brussels: Vrije Universiteit Brussel.
Verweij, C.A. (2011). Synchromodaal transport: Efficiënt en duurzaam transport via netwerkregie [Synchromodal transport: Efficient and sustainable transport via

networkmanagement]. Vervoerslogistieke werkdagen, Antwerp, 1–2 December 2011.

Vlaams Instituut voor Mobiliteit (VIM) (2012). Eindrapport Modelproject en Distributieanalyse Build over Water [Final report of the project and distribution-analysis Build over Water]. Project nr. P029, Diepenbeek, Belgium: VIM.

Vrije Universiteit Brussel (VUB) and COMiSOL (2006). Haalbaarheidsstudie voor de concrete implementatie van de binnenvaart voor vervoer van pallets en de daarmee verbonden stadsbevoorrading [Feasibility-analysis for the concrete implementation of pallet transport via the inland waterways and the related city distribution]. Brussels.

Waterwegen en Zeekanaal NV and NV De Scheepvaart (2011). Steunmaatregel voor het vervoer van palletten via de waterwegen: Handleiding voor de gebruiker [Aid for transport of pallets via the inland waterways: manual for the user]. Retrieved from: www.binnenvaart.be/documents/HandleidingSteunmaatregelPalletvervoer.pdf (accessed 30 June 2012).

9 Policies for inland waterway transport

Needs and perspectives

Vladislav Maraš

Inland Waterway Transport (IWT) is organized in those parts of the world where a natural infrastructure, i.e. waterways, exists or canals have been built. From the economic point of view, the most important areas with such infrastructure are parts of Europe with the Rhine, Danube and their tributaries, the US with the Mississippi and the Great Lakes area, and China with the Yangtze and the Pearl. However, in order to increase its importance and share in worldwide transport flows, new markets have to be addressed by developing new waterway connections and canals, as well as through improved integration of IWT in door-to-door supply chains. This clearly puts emphasis on the importance of adequate policy approaches for the growth prospects of inland navigation. The European IWT policy framework has been developed to contribute to the general objectives of EU (European Union) policy. According to the Europe 2020 Strategy, the EU strives for smart, sustainable and inclusive economic growth. This means a resource-efficient and green economy, with a high level of employment, based on knowledge and innovation and delivering social and territorial cohesion. Obviously, any policy intended to result in sustainable economic development requires a multidisciplinary approach, covering the entire process from setting up a policy mission, focus and relevant goals, to identifying needs and perspectives. Transport activities are generally considered essential for achieving sustainable economic growth (EC, 2011). The Transport White Paper calls for the European transport system to be united, efficient and to enable the successful integration of Europe and its regions into the world economy. In that sense, Europe, through its Trans-European transport network (TEN-T[1]) aims for territorial cohesion of its transport system.

IWT, with its low transport costs, high reliability, low external cost, energy efficiency, safety levels and operational efficiency, is characterized with significant potential to contribute to the goals of the Europe 2020 Strategy. The substantial unused transport capacity of inland waterways may accommodate existing as well as any future growth in freight flows. The Transport White Paper (EC, 2011) recognizes this and calls for an increasing role of IWT in the transport of cargos to the European hinterland and in connecting European seas.

In addition, the EC prepared in 2013 the NAIADES II programme 'Towards quality inland waterway transport' (EC, 2013a), aiming to align European IWT policy with the objectives of the Transport White Paper, such as a modal shift in favour of rail and IWT and emissions reduction. This chapter analyses the effectiveness of the NAIADES II action programme for the European IWT sector by applying a theory-based evaluation (TBE) technique. The rest of this chapter is organized as follows: the NAIADES II programme, as European IWT policy, is presented in Section 9.1. The next section introduces an approach that will be used for the evaluation of the IWT policy, corresponding evaluation criteria and the policy theory behind the NAIADES II. Evaluation results are given in Section 9.3. Relevant findings conclude the chapter.

9.1 European IWT master policy programme: an overview

The current European IWT action and development programme – NAIADES II – represents an update of the EC Communication on the promotion of inland waterway transport 'NAIADES', published in 2006 (EC, 2006). It is structured so as to enable the IWT sector to be in conformity with the Europe 2020 Strategy targets. Therefore, NAIADES II set out the guidelines for the further development of IWT. The programme defines key areas of intervention, elaborates on responsibilities for implementation of these interventions, puts in place a new approach to governance and identifies financing sources for support of policy actions. The key intervention areas, set up in the programme to pursue quality, are the following: quality infrastructure; quality through innovation; smooth functioning of the market; environmental quality through low emissions; skilled workforce and quality jobs; and the integration of IWT into the multimodal logistic chains.

Quality infrastructure aims at full implementation of TEN-T corridors through improving inland waterways connections, clearing important bottlenecks, deploying innovative technologies, improving intermodal accesses to waterways, i.e. transhipment facilities in inland ports, and developing smart infrastructure. Quality through innovation calls for the identification of research and innovation needs and the uptake of innovation. It should come from the increased innovation rate in the sector, reduced fragmentation of the market, an improved innovation culture, strengthening the financial situation of IWT operators etc. The internalization of external costs, a level playing field, equal technical requirements among vessels, matching supply with demand and improving the legislative framework for further development of inland ports are preconditions for the harmonization of IWT operational conditions and therefore a smooth functioning of the market. Environmental quality through low emissions, as the fourth intervention area, aims at reducing air pollution in the IWT sector. This is to be achieved by imposing new emissions limits for inland navigation, overcoming regulatory, financial, technical and infrastructural barriers for LNG (Liquefied Natural Gas) bunkering and use as a fuel and providing financial support to efforts towards reduced emissions. A skilled workforce and quality jobs should bring reduced barriers to labour access and mobility in the IWT sector. Facilitating access to the profession, recognizing qualifications for IWT workers, making it easier to prove sailing experience, improving working conditions on-board vessels, organizing vocational training for IWT workers and fostering the use of innovative technologies and entrepreneurial skills represent required needs and tasks within this intervention area. The integration of the IWT infrastructure, services and information streams into multimodal logistic chains is the sixth intervention area. It requires land use planning providing enough land along rivers to support logistics activities that include IWT, incorporation of IWT and waste collection from vessels into SUMPs (Sustainable Urban Mobility Plans) and city logistics strategies, as well as the integration and exchange of RIS (River Information Services) data with information streams of other transport modes – e-freight concept.

Therefore, the IWT sector mission, according to the European IWT policy, is to contribute to the smart, sustainable and inclusive growth of the European economy. In order to achieve this, NAIADES II puts forward conditions for the sector to become a quality transport mode in the period up to 2020, i.e. it sees IWT as 'well-governed, efficient, safe, integrated into the intermodal chain, with quality jobs occupied by a skilled workforce, and adhering to high environmental standards' (EC, 2013a). Having considered NAIADES II as the European IWT master policy programme, it will be taken as a framework for providing insights, evaluation and an understanding of different European IWT policies, instruments and strategies.

9.2   An approach for the evaluation of European IWT policy needs and perspectives

The effectiveness of NAIADES II, as the European IWT action and development programme, will be assessed in this chapter by adopting the TBE approach. This methodology works by creating and evaluating every step in the causal path from any policy or programme intervention area to the desired outcome (Abdul-Manan *et al.*, 2015). It underlines the mechanisms that will make the intervention successful. Such an analysis is usually based on surveying and utilizing appropriate scientific knowledge and achievements, scientific evidence, expert knowledge, all kinds of formal and informal documents and guidelines etc. Therefore, by applying this approach, the cause-effect chain, including parallel actions, for all NAIADES II key intervention areas is modelled (Figure 9.1).

The evaluation of the NAIADES II key intervention areas is performed based on the adopted evaluation criteria:

* optimal use of resources
* social welfare

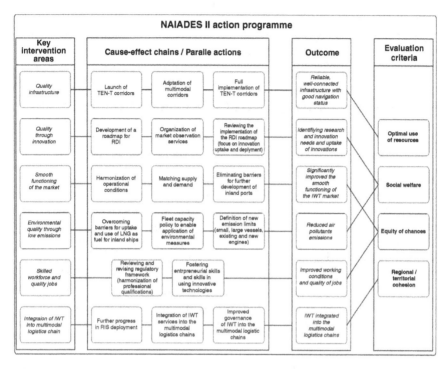

Figure 9.1 Policy-theory of the NAIADES II action programme (Source: NAIADES II; own elaboration)

- regional and territorial cohesion
- equity of chances.

These evaluation criteria refer to the identified focuses of the NAIADES II action programme. Achieving the optimal use of available resources (primarily inland waterways and fleet) has an important role in pursuing quality in the IWT sector. The safety level and environmental friendliness impact the prosperity and well-being of all stakeholders as well as wider society, so, in this context, social welfare is of particular importance. The integration of IWT into multimodal chains as well as spare or unused infrastructure capacities indicate potentials for modal shift and the accommodation of international transport flows on inland waterways. This will provide for the increased integration of the IWT network within and between countries, contributing therefore to the regional and territorial cohesion of the EU. All these processes, as well as the recognition and modernization of professional qualifications of IWT staff, the increased quality of jobs, the harmonization of operational conditions or matching supply with demand are expected to lead into the smooth functioning of the market providing for equity of chances in the IWT sector.

As a result, this evaluation approach enables the evaluator to analyse the design of the NAIADES II action programme and its ability to produce the desired outcome. In addition, based on the evaluation findings, suggestions for further and possible improvements of the existing European IWT policy framework may be given.

9.3   Findings of the European IWT policy evaluation

9.3.1   *Intervention 1: Quality infrastructure – maintenance and improvements of waterway network / TEN-T development*

The competitive position of IWT compared to road or rail transport is mainly determined by its cost levels and service quality. These determinants are dependent on the cargo availability, the carrying capacity of vessels, time reliability, service speed etc. Most of these parameters are directly affected by the quality of inland waterways. Therefore, measures such as maintenance of the fairway's guaranteed or recommended depth, improvements aiming to reach the requirements of the higher CEMT[2] waterway class and construction of new waterways, i.e. the so-called 'missing links' (AGN[3]) of the inland waterways are of significant importance for increasing the modal share of IWT. Improvement activities are also intended to reduce the impact of extreme weather events on the efficiency and costs of IWT (Siedl and Schweighofer, 2014).

Development of the European inland waterway network may be considered an important segment of the existing TEN-T. As of January 2014, the new TEN-T regulation was adopted as a new EU transport infrastructure policy to be developed by 2030 and 2050. TEN-T is targeted to improve territorial, economic and social cohesion by linking all EU regions through 'interconnecting and interoperable national networks by land, air, sea and inland waterways'[4] and includes certain aspects of the European satellite navigating system Galileo.

TEN-T comprises two planning layers:[5] the 'comprehensive network' and the 'core network'. The comprehensive network has been defined as a multimodal network of relatively high density targeted to support the development of all European regions (EC, 2013). The 'core network' is also a multimodal network made of nine TEN-T Core Network Corridors.[6] The network includes the most important nodes and links of the comprehensive network. These nodes and links are determined by their strategic importance for European and global transport flows.[7] With regards to inland waterways, the core network is identical to the comprehensive network (EC, 2013b). It is also worth mentioning that more than half of the approximately 1,500 inland ports on the European continent are located along the main corridors of the TEN-T inland waterways network (Siedl and Schweighofer, 2014).

The TEN-T programme is made of hundreds of projects – defined as studies or works – which are located in every EU member state and involve all modes of transport (road, rail, maritime, inland waterways, air) plus horizontal priorities such as logistics, co-modality and innovation. Thirty Priority Projects (either transport axes or other horizontal priorities) have been established to focus on European integration and development (SuperGreen D2.1, 2010; EC, 2010). Further deployment of 'River Information Services' and 'clean fuel infrastructure' are defined as the priority projects for EU waterway investment within TEN-T.

The CEF (Connecting Europe Facility)[8] tool has been developed for financing TEN-T implementation. Up to 2020, a budget of €26 billion within CEF, as well as funds from other EU sources, is devoted to the realization of this EU transport infrastructure policy. With regards to IWT, CEF will address the challenges and problems related to bottlenecks and missing links, i.e. projects of strategic importance for the future development of IWT.

Waterways included in the TEN-T network should be provided with minimal technical characteristics for the CEMT class IV waterway, for 365 days per year. This means passage of a vessel 80–85 m long, with a maximum width of 9.5 m, minimum draught of 2.5 m and tonnage of 1,000–1,500 tons. Minimum height under bridges is 5.25/7.00 m.

Furthermore, a number of agreements and regulations addressing European fairway conditions and parameters have been adopted and implemented so far. AGN and Danube Commission Recommendations from 1998 and 2013, respectively, deserve to be particularly mentioned in this context. AGN's 'network of inland waterways of international importance' or 'E waterway network' is made of 'inland waterways and coastal routes used by sea-river vessels as well as of ports of international importance situated on these waterways and routes' (AGN, 1996).

As may be concluded, stable nautical conditions are to be achieved only by significant and sustainable investments in waterway infrastructure. The cost-efficiency and reliability of the transport process is highly dependent on these activities. Enabling vessels with a 2.5 m draught, as required by the AGN regulation and TEN-T guidelines, is a very important aspect of reducing transport costs. Improved fairway conditions are usually considered as a way to enable better vessel utilization, more efficient operations and more competitive market prices (NEA, 2011a). However, providing required levels of fairway depth will not be enough to guarantee satisfactory fairway utilization, if transport demand is not significant to lead a modal shift towards IWT. Therefore, favourable navigational conditions are necessary but insufficient conditions for the higher utilization of the existing fleet as well as for investments in new vessels to take place.

Inland ports, as an infrastructure component of IWT, have also been elaborated in both the NAIADES II communication (EC, 2013a) and the TEN-T guidelines (EC, 2013b). TEN-T regulation introduces criteria for the inclusion of inland ports in both comprehensive (annual freight transshipment volume over 500,000 tons) and core networks. It emphasizes the role of inland ports in strengthening and utilizing the potential of multimodal transport across Europe. On the other side, NAIADES II, in the section dealing with infrastructure quality, points out the importance of the 'inland waterway-friendly access' of seaports for both seaport authorities and IWT operators. As one of the determinants of the quality of the transport services to or from the seaports' hinterlands, it impacts their competitive position. In addition, IWT-friendly access of seaports may improve the modal share of IWT in the seaports by reducing the handling time of vessels and the improving quality of IWT activities.

TEN-T guidelines recognize also the importance of cooperation between EU member states and their neighbours, so-called third countries in terms of connecting their transport infrastructure through the support and funding of common projects. Facilitation of IWT with these third countries is particularly highlighted. It may be considered important for the further and equable development of IWT, as vessel routes usually cross borders of both the EU member and neighbouring states. As an example, the NEWADA Duo project (NEWADA Duo, 2014) supports the cooperation of the waterway management authorities of the Danube riparian countries (not all of them are EU member states) and focuses on efficient and effective waterway infrastructure maintenance as well as customer-oriented services. The budget given to waterway agencies for maintaining and increasing the availability of the waterways directly impacts the utilization rate and level of transport costs of inland navigation. Therefore, EU waterway infrastructure policy and the legislative framework will deliver the expected results if only it spans and encompasses entire river basins and networks.

Siedl and Schweighofer (2014) point out that infrastructure development works on inland waterways should always take into account the following two aspects: economics of inland navigation (connection between the existing waterway infrastructure and the efficiency of transport) and ecological effects of infrastructure works (balancing environmental needs and the objectives of inland navigation – integrated planning process). The integrated planning process, i.e. ecology-oriented river engineering, allows for the integration of environmental objectives into the IWT project design with an aim to achieve greater understanding between IWT project planners and environmental authorities.

TEN-T guidelines clearly recognize the importance of the sustainability in the waterway infrastructure project.[9] It states that EU-funded transport infrastructure projects of common interest are requested to take into account an analysis of environmental benefits and costs. Specific to IWT, protection of the environment and biodiversity is pointed out. The guidelines also lay out twofold targets for maintaining inland waterways. Besides preserving a good navigational status, such works are required to respect relevant environmental laws as well. This approach has become a common practice in a number of European countries such as Austria, Belgium, Denmark, Germany, the Netherlands and Switzerland. However, the NAIADES II communication does not clearly specify the importance of this approach in its section devoted to the 'Quality infrastructure'. On the other side, inland waterway infrastructure policy, in this segment of the TEN-T guidelines, may be considered as well designed and takes into account the relevant knowledge and achievements.

9.3.2 *Intervention 2: Quality through innovation*

In order to improve its competitive advantages, IWT, as well as any other transport sector, is required to innovate. However, IWT innovation activities have been rather limited so far (EC, 2013a). Even though IWT is often considered to be one of the most sustainable transport modes, its position as such may be jeopardized by low levels of investment in innovation. Consequently, further greening of the sector is one of the future research, development and innovation (RDI) priorities identified in the NAIADES II programme. Other competitive advantages of IWT, like cost-efficiency or safety, may also be lost due to a lower rate of innovation. These trends will weaken IWT's position to contribute actively – particularly in terms of its cost and emissions advantages – to the quality of the European economy and society. This will also prevent IWT from adequately addressing the aims of the White Paper on Transport (EC, 2011) calling for a modal shift and reduced emissions in transport.

Several factors may be identified as the most important reasons behind the low level of innovation activities in IWT. Long depreciation times for inland vessels and other IWT equipment (lowering the renewal rate of vessels), market fragmentation, lack of an innovation culture and a weak financial situation among IWT operators have all been mentioned in NAIADES II. In addition, fleet overcapacity contributes to the low innovation rate, as it creates no demand for new vessels in the short term (NEA, 2011a). Furthermore, van Kester (2014) finds that the existing regulative framework does not provide enough support for innovation in the IWT sector.

In an effort to enable IWT to contribute actively to the aims of the European transport policy and overcome all possible issues brought about by a low rate of innovation, the vision 'Towards a Strategic Research and Innovation Agenda for Inland Waterway Transport' – in short 'Navigator 2020' – has been developed within the PLATINA[10] project (Navigator 2020, 2014). With an aim to achieve visible results within a short time frame, Navigator 2020 covers a period of eight years. It has two primary objectives: to identify innovations that will contribute to the integration of IWT into multimodal chains in a clean and green way and to assess barriers to the further spread of strategic innovations (Fastenbauer *et al.*, 2014). In that context, the vision has identified the following four action areas:

1   logistics efficiency – aiming for smart and intelligent logistics solutions as well as cost-efficient transhipment;
2   infrastructure – aiming for a well maintained and climate-change-resilient inland waterway network;

3   vessels – aiming for a new generation of smart, clean, innovative and climate-change-adapted vessels;
4   education and qualification – aiming for highly qualified and skilled crews.

Due to their interactivity, all four action areas are to be considered integrally. As such, each part will be able to realize its full potential (Navigator 2020, 2014). Navigator 2020 has also identified three future challenges and relevant targets related to innovation in the IWT sector. Strengthening the competitive position of IWT within the EU transport system is defined as the first challenge. Its targets are set as an increase in transport performance by 15 per cent by 2020 and by 56 per cent by 2040. The second challenge strives for long-lasting green excellence within IWT. Reducing emissions of greenhouse gases per ton-kilometre by 20 per cent by 2020 and reducing air pollution emissions to nearly zero are defined as targets. The creation of a supporting governance capability for innovation in IWT is the third challenge the sector will face within the forthcoming period. These targets envision a fully functioning private-public research and innovation cluster for inland navigation as well as a pro-competitive investment climate by 2020.

Navigator 2020 foresees that the EC, through its financial instruments such as Horizon 2020 or CEF, should support the development and market uptake of innovation in the IWT sector. According to NAIADES II, the sector itself – i.e. the industry and market players – is required to take a more pro-active role in RDI and subsequent implementation activities. The role of the EC is to facilitate this process. However, given all the reasons behind the current low innovation rate in the sector, the EC needs to build a favourable market environment for innovation and to support relevant projects adequately. An innovation-supportive IWT market can be enabled only by defining long-term policies that take into account all characteristics of the sector and ways to overcome barriers preventing successful innovation activities. A strengthening of the existing EU innovation policy is therefore needed for further modernization of the IWT sector.

9.3.3   Intervention 3: Smooth functioning of the market

9.3.3.1   Harmonization of IWT operational conditions

The EC, through its NAIADES II communication, calls for harmonization as a necessary action to overcome barriers and allow for effective functioning of the internal inland waterway market. Ultimately this will lead to fair competition between operators of IWT vessels. This harmonization process has been complicated so far by the fact that there are several organizations regulating operational conditions in IWT whose jurisdictions often overlap and relate to specific rivers. While the UNECE (United Nations Economic Commission for Europe) has the biggest geographical scope, its resolutions, not binding on its members states, are characterized by the lowest level of harmonization. Furthermore, in the EU, the IWT regulatory framework is not at the desired level because of the rather fragmented legislative and institutional framework both regionally and domestically (van Weenen *et al.*, 2013). Its IWT-related directives, as well as CCNR (Central Commission for the Navigation of the Rhine) Regulations, are, however, binding (contrary to the Danube Commission [DC] recommendations and International Sava River Basin Commission [ISRBC] Rules) for all member states. Non-EU member states put in place their own IWT regulations, often relying on the provisions of these five regulatory frameworks. Even though there is no clear distinction between their hierarchy and jurisdiction, these bodies often work together to harmonize operational and navigational conditions on the European inland waterway network.[11] Therefore, harmonization is required to avoid possible distortions of competition caused by different national, as well as regional regulative frameworks.

9.3.3.1.1 EQUAL TECHNICAL REQUIREMENTS FOR INLAND
WATERWAY VESSELS

Important work on setting out technical requirements for inland waterway vessels has been done by CCNR (The Rhine Vessel Inspection Regulations – RVIR), UNECE (Resolution no. 61 revised) and the EC (Directive 82/714/ EC superseded by Directive 2006/87/EC and its amending acts). Further, European national legislations have more or less adopted the provisions of these regulations and directives (e.g. Germany, the Netherlands etc.). NAIADES II recognizes that the harmonization of technical requirements for vessels, particularly regarding cost and safety aspects, will contribute to the smooth functioning of the market. The 2013 Administrative Arrangement is a step in this process and defines that the harmonization of different standards maintained by the EC and CCNR will include, in the first phase, the technical requirements for inland waterway vessels. In general, technical requirements for vessels set out conditions to which the vessels are subject before being licensed and allowed to navigate on European inland waterways. Therefore, the harmonization of technical requirements for vessels should primarily prevent distortions of fair competition and maintain the equivalence of inland navigation certificates as well as increase the safety of navigation, protection of environment, quality of services and modal share of IWT. NEA (2011b) asserts that technical requirements for inland waterway vessels should be published by one body, be binding for all countries and be regularly updated. In that context, the European Committee for drawing up Standards in Inland Navigation (CESNI) was established in 2015 by the European Council with an aim to develop standards (including technical requirements for inland waterway vessels) to which the EU and CCNR will refer in their IWT regulative frameworks.

9.3.3.1.2   EQUAL REGULATIONS FOR WORKING CIRCUMSTANCES
ON IWT VESSELS

Working circumstances in the IWT sector vary from country to country across Europe. The conditions on board vessels depend on the flag of the vessels, the relationship between the owner and the operator of the vessels and applicable legislation. Employment and collective agreements, wages, working times or manning levels are among the most important issues in the context of working circumstances in the IWT sector (van Weenen *et al.*, 2013). Even though the employment agreements are subject to provisions of collective agreement, they are also negotiated between IWT crew members and vessel owners. Collective agreements regulate working conditions of IWT staff in most of the European countries. Different rules may apply for employment agreements, but generally they regulate working times, annual leave, wages, pension schemes, disability benefits etc. These agreements can be seasonal, self-employed or based on a strict contract depending on the nature of crew members' work on-board vessels (van Weenen *et al.*, 2013). Furthermore, wages levels and related aspects in the IWT sector may be summarized as follows (van Weenen *et al.*, 2013):

- wages depend on the experience, age and on-board position of workers;
- wages vary from country to country in European inland navigation – Eastern Europeans earn less compared to their colleagues from Western Europe;
- due to higher wages, many Eastern Europe IWT crew members have migrated to work for Western Europe IWT operators.

Working time is regulated by national laws or collective agreements in most European countries. In addition, ILO (International Labour Organization) Recommendation no. 8 of 1920 on the Limitation of Hours of Work in Inland Navigation is an instrument regulating working time. UNECE Resolution no. 61 recognizes three operating modes (A1, A2 and B) of IWT vessels and rest periods for crew members.[12] The EC, in collaboration with the EBU (European Barge Union), ESO (European Skippers' Organization) and ETF (European Transport Workers' Federation), has also been dealing with working time rules in the IWT sector (van Weenen *et al.*, 2013). Manning levels for IWT vessels depend on the size of the vessel,[13] operating mode and available on-board equipment.[14] The most comprehensive manning requirements are set out in UNECE Resolution no. 61. The provisions of this Resolution are almost the same as CCNR requirements. The Resolution is also used by DC and ISRBC as vessel manning recommendations for their member states. However, in addition to working time and manning levels, education, training and certification of IWT staff should also be elaborated and harmonized across Europe.

9.3.3.1.3 EQUAL FISCAL REGIMES

The harmonization of fiscal regimes and tax levels are considered important conditions for further integration of European IWT markets (ECMT, 2006). Differences in this context continue to exist across Europe. With certain countries having low to no taxes for business and personnel, tax credits for investments etc., the re-flagging of IWT vessels has become commonplace. The flags of Malta and Cyprus, for example, are popular on European inland waterways. The number of vessels flying the Luxembourg flag has also recently increased for the same reasons (van Weenen *et al.*, 2013). In general, the taxing rights of countries and the social security benefits of IWT employees depend on the domicile of IWT enterprises. Thus fiscal regimes impact ship operators' decisions regarding the domicile of their enterprises. It may be concluded that the harmonization of fiscal regimes and relevant rules is a step towards further development of the IWT market. Limiting the right of ship owners to register the vessels in countries with no geographical links to the inland waterway network is among the required activities in this area.

9.3.3.1.4 INTERNALIZATION OF EXTERNAL COSTS

The transportation process implies costs borne either by those directly benefiting from it (direct stakeholders: carriers, shippers etc.) – internal or private costs – or by the wider society, which is generally not linked with the passenger or freight movements – external costs. The most important external cost categories in transport are (Macharis, *et al.*, 2010; NEA, 2011b; Caris *et al.*, 2014):

- *accidents* (e.g. fatalities and injuries);
- *noise* (external noise costs for IWT may be taken as zero);
- *air pollution* (estimated by multiplying the emissions per tkm with so-called shadow prices – constructed prices for goods or production factors that are not traded in actual markets);
- *climate change* (shadow prices for CO_2 emissions);
- *congestion* (depends heavily on case-specific factors, i.e. available infrastructure, total vehicle kilometres and governmental policies on congestion; show a linear relationship with total vehicle kilometres).

In general, transportation costs should take into account the realistic impact on society. Consequently, the 'internalization of external costs' is a policy instrument that is being considered as a way to assure application of the 'polluter pays' principle in transport. This means that the monetary value of external costs have to be determined and added to the internal costs in order to establish fair pricing for all transport modes. The internalization of external costs is particularly important for efficient use of the transport infrastructure (Macharis, *et al.*, 2010). The NEA (2011b) have suggested economic instruments for the internalization of external costs in IWT. These instruments are based on the pricing principles designed according to the policy objective to be met. The following economic instruments and their applicability were analysed:

- *subsidies* (programmes to accelerate the introduction of CCNR-2 engines, DPFs and SCR catalysts;[15] scrapping schemes);
- *fuel taxes* (as CO_2 emissions are proportional to the amount of fuel used);
- *emission taxation* (NO_x tax and NO_x fund – taxes are paid to the fund not to a government; the fund is committed to reduce NO_x emissions);
- *emission trading system* (to internalize the external CO_2 costs and hence reduce the CO_2 impact);
- *(differentiated) kilometre charges* (provides an incentive to reduce transport demand);
- *differentiated port dues* (discount offered by ports if vessels are equipped with clean engines);
- *combination of different types of instrument* (reaching various objectives, e.g. internalization or the reduction of both CO_2 and air pollutant emissions, will probably require a combination of policy instruments).

According to the White Paper on Transport (EC, 2011), an approach for the internalization of external costs in IWT will be developed by 2020. This is a complex task as it has to take into account the numerous functions of the waterways (nature, flood protection, recreation etc.). The EC will also examine its mandatory applicability on all EU waterways. Therefore, reducing the externalities of IWT is gaining importance as internalization charges are expected to go in favour of improving the market position of more environmentally friendly modes like IWT. Particular attention should be given to the reduction of air pollution emissions as the most significant external cost category for IWT (NEA, 2011a). However, NAIADES II recognizes infrastructure charging as a way to internalize the external costs in IWT. Inland waterways are usually being used free of charge, so such new charges may reduce the capabilities of IWT for modal shift. Obviously, a clear distinction between infrastructure charging and the internalization of external costs is needed in this area.

9.3.3.2 *Matching supply and demand in IWT*

Market conditions, i.e. the ratio between supply and demand, influence the level of freight rates in IWT, lead to fierce price competition and impact the competitive position of the sector. The competitiveness of the sector is also highly impacted by the ownership structure of the IWT enterprises. The majority of these enterprises are owned by owner-operators. Ecorys and NEA-Panteia (2013) report that, in 2010, there were 9,645 enterprises in the IWT sector in the EU. Most IWT enterprises are enterprises with fewer than

Table 9.1 Average utilization rates, available and required tonnage of the Western European inland navigation fleet (in millions of tons)

		2004	2005	2006	2007	2008	2009	2010	2011	2012	2013
Dry shipping	Total required tonnage	8.06	8.14	8.24	8.65	8.64	7.50	7.81	8.38	7.70	7.88
	Total available loading tonnage	9.22	9.20	9.30	9.42	9.53	10.23	10.30	10.29	10.24	10.26
	Average utilization rate (%)	87	88	89	92	91	73	76	81	75	77
Tanker shipping	Total required tonnage	1.53	1.72	1.73	1.64	1.79	1.67	1.65	1.82	1.69	1.69
	Total available loading tonnage	1.91	2.19	2.29	2.32	2.34	2.56	2.89	3.01	3.04	3.07
	Average utilization rate (%)	80	78	76	71	76	65	57	60	56	55

Source: CCNR, EC, Panteia (2014)

ten workers. Around 45 per cent of these companies are Dutch-based inland navigation companies, with only two crew members on each vessel (around 90 per cent of companies have only one vessel; 5 per cent have more than two vessels). This practice limits them to daytime-only or to semi-continuous operations mainly in dry-cargo transport. IWT companies with more than two vessels are more common in the tanker, container or passenger markets, i.e. markets requiring specialized transport means (Ecorys and NEA-Panteia, 2013). However, such a supply structure makes competition in the sector strong. The supply side in IWT has also recently witnessed the issue of fleet overcapacity (particularly in dry and tanker shipping), clearly hampering IWT's competitiveness and its position in relation to other transport modes (CCNR, EC, Panteia, 2014). Data on capacity utilization rates of the fleet, as well as on required and available tonnage of the fleet are given in Table 9.1.

By analysing the data from Table 9.1 it may be concluded that the problem of fleet overcapacity has increased, particularly since 2008 and the start of the economic crisis. Favourable market conditions triggered the orders of new and larger ships in the years before the crisis. These ships were put into service during the period of crisis and this trend continued in the years to follow.

ADN provisions requiring the replacement of single-hull by double-hull tankers may increase the importance of the overcapacity problem due to utilization of both types of tankers in the period before 2019.[16] However, gradual phasing out of single-hull vessels will reduce the significance of the overcapacity in the tanker sector. In order to deal with such serious disturbances in the IWT market, the EC introduced, in 1999, Regulation 718/1999 as a Community-fleet capacity policy. This Regulation adopted the 'old-for-new' ratio intended to regulate fleet capacity in the member states. The ratio has been set to zero and, as a standby mechanism, may be re-activated in case of disturbances defined in Article 7 of Directive 96/75/EC. The Regulation also obliges each member state with inland waterways linked to those of another member state and with a total fleet tonnage of over 100,000 tons to set up an Inland Waterway Fund. The Fund serves as a reserve fund that may be used if intervention in the market proves necessary. The Regulation also adopts the possibility for financing, through the Fund, a set of social measures, intended to help workers who wish to leave IWT or to retrain for jobs in another sector, as well as measures to improve the working environment and safety on board vessels. This section of the Regulation has been amended by Regulation 546/2014, encouraging innovation and environmental friendliness in the sector. Obviously, all these issues contribute to the supply fragmentation and therefore it is more difficult to match it with transport demands (EC, 2013a). These characteristics as well as the presence of other market players make for fierce price competition and lower the ability of IWT enterprises to make profits and to invest in new capacities or in innovation. Obviously, short-term actions intended to reduce fragmentation among IWT market players need to be adopted and implemented by relevant European institutional bodies (EC, UNECE, CCNR, DC, ISRBC, Moselle Commission). In such context,

NAIADES II (EC, 2013a) recognizes joint purchasing, joint innovation and further consolidation as possible measures to achieve synergies between IWT enterprises.

9.3.3.3   *Further development of inland ports*

NAIADES II points out that inland ports have not been adequately elaborated in the several existing port regulations of the EC (e.g. 'Ports: an engine for growth', 'Proposal for a regulation establishing a framework on market access to port services and financial transparency of ports'). Besides NAIADES II, the position of the EU towards inland ports has also been explained in other documents such as the White Paper on Transport (EC, 2011), the TEN-T Guidelines (EC, 2013b) and the Combined Transport Directive. However, NAIADES II also calls for the assessment of barriers to the further development of inland ports, as well as the appraisal of needs for a relevant legislative framework regulating the operational conditions and infrastructural development of inland ports.

9.3.4   Intervention 4: Environmental quality through low emissions

NAIADES II has recognized the improvement of IWT environmental performance as a condition to increase the quality of the sector's operating conditions. In this regard, the improvement of energy efficiency in the IWT field, the development of more stringent emission standards and an analysis of climate change impacts are needed and as a targeted approach should increase the acceptability of intermodal chains using inland navigation.

9.3.4.1   *Energy efficient IWT operations*

Energy efficiency in inland navigation is high compared to other, land-based transport modes. As such, it contributes to the goals set out in the White Paper on Transport regarding low carbon economy (EC, 2013a). Its energy efficiency, as well as the relatively low modal share of IWT, results in the sector's notably lower contribution to the total GHG emissions (particularly CO_2 emissions) compared to road transport. The energy efficiency of inland navigation vessels could be increased even more by the application of technical measures or by improving the characteristics of waterways. For example, Advising Tempomaat (ATM) is an electronic control system that contributes to the reduction of fuel consumption and emissions (expected around 10 per cent separately for NO_x, PM, FC and CO_2) by training and advising crew members on the optimal speed for any water conditions. Further, the application of RIS technologies will improve the voyage planning and scheduling of vessels and therefore contribute to the reduction of fuel consumption and increase energy efficiency. The dimensions of waterways impact the fuel consumption of vessels as well, so improvements in this area also influence the environmental performance of

IWT and the energy efficiency of vessels. All these advances will enable IWT to maintain its advantages with regards to CO_2 emissions compared to other, land-based modes. China has also identified key technologies for increasing energy saving and efficiency in the IWT sector. These include ship design optimization (optimal matching of vessel, engine, propeller and rudder, and the power device, improving propulsion efficiency, reducing fuel consumption and operating costs) and the optimization of a vessel's power instruments (e.g. developing more efficient engines and new fuel additives, making use of the main engine's exhaust gas for saving energy, utilizing electronic fuel injection systems, optimizing the arrangement of the engine room). Beside the application of energy saving technologies, it is recognized that energy efficiency increases may be achieved through improvement of the waterway network and the utilization of larger and high-efficiency vessels. However, policy-related problems raise some difficulties for energy saving processes in IWT in China. These include the non existence of rules, not enough policies to encourage the implementation of energy saving regulations and a lack of standards and rules for introducing improvements and technology in regard to vessels' energy saving (Wang *et al.*, 2014).

9.3.4.2   *Development of emission standards*

When addressing the emission levels of IWT, it may be necessary to differentiate between existing and new engines powered by diesel fuel (NAIADES II; Panteia, 2013; van Zeebroeck *et al.*, 2014). The longevity of IWT engines means that the emission performances of existing engines (particularly regarding NO_x and PM), after e.g. 10 or 20 years of service, are not on the level of the corresponding components of new-built vessels as well as of trucks and other NRMM (non-road mobile machinery). Therefore, limiting only the emissions on new IWT engines will not provide satisfactory results, so it is necessary to adopt instruments to reduce the emissions of existing engines as well. Another important determinant in this process is the less stringent emission standards in inland navigation compared to those of other, land-based modes. The EU, CCNR or EUROMOT (European Association of Internal Combustion Engine Manufacturers) have been dealing with IWT emission standards and limits for years. The actual emission standards (in 2015) for new IWT engines, determined as Stage IIIA, impose limits for the emissions of CO, HC (in combination with NO_x) and PM.[17] Both Stage IIIA and valid CCNR regulations on emissions, CCNR II, have been in force since 2007 (NEA, 2011b). EUROMOT and CCNR have also set up their own proposals for further emission limits – stages IIIB and IV (van Zeebroeck *et al.*, 2014). The proposed NRMM Stage IIIb limits are aligned with IMO (International Maritime Organization) Tier 3 engines (for engines <600 kW, with SCR – Selective Catalyst Reduction – and without DOC – Diesel Oxidation Catalyst) and with the US EPA (US Environmental Protection Agency) Tier 4 (for engines >600 kW, with SCR and an upstream

DOC). So far, China has not introduced initiatives to follow these European standards (van Zeebroeck *et al.*, 2014). In order to enable existing engines to meet the next emission stage, reductions by 80 per cent for NO_x and 90 per cent for PM (NO_x and PM strongly determine the performance of IWT in terms of external costs) are needed. Several innovative technical measures can be applied to bring the existing engines into line with these stricter emissions standards, such as (Panteia, 2013):

- SCR possibly combined with a DOC – reduction of NO_x, HC and CO levels;
- application of (diesel) particulate filters (DPF) – reduction of PM levels;
- engines running on LNG: Dual Fuel LNG (DF LNG);[18]
- other possible solutions (Fuel-Water Emulsion (FWE); methanol instead of LNG as fuel; hydrogen fuel emulsification; diesel electric configurations; monofuel LNG application).

LNG, as an alternative fuel type, enables the significant reduction of air emissions (CO_2: -10 to -20 per cent; NO_x: -80 to -90 per cent, PM and SO_x: almost zero – Seitz, 2015). However, the uptake of LNG by IWT is limited by numerous barriers. With regard to the policy aspects, the most important problems for the breakthrough of LNG in inland navigation are bans on using LNG as fuel as well as on transporting LNG as a cargo. According to Directive 2006/87/EC, fuels with a flashpoint of below 55°, like LNG (the flashpoint is around -181°C), are forbidden to be used on inland ships. Such provision is taken over from the CCNR's Rhine vessel inspection regulations (RVIR). RIVR has been published together with ADN, whose previous editions contained the same prohibition as well as prohibition of LNG transport as cargo through inland waterways (de van Ven, 2014). Obviously, the mentioned prohibitions have been preventing and still impede the occurrence of any significant demand for LNG on inland waterways. On the one hand, Directive 2014/94/EU on the deployment of an alternative fuels infrastructure states that a number of refuelling points for LNG will be put in place at inland ports throughout the TEN-T Core Network by 31 December 2030. Therefore, amendments to the relevant regulatory framework will precede investments by vessel owners and inland ports in LNG-fuelled ships and the appropriate installations. As a step in this process, the large-scale carriage of LNG on inland waterways has been allowed, as of January 2015, by the amended ADN. In addition, CCNR has initiated the process of amending RIVR so as to include and allow LNG as a fuel for inland ships. The new provisions are expected to enter into force by mid-2016.[19]

The relatively small size of the IWT market (particularly in terms of orders for new vessels and engines), the small potential for application of IWT innovation, an inadequate regulatory framework or lack of relevant incentives all lead towards a low re-investment capacity among IWT enterprises and limited research and innovation activities in the sector. The introduction of new technologies, like LNG, may therefore impose substantial subsidies in the initial phases of technology development or implementation. As an example, Directive 2014/94/EU calls for adoption of a National Policy Framework intended to enable the development of an alternative fuels market in the transport sector. This Framework should contain various policy measures supporting the use of alternative fuels such as: direct incentives for the purchase of transport vehicles using alternative fuels or building an adequate infrastructure, a tax incentive to promote such vehicles and infrastructure, public procurement in support of alternative fuels, demand-side non-financial incentives, support measures for research and development. However, such a situation may bring about a transfer of wealth from all taxpayers or from a wide range of IWT stakeholders (depending on who is expected to bear these costs) to the technology developers and in the short term jeopardize the goals towards enhanced social well-being. It is therefore important that such support is of a temporary character, technology neutral and provides for transition towards the implementation of new technologies. If the IWT sector aims to maintain its environmental advantages and impose much stricter emission standards, a new emission regulatory framework is needed.

9.3.4.3   Anticipation of climate change

The impact of climate change on IWT may be substantial. Disturbances in waterway hydrology, particularly lowering water levels in rivers, should be particularly emphasized. Low water levels reduce the utilization rate of a vessel's carrying capacity and thus increase the transportation costs. On the other hand, high water levels limit a vessel's air draught and consequently its load factor as well and in some cases lead to blockages in IWT due to safety reasons (Caris *et al.*, 2014). Jonkeren (2009) and Jonkeren *et al.* (2011) differentiate between climate change impacts on IWT in winter and summer periods. An increase in high water levels may be expected in winters due to more precipitation directly entering rivers (as a result of smaller snow levels in the mountains caused by higher temperatures and an increase in precipitation). Low water levels, on the other hand, will occur more often during the summer as a consequence of less precipitation and more evaporation caused by the expected temperature increases. Therefore, load factors of vessels will decrease, leading to a rise in the cost per ton transported. It may be assumed[20] that such a rise will be equal to the increase in price per ton. Consequently, IWT will lose its competitive advantages compared to road or rail transport. However, several studies (Jonkeren *et al.*, 2011; Beuthe *et al.*, 2014) indicate that, in the long term, e.g. up to 2050, the forecasted climate changes and their impact on hydrology are likely to induce a rather limited shift in modal split on the Rhine and Danube. Nevertheless, even such a small change in the modal split is not in line with the declared policy goal of the EC to shift cargo from road to rail and IWT. In that context, the projects ECCONET, EWENT,

WEATHER and Knowledge for Climate have proposed the following set of policy actions with an aim to overcome climate change impacts on IWT (Siedl and Schweighofer, 2014):

- continuous observation of and research into climate change impacts on IWT;
- support for adaptation and the modernization of the IWT fleet;
- development of adaptation measures for infrastructure planning and maintenance;
- stronger cooperation of waterway administrations;
- permanent and pro-active cooperation of river commissions;
- preparation of ports for efficient handling of adapted/modernized vessels;
- enhanced use of ICT (Information and Communication Technology) – 'smart waterways';
- improved hydrological predictions;
- improved logistic management.

9.3.5 Intervention 5: Skilled workforce and quality jobs – employment and education in the IWT sector

The efficiency and performance of IWT is highly dependent on its competitive advantages compared to other transport modes, as well as possibilities to cooperate with these modes. The complexity of these links and dependences seeks the staff with adequate levels of professional and entrepreneurial skills and expertise. It becomes obvious that quality employment and education in the IWT sector, as conditions for a skilled workforce and quality jobs, are gaining importance. Therefore, this section is structured to give a short but comprehensive evaluation of numerous aspects of and issues related to employment and education in inland navigation across Europe.

9.3.5.1 Employment in the IWT sector

Employment in IWT – including owner-operators, part-time and temporary employment, but excluding land-based personnel – in Europe has reached 42,800 people in 2011, out of which, according to the IWT agreement,[21] around 29,500 (close to 70 per cent) are mobile workers[22] (Ecorys and NEA-Panteia, 2013). The countries linked to the Rhine-Main-Danube waterway network account for around 84 per cent of the total number of mobile workers (most of the IWT mobile workers come from the Netherlands, Germany, France, Luxembourg, Italy, Belgium and Romania, i.e. around 78 per cent of the total IWT mobile labour force in the EU). Self-employed workers mostly come from the following five countries: the Netherlands, Bulgaria, Belgium, Italy and Germany. In 2011, they account for more than 86 per cent of total self-employed workers (van Weenen *et al.*, 2013). With regard to future requirements, NEA (2011a) forecasted a growth of transport performance

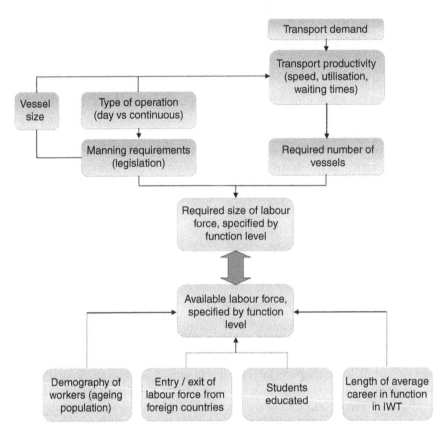

Figure 9.2 IWT labour calculation model (IWT-LCM) – required vs available labour
force (Sources: NEA 2011a; Ecorys and NEA-Panteia 2013)

in IWT for the periods 2007–2020 (7–23 per cent) and 2020–2040 (23–47 per
cent). On the other hand, the expected introduction of fully or almost-fully
automated vessels in IWT in the coming decades will reduce the demand
for nautical personnel (NEA, 2011a). The same report presented the most
important factors for analysing required vs available workers in the IWT
sector (Figure 9.2). The authors claim that between 300 to 800 people would
be needed annually to cope with the growth in IWT transport demand.
Ecorys and NEA-Panteia (2013) used the same model (Figure 9.2) to estimate
the required and available number of IWT mobile workers for EU28 for the
period 2012–2050. From the application of this IWT Labour Calculation
Model (IWT-LCM) in the long term, it may be concluded that the required
number of mobile workers is expected to increase (due to, e.g., increasing
demand for transport), while the available labour force will decrease (due to
ageing or unattractive prospects in the IWT sector for young people). The

size of this gap between the required and available workers, i.e. the shortage, is projected to reach 5,000 mobile workers in 2050. The shortage of workers should be addressed by increasing the attractiveness of jobs in the IWT sector for young people, as well as through the improvement of the IWT education system. Job attractiveness may be considered as closely linked with job quality, so an increase in job quality increases the job attractiveness (Panteia, 2014a). The European Parliament (2009) and Panteia (2014a) identify the determinants of job quality as related to employment quality and work quality. The first group of determinants deals with the contractual relationship between employer and employee and encompasses remuneration and social benefits, job flexibility (working hours, working time arrangements and time flexibility), job security, employee participation and skills development. Work quality determinants relate to the conditions for performing certain tasks as well as the characteristics of the tasks themselves. They comprise work autonomy, physical working conditions, health variables and risks of accidents, psychosocial risk factors, intensity of work and meaningfulness of work. Obviously, both employment and work quality-related determinants should be taken into account in an effort to increase job attractiveness in the IWT sector.

The current situation as well as future estimations of the IWT labour market require the facilitation of labour access to European waterways and improved labour mobility. EC Directives dealing with the issue of labour mobility are: 91/672/EEC, 96/50/EC, 2005/36/EC. Directive 91/672/EEC regulates the reciprocal recognition of national boatmaster certificates. In addition, as an effort to reduce barriers to labour access and mobility, Directive 96/50/EC regulates mutual recognition and the modernization of professional qualifications in inland navigation. However, it concerns boatmasters only, is limited in scope to the Rhine and Danube and does not cover non-EU member states (Panteia, 2014b). IWT professions other than boatmaster are hardly addressed in any EU Directive. Even 2005/36/EC does not deal with the recognition of professional qualifications of IWT crew members, but only mentions IWT in a general way. Therefore, the harmonization of professional qualifications, descriptions and names of IWT crew functions (sailing ranks) and the mutual recognition of relevant certificates is needed in this area (Panteia, 2014a).

Existing EC Directives dealing with the modernization and recognition of professional qualifications are mostly based on the provisions of relevant CCNR Regulations. CCNR has adopted and implemented several mechanisms and instruments addressing IWT labour mobility issues. Regulations for Rhine navigation personnel (RPN) affect all IWT staff working on the Rhine and represent a framework for the mutual recognition of professional qualifications (Panteia, 2014b). The modernization of professional qualifications has also been elaborated in the 2013 Administrative Agreement. In addition, CCNR has established several bilateral agreements and one multilateral agreement with some Central European countries that are given the status of observer in the CCNR. These agreements address the issues of the mutual recognition of boatmaster certificates and service record books (Panteia, 2014a). The reviewing, harmonization and modernization of legal requirements for professional qualifications of IWT staff in Europe is a necessary step forward in this area. It is expected to improve the knowledge and skills (including entrepreneurial skills) in the sector, facilitate the implementation and usage of innovative technologies, contribute to the reduction of administrative costs and increase the quality of services in the IWT sector.

9.3.5.2   Education of IWT staff

The complexity of the required knowledge of IWT staff has recently considerably increased with additional growth prospects in the future. Vessels with fully or semi-automated operations, as well as the application of innovative technical and electronic advances should be particularly emphasized in this context. Such innovations will lower the crew requirements, but may impact safety. The complexity will also be increased by requirements for energy-efficient navigation, i.e. reduced energy consumption. On the other hand, a lack of sufficiently qualified on-board workers is noticeable in the IWT sector. The majority of vocational trainees in German IWT have acquired only a low or medium school education (in 2009, only 1.3 per cent have graduated from university – NEA, 2011a; van Weenen *et al.*, 2013). Therefore, new IWT education curriculums and training approaches and tools, adopted to technical, technological and electronic advances, need to be implemented in a harmonized manner at national, regional and European levels (Navigator 2020, 2014). Within the PLATINA project, efforts have already been made to harmonize IWT education and training schemes through establishing IWT educational network EDINNA – Education in Inland Navigation.[23] As an international organization EDINNA, founded in 2009, brings together inland waterway navigation schools and training institutes. In an effort to harmonize the professional competences and strengthen labour market mobility in the IWT sector in Europe, EDINNA has introduced the Standards of Training and Certification in Inland Navigation (STCIN). This standardized training is intended to contribute to the improvement of the quality of workers and safety in inland navigation, as well as to facilitate labour mobility.

The application of more advanced transport technologies and ICT will increase the need for staff (not only navigational) with higher professional and academic education. The relevant knowledge to deal with the challenges of further integration of IWT in intermodal transport chains will become a basic requirement. Due to its importance, a specific knowledge of the climate change and environmental impacts on IWT and vice versa as well as strategies to mitigate these impacts has to be incorporated into existing and future education programmes in the IWT sector (particularly at the university level). An increased share of foreign workers on-board IWT vessels and safety aspects put additional emphasis on linguistic capabilities and legal problems. All above-mentioned IWT-related issues are still barely incorporated in the educational systems in most European countries (particularly in the Danube region). Education in IWT should therefore be more oriented towards increasing the knowledge of staff at any decision-making level, including personnel on-board vessels, with regard to transport technologies (particularly barge) and ICT.

9.3.6 *Intervention 6: Integration of IWT into the multimodal logistic chains*

Worldwide economic and structural market changes increase the share of transport of semi-final and final products in the total transport flows. These trends have required a raising of the service quality offered by IWT. IWT container services have proved to be particularly important here, as well as for the inclusion of IWT in intermodal transport chains (Konings, 2009). The modal share of road transport in European countries is significantly higher compared to that of rail and IWT.[24] However, the continued growth of transport flows, as well as environmental issues, better performances in congestion, noise, energy use and CO_2 emissions are forcing the European Commission, as well as the national and regional governments of European countries, to impose measures that will contribute to shifts in modal share towards rail and IWT transport (as more sustainable transport modes), in particular benefiting intermodal transport.[25] By having IWT more heavily involved in the multimodal transport and logistics chains, the competitiveness of the European industry will benefit from all IWT advantages, particularly in terms of cost-efficiency and safety (Fastenbauer *et al.*, 2014). At the same time, impacts on the environment will be reduced, leading to the increased sustainability of transport chains spanning Europe. The integration of IWT into multimodal logistic chains refers not only to IWT services, but also to the infrastructure of inland ports, as multimodal connecting points. The capacities and available equipment of these ports are required to enable such integration, absorb more freight and increase the modal share of IWT. An important role for inland ports in this context, i.e. to enhance multimodal transport capacities in Europe, has also been recognized in the TEN-T Regulation (EC, 2013b). Furthermore, the development and application of ICTs on European inland waterways has witnessed significant progress in recent years. Nowadays, these technologies can be found in all technical subsystems of inland navigation, i.e. waterways, fleets, ports and harbours, and navigational safety services. This trend is mainly based on the implementation of RIS which has notably increased the level of inland navigation safety. RIS is intended to facilitate seamless connections between the transport modes, as well as between regional and local transport systems. The TEN-T Regulation (EC, 2013b) foresees the full implementation of RIS on main European waterways. RIS is a concept of harmonized communication services and information systems supporting inland navigation and interfacing to other transport modes. Based on the application of contemporary technologies, it shapes and directs data exchange processes between entities in inland navigation. Implementation of the RIS concept took off after 2005. Since then, the EU has been working on the process of implementing the RIS concept in all EU member states, as well as other non-EU countries that are connected to the EU waterways network. The legal framework of RIS is primarily based on Directive 2005/44/EC on Harmonized River Information Services (RIS) on Inland Waterways of the Community ('RIS Directive'). This Directive establishes a Europe-wide framework for the harmonized deployment of RIS, and the compatibility and interoperability of actual and new systems. The inland waterways of CEMT class IV and above of those EU countries involved (Austria, Belgium, Bulgaria, Czech Republic, Germany, France, Hungary, Luxembourg, the Netherlands, Poland, Romania, Croatia and the Slovak Republic) – or about 37 per cent of their total navigable waterway network – are subject to the RIS Directive, (Panteia, 2014c). Several other countries, including Italy, Serbia, Sweden, Switzerland and Ukraine, have also participated in the process of defining and implementing adequate RIS technologies. These technologies have been gaining importance in the IWT policy agendas of countries outside Europe and the EU as well, including Brazil, China, India and the United States.

9.4   Conclusion

This chapter applies a TBE approach to assess the effectiveness of the NAIADES II programme of the EC. The abilities of the programme's key intervention areas to produce the desired outcomes are analysed. Therefore, in an effort to emphasize the possibilities of the IWT sector to contribute to the smart, sustainable and inclusive growth of the European economy, this chapter elaborates the maintenance and improvement aspects of the European waterways network, innovation activities and possibilities, conditions for smooth functioning of the IWT market, environmental performances of the sector, employment and educational needs and integration capabilities of IWT into the multimodal logistic chains. Based on the performed analysis, relevant conclusions may be derived for each of these intervention areas.

The first key intervention area of the NAIADES II action programme deals with the inland waterways network. Several prerequisites for the successful implementation of this intervention area have been identified. It is pointed out that only Europe-wide waterway infrastructure policy and legislative frameworks will deliver the expected results. These frameworks have to be based on integrated planning processes, i.e. they have to take into account both economic and ecological aspects of infrastructure development works. Furthermore, appropriate budget and defined investment strategies are needed to allow waterway agencies to maintain or improve the fairway conditions. However, it has been emphasized that a satisfactory level of fairway utilization will not be achieved only through quality infrastructure, but should be followed with increased transport demand and a modal shift towards IWT.

Overcapacity, the lack of a culture of innovation, the low access to capital and re-investment capacity of IWT enterprises, existing regulatory and policy frameworks are identified as obstacles for IWT to pursue quality through innovation. As a step in the right direction, the roadmap for RDI, intended to increase the innovation rate in the sector, has been developed. However, EC financial instruments supporting the development and uptake of innovations, pro-active roles among industry and market players, as well as long-term regulatory and policy frameworks are needed to overcome the existing barriers preventing successful innovation activities in the IWT sector.

The smooth functioning of the IWT market requires the harmonization of operational conditions, matching supply and demand, and the further development of inland ports. Harmonization aims at providing fair competition between IWT operators, an increased quality of services and an improved modal share of IWT. In that context, a clear distinction between jurisdictions and the hierarchy of several regulatory bodies in Europe (UNECE, EC, CCNR, DC, ISRBC), as well as their common work, represents an important requirement for the harmonization of IWT operational conditions. All of these institutional bodies should invest efforts to reduce fleet overcapacity and fragmentation among IWT market players so as to match the supply with demand in the IWT market. In addition, an approach for the internalization of external costs based on infrastructure charging may go in favour of other transport modes. Nevertheless, if IWT still performs better with regard to the internalization of external costs after 2020, public policy may support the promotion of and investments in IWT and therefore increase its modal share. This will enable significant benefits for the society through less congestion, fewer accidents, less noise and less pollution.

Pursuing environmental quality through low emissions is also one of the key intervention areas of the NAIADES II programme. This area requires particular attention to be paid to energy efficiency in IWT operations, the development of more stringent emission standards and the anticipation of climate change impacts on IWT. The development and implementation of innovative technologies, like LNG, will contribute to the reduction of fuel consumption and emissions from IWT vessels. A relevant regulatory framework has to follow these advances in order to enable and promote their uptake on the market. However, substantial subsidies are often required in the initial phases of technology implementation. Since subsidies mean transfer of welfare to the technology developers, these forms of support should only be set as temporary. Furthermore, climate change impacts call for a set of measures to be applied in the IWT sector.

Improved employment conditions and education in the IWT sector will result in quality jobs and a skilled workforce. The expected shortage of IWT workers demands increases in job attractiveness in the IWT sector. This should be achieved by addressing both employment quality- and work quality-related determinants of any IWT job. Further, this situation requires the facilitation of labour access to European waterways and improved labour mobility through the mutual recognition of professional qualifications and certificates in this sector. IWT education curriculums need to follow technological and operational advances in the sector. The education of IWT staff, at any decision-making level, should particularly be focused on extending knowledge on transport technologies and ICT applications.

The sixth key intervention area calls for the integration of IWT into the multimodal logistics chains. Numerous policy measures have been developed in this context. They are intended to contribute to the shifts in modal share towards IWT. At the policy level as well, RIS is considered one of the preconditions of increased IWT modal share. The further development orientation of RIS takes into account links between this service, market observation and the TEN-T tool on the one hand, and information streams of other transport modes, through the e-freight concept, on the other. This will contribute to paperless transport as well as to the increase of interoperability between modes and the quality of IWT services.

Notes

1 Regulation (EU) No. 1315/2013 of the European Parliament and of the Council of 11 December 2013 on Union guidelines for the development of the trans-European transport network (TEN-T Guidelines) and Regulation (EU) No. 1316/2013 of the European Parliament and the Council of 11 December 2013 establishing the Connecting Europe Facility, amending Regulation (EU) No. 913/2010 and repealing Regulation (EC) No. 680/2007 and (EC) No. 67/2010 (CEF Regulation).
2 The Classification of European Inland Waterways created by the European Conference of Ministers of Transport (ECMT; French: Conférence Européenne des Ministres des Transports, CEMT) in 1992 – Resolution No. 92/2 on New Classification of Inland Waterways.
3 AGN – European Agreement on Main Inland Waterways of International Importance. This is a United Nations treaty adopted by the UNECE Inland Transport Committee in 1996 setting out a pan-European network of inland waterways of international importance ('E waterways'). This agreement entered into force on 26 July 1999 and, as of 10 January 2014 (Serbia's accession to the AGN), counts 18 Contracting Parties.
4 http://ec.europa.eu/ [accessed 25 January 2015].
5 http://ec.europa.eu/transport/themes/infrastructure/ten-t-guidelines/maps_en.htm [accessed 24 December 2014].
6 Annex 1 of the CEF Regulation provides the alignment of the nine TEN-T Core Network corridors.
7 http://ec.europa.eu/transport/themes/infrastructure/ten-t-guidelines/maps_en.htm [accessed 24 December 2014].
8 CEF is an EU programme for investing in transport, energy and telecommunications infrastructure priorities in the period 2014–2020.
9 Besides PLATINA Manual (2010), advantages of the integrated planning process have been pointed out in a number of ways like the Joint Statement process in the Danube area (2007); the PIANC publication 'Working with Nature' (2008) or concrete projects such as the Integrated River Engineering Project on the Danube east of Vienna.
10 PLATINA 1 is a FP7 project (delivered in the period 2008–2012) that aims to support the NAIADES 1 action programme. The successor project, PLATINA 2, is also a FP7 research and coordination action (to be performed between 2013 and

2016) created to support the implementation of the NAIADES II policy package 'Towards Quality Inland Waterway Transport' (www.naiades.info/ [accessed 26 July 2015]).

11 Cooperation between the CCNR and the EU Commission is set out through the 2013 Administrative Arrangement concerning a Framework for Cooperation between the Secretariat of the CCNR and the Directorate-General for Mobility and Transport of the European Commission (DG Move); www.ccrzkr.org/files/conventions/Administrative_Arrangement_CCNR_CE_en.pdf [accessed 23 January 2015].

12 A1 – daytime navigation of no more than 14 hours (all crew members shall have eight hours of uninterrupted rest outside sailing time); A2 – semi-continuous navigation for no more than 18 hours (all crew members shall have eight hours' rest, including six hours of uninterrupted rest outside sailing times); B – continuous navigation for 24 hours or more (all crew members shall have a 24 hours' rest time per 48-hour period, including two six-hour periods of uninterrupted rest).

13 Manning levels are determined for the following four categories of vessels: vessels shorter than 55 m; vessels between 55 and 70 m; vessels between 70 and 86 m; vessels longer than 86 m.

14 Manning requirements are determined for the two types of on-board equipment, categorized as S1 and S2. Category S1 comprises basic equipment, while S2 requires that the vessel or pushed convoy should be equipped with an active bow-rudder and mechanical winches if it is to push other vessels or convoys.

15 DPF – Diesel Particulate Filter; SCR – Selective Catalytic Reduction – technologies reducing pollutant emissions.

16 ADN prescribes that replacement of single-hull by double-hull tankers must be completed before 2019.

17 Special focus on EU Directives 97/68/EC, 2004/26/EC and 2006/87/EC.

18 Application of LNG in combination with SCR and DPF is taken as Stage V of engine emission limits in IWT. It would bring down these limits to values similar to those applied in the Euro VI standards for Heavy Duty Vehicles on the road. However, engine manufacturers are not sure that the production of Stage V diesel engines will be possible, due to the high investment costs and relatively small engine market.

19 www.green4sea.com/lng-promising-fuel-for-inland-shipping/ [accessed 24 August 2015].

20 The inland waterway transport market can be characterized as a perfectly competitive market.

21 The Agreement between the European Barge Union (EBU), the European Skippers Organisation (ESO) and the European Transport Workers' Federation (ETF), adopted at Brussels, 15 February 2012. The Agreement applies to all navigation personnel (crew members) or shipboard personnel (in another function) on board a ship, i.e. mobile workers who are not self-employed.

22 Crew members in inland waterway transport can be considered self-employed members and mobile workers. Owner-operators either registered or not as employees for social security purposes and crew members and other shipboard personnel that are self-employed according to national definitions belong to the self-employed members group. Mobile workers are those workers, constituting part of the travelling staff, who are in the service of an IWT undertaking.

23 www.edinna.eu/ [accessed 30 January 2015].

24 EU28 modal split in transport for 2012: 75.1 per cent road; 18.2 per cent rail; 6.7 per cent inland waterway transport (EUROSTAT).

25 Intermodal transport, incorporating more environmental modes such as barge, rail and short sea shipping, has lower external costs then unimodal road transport in most of the trajectories (Kreutzberger *et al.*, 2006).

References

Abdul-Manan, A.M.N., Baharuddin, A., Chang, LW. (2015). Application of theory-based evaluation for the critical analysis of national biofuel policy: A case study in Malaysia, *Evaluation and Program Planning*, 52, 39–49.

AGN (1996). European Agreement on Main Inland Waterways of International Importance, UNECE, Inland Transport Committee, Geneva.

Beuthe, M., Jourquin, B., Urbain, N., Lingemann, I., Ubbels, B. (2014). Climate change impacts on transport on the Rhine and Danube: A multimodal approach, *Transportation Research Part D*, 27, 6–11.

Caris, A., Limbourg, S., Macharis, C., van Lier, T., Cools, M. (2014). Integration of inland waterway transport in the intermodal supply chain: A taxonomy of research challenges, *Journal of Transport Geography*, 41, 126–136.

CCNR, EC, Panteia (2014). Inland Navigation in Europe: Market Observation Report No. 18, The Inland Navigation Market in 2013 and Perspective for 2014/2015.

de van Ven, M. (2014). LNG Bunkering: Regulatory Framework, Safety Study LNG Masterplan, Rhine Port Group.

ECMT (2006). Strengthening Inland Waterway Transport: Pan-European Co-operation for Progress, European Conference of Ministries of Transport, OECD Publication Service, France.

Ecorys and NEA-Panteia (2013). Study on the Costs and Benefits of the Implementation of the European Agreement on Working Time in Inland Waterway Transport: A Comparison with the Status Quo, Final Report, European Commission, Directorate-General for Employment, Social Affairs and Inclusion, Brussels.

European Commission (2006). NAIADES Action Programme: Communication on the Promotion of Inland Waterway Transport.

European Commission (2010). Trans-European Transport Network Executive Agency, http://tentea.ec.europa.eu/en/ten-t_projects [accessed 24.12.2014].

European Commission (2011). *Roadmap to a Single European Transport Area: Towards a Competitive and Resource Efficient Transport System*, White Paper on Transport, Brussels.

European Commission (2013a). NAIADES II Communication: Towards Quality Inland Waterway Transport.

European Commission (2013b). The Planning Methodology for the Trans-European Transport Network (TEN-T), Commission Staff Working Document.

European Parliament (2009). Indicators of Job Quality in the European Union, Directorate-General for Internal Policies, Economic Department A, Economic and Scientific Policy.

Fastenbauer, M., Bäck, A., Maierbrugger, G. (2014). Navigator 2020: Innovation in Inland Waterway Transport, Transport Research Arena 2014, Paris.

Joint Statement Process in the Danube Area (2007). Joint Statement on Guiding Principles for the Development of Inland Navigation and Environmental Protection in the Danube River Basin, ICPDR (International Commission for the Protection of the Danube River), Danube Commission and ISRBC (International Sava River Basin Commission).

Jonkeren, O. (2009). Adaptation to Climate Change In Inland Waterway Transport, PhD Thesis, Free University of Amsterdam.

Jonkeren, O., Jourquin, B., Rietveld, P. (2011). Modal-split effects of climate change: The effect of low water levels on the competitive position of inland waterway transport in the river Rhine area, *Transportation Research Part A*, 45, 1007–1019.

Konings, R. (2009). Intermodal Barge Transport: Network Design, Nodes and Competitiveness, PhD Thesis, Technische Universiteit Delft.

Kreutzberger, E., Macharis, C., Woxenius, J. (2006). Intermodal versus unimodal road freight transport – a review of comparisons of the external costs, in: Jourquin, B., Rietveld, P., Westin, L. (eds), *Towards Better Performing Transport Systems*. Routledge, London, 17–42.

Macharis, C., Van Hoeck, E., Pekin, E., van Lier, T. (2010). A decision analysis framework for intermodal transport: Comparing fuel price increases and the internalisation of external costs, *Transportation Research Part A*, 44, 550–561.

Navigator 2020 (2014). Towards a Strategic Research and Innovation Agenda for Inland Waterway Transport, PLATINA, FP7 Project, European Commission.

NEA (2011a). Medium and Long Term Perspectives of IWT in the European Union, Final Report – Main Report.

NEA (2011b). Medium and Long Term Perspectives of IWT in the European Union, Final Report – Annex Report.

NEWADA Duo (2014). Set of Performance Indicators and Common Minimum Level of Service for Waterway Management on the Danube, Final Report, South East Europe Transnational Cooperation Programme.

Panteia (2013). Contribution to Impact Assessment of Measures for Reducing Emissions of Inland Navigation, European Commission.

Panteia (2014a). Recognition and Modernisation of Professional Qualifications in Inland Navigation, Technical Support for an Impact Assessment, Final Report.

Panteia (2014b). Evaluation of the Relevant Directives Related to the Initiative on Recognition and Modernisation of Professional Qualifications in Inland Navigation (Directives 91/672/EEC and 95/50/EC), Final Report.

Panteia (2014c). Evaluation of RIS Implementation for the Period 2006–2011, Main Report, EC DG Move.

PIANC (2008). Working with Nature, The World Association for Waterborne Transport Infrastructure (PIANC).

PLATINA Manual (2010). Manual on Good Practices in Sustainable Waterway Planning, PLATINA, FP7 Project.

Seitz, M. (2015). Masterplan for LNG on Rhine-Main-Danube Axis: Building a Pioneer Market and LNG Artery for Europe, LNG Masterplan: Status April 2015.

Siedl, N., Schweighofer. J. (2014). Guidebook for Enhancing Resilience of European Inland Waterway Transport in Extreme Weather Events, FP7 Project MOVE-IT.

SuperGreen D2.1 (2010). Selection of Corridors, SuperGreen – Supporting EU's Freight Transport Logistics Action Plan on Green Corridors Issues, FP7 project, European Commission.

van Kester, T.G.A.. (2014). Modes of Exploitation and Manning Regulations of Inland Waterway Transportation, Master's thesis, Erasmus University Rotterdam.

van Weenen, R.L., Ferencz, J., Chin, S., van der Geest, W. (2013). Living and Working Conditions in Inland Navigation in Europe, International Labour Office, Geneva, December 2013.

van Zeebroeck, B., Vanhove, F., Franckx, L. (2014). Impact Assessment Study: Reviewing Directive 97/68/EC Emissions from Non-road Mobile Machinery, Final Report, EC DG Enterprise and Industry.

Wang, Y.F., Li, K.P., Xu, X.M., Zhang, Y.R. (2014). Transport energy consumption and saving in China, *Renewable and Sustainable Energy Reviews*, 29, 641–655.

Index

agri industry 29, 30
agribulk sector 30–1, 73
air draught 23, 99, 104, 120, 206
Amazon River 4
Austria 4, 6, 8, 33, 55, 91, 95, 184–5, 194, 212

Barge Truck 117, 123, 157
beam of inland vessels 100, 118
Beerboat 170, 178
Belgium 4–6, 8, 16, 32, 89, 91, 94–5, 107, 114, 123, 132–3, 157, 164, 170–1, 177–8, 180, 184–5, 187, 194, 207, 212
benchmarking 20–1, 34
Brazil 3–4, 8, 12–13, 142, 212
bridge height 99, 110, 112, 115
Build-over-Water project 178, 182
bulk traffic 129, 131, 137–8

canal enlargement 23
capacity of waterways 9
capital costs 25, 28, 42, 59, 151
cargo capacity 4, 78, 90, 107
cargo flows for inland waterway transport 9
CCNR (Central Commission for Navigation on the Rhine) 63, 68, 118, 143–5, 152–3, 155, 157–8, 166, 197–8, 200–2, 204–5, 209, 210, 213, 215–16
CEMT-1992 (classification for inland waterways) 108–10, 114
China 3–7, 9, 10–11, 16–17, 21, 32–3, 65, 80, 136–7, 140, 142–4, 146, 154, 165, 167, 188, 204–5, 212, 217
classification of inland waterways 108
cleaner fuels 152
climate change 14, 46, 67, 74, 97, 139, 151, 153, 167, 177, 182, 195–6, 199, 203, 206, 207, 210, 213, 216
coal 9, 10, 13, 29, 30, 36, 42, 62, 127

coasters 104
competitiveness of inland waterway transport 18, 157
Congo 3, 100
Connecting Europe Facility 193, 214
container barge traffic 11
container barge transport 9, 11, 12, 102, 114, 120, 140
container terminal 13–14, 57, 60, 114, 132, 135, 169
container transport 9, 11, 13, 31–2, 37–8, 60, 66, 75, 102, 108, 110, 112, 114, 118, 120–1, 133, 146, 169, 179, 184
continental container transport 112, 114, 121
continental transport 11
cost-competitiveness of inland waterway transport 12
customization 41, 43, 60

Danube 4, 6, 59, 102, 142–4, 160, 164, 188, 193, 194, 197, 206–7, 209, 211, 214, 216–7
Danube commission 193, 197, 216
Data Envelopment Analysis 21, 33
dedicated vessels 29, 30, 60, 133, 152–3, 161, 163, 169
demand for inland waterway transport 18, 32, 71, 87
demolition actions 89, 90–1, 93
demolition market 86–7
demolition rules 72–3, 79, 81, 88, 91
distortions in competition 26
Distrivaart 161, 163, 170, 175, 186
Don 4
door-to-door transit times 32
Dortmund–Ems Canal 108
dry bulk 26, 29, 30, 32, 58, 95, 145–6, 152, 161, 166
dry cargo market 71–2, 74, 83

dry cargo sector 73, 75, 77, 81, 83, 90–1
dry ports 126

economic development 6, 7, 27, 41–3, 70, 97, 188
economic performance 18
education of staff 210, 214
Elbe 5, 108–9
electrically propelled vessel 162
emission standards 152, 203–4, 206, 213
emission taxation 200
employment in the inland waterway transport sector 207
Ems 5, 108
energy consumptions 158–60, 210, 217
energy use 22, 39, 211
environmental conditions 104
environmental costs of transport 27
estuary vessels 104
export market 86
external costs 41–6, 67, 158, 173, 180–2, 189, 199, 200, 205, 213, 215

fairway depth 6, 30, 193
Festfrachten 89
fiscal regimes 199
France 3–8, 11, 89, 91, 95, 107, 184–5, 207, 212, 216, 217
freight forwarders 18, 32
freight market 80, 85–7
freight tariffs 71
freighting in rotation 89
fuel costs 26, 151, 159
functional quality 22

Gambia 100
Germany 3–6, 8, 11–12, 27, 41–2, 54, 69, 74, 89, 91–2, 95, 108, 133, 140, 164, 184–5, 194, 197, 207, 212, 217
gravel 9, 62, 127
green logistics 46, 60, 63
greenhouse gas emissions 22, 35, 46

hinterland container transport 11
hinterland transport xiii, 11, 13, 32, 36, 60, 140
historical value of waterways 2
Hungary 4, 6, 8, 123, 167, 184, 212

Inlanav project 157
inland ports 14, 16–17, 23, 25, 54–5, 61, 125–9, 130–4, 136, 138–9, 140–1, 189, 191–3, 203, 205, 211, 213
inland vessel design 142, 149, 159

inland waterway characteristics 99
Inland Waterway Fund 202
inland waterway network 6, 15, 39, 97, 124, 166, 180–1, 192, 195, 197, 199
inland waterway transport of pallets 170, 174, 177, 183
inland waterway transport policy evaluation 192
innovation characteristics 149
Intelligent Transport Systems xiv, 64, 67, 69, 70
interconnectivity 14
intermodal traffic 138
internalization of external costs 46, 173, 189, 199, 200, 213
interoperability 14, 46, 69, 124, 212, 214
intracoastal waterways 24

Kama 4
Kondratieff waves 112–13
koppelverband 110

labour costs 25–6
lay-up of vessels 78, 80–1, 83, 92
life cycle cost 150
liquid bulk 18–19, 26, 29, 31–2, 58, 71, 73, 77–8, 127, 129, 145
LNG propulsion 160
LNG-fuelled ships 205
locks 6, 14–15, 19, 23–5, 38, 57, 59, 100–1, 104, 107–8, 112, 115, 120, 122, 156, 177
logistic operations 6
logistical features of inland waterway transport 36
logistics service providers 18, 32, 38, 41, 43, 49, 50, 53–4, 56–8, 61, 64, 76
logistics trends 41, 61

Main 5, 160, 207, 217
maintenance of the infrastructure 18–19
market share 7, 11, 23, 29, 110, 116, 132
Mississippi 4, 6, 12–13, 16, 101, 125–6, 128, 137–99, 142–3, 157, 188
modal share 7, 8, 169, 192, 194, 197, 203, 211, 213–14
modal split 9, 11, 13, 206, 215–16
Mokum Mariteam 170, 178
Mosel 5, 14, 133, 202

NAIADES II programme 189, 195, 212–213
navigability 3, 95, 100
navigable quality of the waterways 8

navigation conditions 11, 153
Neckar 5
Netherlands 4–8, 12, 19, 23–4, 27, 32, 67, 69, 86, 89, 91–2, 94–5, 97, 107, 123, 132–5, 157, 161, 163–4, 166, 171, 175, 178–9, 185–6, 194, 197, 207, 212
network connectivity 22, 37–9
Neva 4
Niger 3, 81, 86, 100
Nile 6, 102
non-transport-related functions 1

Oder 5, 102
Ohio 4, 16, 24
Ohio River 16, 24
old-for-new actions 87–9, 90
old-for-new regulation 72, 74, 91, 93
old-for-new rules 73, 76, 79, 91
ores 9, 10, 30, 127

Pallet Shuttle Barge 175–6
palletized cargoes 161
pallet-wide containers 112, 122–3
Paraguai 4
Parano – Tiete 4
passenger transport 6, 12, 28, 106, 166
Peniche 107, 109, 158–9
petroleum and chemical industry 31, 73
PIANC 16, 108, 115, 124, 214, 217
PLATINA project 195, 210
port dues 20, 25, 200
port–city relationships 130
power generation industry 29
pre- and end-haulage 18, 114
pre- and post-haulage costs 172
push barge convoys 30–1, 73
push boat 29
push convoys 29
pushtows 142, 144–5, 153, 157–8

Q-barge 157
quality of waterways 5, 7

rail freight transport 28, 43
regulated markets 89, 96
regulations for working circumstances 198
relational quality 22
Rhine 4–6, 8, 11, 13, 17, 29, 30, 32, 55, 59, 67–8, 74, 89, 95, 97, 100–2, 106–9, 114, 118, 121–2, 124–9, 131–4, 137–9, 140, 142, 144–6, 152–3, 156–7, 160, 163–7, 181, 188, 197, 205–7, 209, 216–17

Rhine–Herne Canal 108, 181
Rhine–Scheldt canal 5–6
Rhône 5, 14
Rijkswaterstaat 69, 107, 109, 110, 118, 123–4
River 1–4, 6, 8, 11, 13, 16–17, 19, 23–5, 33, 35, 37, 44, 47, 51–2, 56–9, 67–9, 70, 95, 97, 99, 100–1, 104, 106–7, 125–9, 131, 133–9, 140–3, 146, 153, 157, 163, 165–7, 175, 190, 193–4, 196–7, 206–7, 212, 214, 216
river hopper 163
River Information Services 35, 44, 52, 67–9, 70, 190, 193, 212
road freight transport 22–3, 28, 217
road-only transport 32
Romania 4, 6, 8, 32–3, 185, 207, 212
Russia 3–8, 104, 142, 166

sand 1, 9, 62, 127
Sao Francisco 4
scrapping action 89
seagoing ships 143, 150, 164
second-hand market 86–7
Seine – Nord Canal 15
Seine 5–6, 15
self-propelled vessels 30, 78, 142, 144–5, 154, 157, 164
Serbia 4, 6, 212, 214
service characteristics 22
service quality criteria 40–1
shippers 6, 11, 13, 18, 22–4, 29, 30–2, 50, 60, 83, 86, 88, 94, 132, 137, 151, 165, 177–9, 182, 199
single-hulled tank vessels 152
small inland waterways 121
St Lawrence–Great Lakes 125–8, 137–8
standard Rhine vessel 108
Standards in Inland Navigation (CESNI) 197
steel industry 13, 29, 30
Stochastic Frontier Analysis 21
structural overcapacity 71
supply and demand characteristics 73
supply of IWI 18–19
synchromodality 36, 47, 60, 63, 179

tank barge sector 75–8, 80, 81, 83–4, 90–1
tank vessels 31, 145, 152, 154, 161
tanker market 71, 81
technical quality 22
technical requirements for inland waterway vessels 197

technological developments 1
TEN-T corridors 189, 191
TEN-T development 192
terminal operators 13, 18–19, 32, 49, 50, 52–3, 55, 64, 132, 134, 139
Thames 100
tonne kilometres 5, 73
tonnes 5, 21, 29, 34, 73–6, 86, 90–1, 94, 101, 107, 116, 175, 180
total logistics costs 172, 180, 185
tour-de-rôle 89, 93, 95
touristic and recreational value 2
transhipment costs 40, 172
transport corridors 7, 135, 141
transport demand 9, 18, 193, 200, 202, 208, 212
transport frequency 22, 37, 39, 40
transport function of inland waterways 2
transport of palletized goods 37, 162, 170, 179, 180, 184, 186
transport of raw materials 7, 30
transport performance 5–8, 19, 35, 67, 158, 196, 207
transport performance measurement 18–19

transport quality 22
transport safety xv, 22, 37, 39, 40, 57, 59
transport security xiv, 22, 37, 39, 66, 68
transport speed 22, 36–7, 39, 40, 61, 173
Transport White Paper 188–9
trekschuit 106–7
trunk-feeder services 133
type of vessel 90, 109, 142–4

urban freight logistics 61
US Army Corps Of Engineers 5, 10, 13, 17, 24, 167

Vert Chez Vous 170
Volga 4, 6, 8
Vracht door de Gracht 170

water management 1, 167
Watertruck 117–18
Weser 5

Yangtze xi, 3, 6, 11, 16, 17, 100, 125–8, 131, 135–9, 140–2, 146, 154, 167, 188
Yellow river 4

Taylor & Francis eBooks

Helping you to choose the right eBooks for your Library

Add Routledge titles to your library's digital collection today. Taylor and Francis ebooks contains over 50,000 titles in the Humanities, Social Sciences, Behavioural Sciences, Built Environment and Law.

Choose from a range of subject packages or create your own!

Benefits for you

>> Free MARC records
>> COUNTER-compliant usage statistics
>> Flexible purchase and pricing options
>> All titles DRM-free.

Benefits for your user

>> Off-site, anytime access via Athens or referring URL
>> Print or copy pages or chapters
>> Full content search
>> Bookmark, highlight and annotate text
>> Access to thousands of pages of quality research at the click of a button.

 REQUEST YOUR **FREE** INSTITUTIONAL TRIAL TODAY **Free Trials Available**
We offer free trials to qualifying academic, corporate and government customers.

eCollections – Choose from over 30 subject eCollections, including:

Archaeology	Language Learning
Architecture	Law
Asian Studies	Literature
Business & Management	Media & Communication
Classical Studies	Middle East Studies
Construction	Music
Creative & Media Arts	Philosophy
Criminology & Criminal Justice	Planning
Economics	Politics
Education	Psychology & Mental Health
Energy	Religion
Engineering	Security
English Language & Linguistics	Social Work
Environment & Sustainability	Sociology
Geography	Sport
Health Studies	Theatre & Performance
History	Tourism, Hospitality & Events

For more information, pricing enquiries or to order a free trial, please contact your local sales team:
www.tandfebooks.com/page/sales

 Routledge
Taylor & Francis Group

The home of
Routledge books

www.tandfebooks.com